CREATIVE
AWAKENING

Recent Titles in
Contributions in Ethnic Studies
Series Editor: Leonard W. Doob

CREATIVE AWAKENING

The Jewish Presence
in
Twentieth-Century American Literature,
1900–1940s

LOUIS HARAP

Published in cooperation with the
American Jewish Archives

FOREWORD BY JACOB RADER MARCUS

Contributions in Ethnic Studies, Number 17

GREENWOOD PRESS
New York • Westport, Connecticut • London

Library of Congress Cataloging-in-Publication Data

Harap, Louis.
    Creative awakening.

    (Contributions in ethnic studies, ISSN 0196-7088 ;
no. 17)
    "Published in cooperation with the American Jewish
Archives."
    Bibliography: p.
    Includes index.
    1. American literature—Jewish authors—History and
criticism.   2. American literature—20th century—
History and criticism.   3. Jews in literature.
I. American Jewish Archives. II. Title. III. Series.
PS173.J4H29   1987   810′.9′8924   86-14986
ISBN 0-313-25386-2 (lib. bdg. : alk. paper)

Library of Congress Catalog Card Number: 86-14986
ISBN: 0-313-25386-2
ISSN: 0196-7088

First published in 1987

Greenwood Press, Inc.
88 Post Road West
Westport, Connecticut 06881

Printed in the United States of America

The paper used in this book complies with the
Permanent Paper Standard issued by the National
Information Standards Organization (Z39.48-1984).

10 9 8 7 6 5 4 3 2 1

Copyright Acknowledgments

The author and publisher gratefully acknowledge permission to use material previously
published:

American Jewish Archives for "Jews and American Drama 1900-1918" by Louis Harap,
American Jewish Archives, November 1984.

Midstream: A Monthly Jewish Review for "The Menorah Journal: A Literary Precursor"
by Louis Harap, *Midstream*, October 1984.

S.U.N.Y. Press for "Mute Inglorious Miltons: Maimie Pinzer and Sidney Greenberg" by
Louis Harap, *Studies in American Jewish Literature*, No. 2 (1982).

Judaism for "The Religious Art of Cynthia Ozick" by Louis Harap, *Judaism*, Vol. 33, No.
3 (Summer 1984).

International Creative Management Inc. for the poem "To be a Jew in the Twentieth Century" by Muriel Rukeyser, Copyright © 1944 and 1968 by Muriel Rukeyser, published in
Beast in View.

Very possibly there may be at this moment
a Russian or Polish Jew, born or bred on
our East Side, who may burst from his
parental Yiddish, and from the local hydrants,
as well as from wells of English undefiled,
slake our drouth of imaginative literature.

—William Dean Howells, 1915

To be a Jew in the twentieth century
Is to be offered a gift. If you refuse,
Wishing to be invisible, you choose
Death of the spirit, the stone insanity.
Accepting, take full life. Full agonies:
Your evening deep in labyrinthine blood
Of those who resist, fail, and resist; and God
Reduced to a hostage among hostages.

The gift is torment. Not alone the still
Torture, isolation; or torture of the flesh.
That may come also. But the accepting wish,
The whole and fertile spirit as guarantee
For every human freedom, suffering to be free,
Daring to live for the impossible.

—Muriel Rukeyser, 1944

Contents

Series Foreword

The Contributions in Ethnic Studies series focuses on the problems that arise when people with different cultures and goals come together and interact productively or tragically. The modes of adjustment or conflict are various, but usually one group dominates or attempts to dominate the other. Eventually some accommodation is reached: the process is likely to be long and, for the weaker group, painful. No one scholarly discipline monopolizes the research necessary to comprehend these intergroup relations. The emerging analysis, consequently, is of interest to historians, social scientists, psychologists, psychiatrists, and scholars in communication studies.

For centuries Jews everywhere have been the victims of prejudice and discrimination while preserving many of the main tenets of their culture and religious beliefs. In these three volumes the treatment of Jews in fiction, serious journals, drama, and poetry by Jewish and non-Jewish authors in the United States during the twentieth century is vividly portrayed. In each case, a concise, arresting, critical summary of the story, plot, or theme follows the salient biographical details concerning the writer himself or herself. The reader thus either can nostalgically recall a book or character he once read or knew, or else he can be stimulated to pursue for the first time a literary experience by dipping or plunging into the publications of a popular or scarcely known writer.

We have in these pages an opportunity to view the impact of changes within American society upon the depiction of Jewish characters and indeed of anti-Semitism among gentile, Black and Jewish authors. In the earlier part of the period conditions in the slums of East Side New York City, for example, impelled many Jews to join the forces supporting unions and the American version of socialism. Then the rise of Nazi ideology in the 1930s and later the depictions of the Holocaust caused Jews and non-Jews alike to appraise anew their own Jewish stereotypes. In addition, as readers we are challenged by a philosophical and social issue that still confronts Jews as well as other minority ethnic groups: should or how can we choose between the now less popular melting-pot objective for these groups, or have we really come to tolerate or favor cultural pluralism?

Louis Harap emphasizes quite rightly what he calls the problems of acculturation and assimilation of Jews as described in the literature and by the writers of the period, particularly when he examines differences between older and younger generations of Jews and also when he analyzes alienation generally in our society. The fiction and other literary creations, therefore, have never been wholly fictitious; perhaps more than scholarly tomes they depict the struggles and the satisfactions of Jews as well as unfriendly and friendly appraisals by other Americans. Simultaneously, moreover, they influence the views of a very large public. We are thus offered a most compelling documentation of the significant interaction between literature and what we too easily call reality: accurately or not, literature both reflects and affects us, or at least some of us.

Leonard W. Doob

Foreword

There are minds which insist on literature as pure artifice, and there are minds which see in literature a reflection not only of literary tradition but also of history and sociology. Louis Harap belongs — has long belonged — to this latter company. Literary merit is not the sole value he seeks when he confronts a work of the imagination. He looks for social value as well. It is important to discern and appreciate in him an accomplished social analyst of literary effort, a scholar who tends to concentrate unfailingly on the (not always so clearly discernible) nexus between a work of literature and the social or psychosocial context in which it was composed.

Dr. Harap is not a literary critic or literary theorist. He is an historian and draws on literature for his work as an historian. He is, more emphatically, a social historian, an historian devoted to the study of social reality with literary expression as a major instrument for his research.

Now to say this is not to suggest the lack in Dr. Harap's work of a *Tendenz* or ideological preference. His work does evince bias and offers a left-of-center perspective — but he is certainly not to be thought of as a ideologue in his judgments. It is Dr. Harap's sensitivity to social experience, not any ideological commitment he may have, that gives his thought a large interest for those concerned, as I am, to find in American-Jewish literary expression some index to how Jews have found their way through the labyrinths of American life.

What Dr. Harap offers in these three new volumes are erudite, forthright, incisive discussions of fiction, discussions which are consistently "socioliterary" — that is, art-for-the-sake-of-art, the purely esthetic, is never his goal or preoccupation. No, it is something else, awareness of the socioeconomic and psychic context, which governs his understanding of the stories and novels he examines so intelligently.

I think worth noting also Dr. Harap's readiness to consider women writers and women characters a major factor in the web of literary expression documenting American-Jewish life. It is impressive to see him calling our attention to Clara Yavner in Abraham Cahan's 1905 novel *The White Terror and the Red*; Clara, he observes, "is among the distinctly new figures . . . in all American fiction" and is "of special interest because she anticipates the new place of the Jewish woman in radical fiction of the first decades of the century — the courageous, effective, able Jewish woman labor organizer and socialist." Dr. Harap notes with approval James Oppenheim's incorporation into his 1911 novel *The Nine-Tenths* of a "recognition that the waistmakers' strike in 1911 had brought forward perhaps for the first time in the United States the 'New Woman,' the active and heroic participant in labor struggles and the struggle for a better world." The illumination of Jewish women by non-Jewish writers is not overlooked. He takes into account, for instance, Albert Edwards (*né* Arthur Bullard), who in 1913 published *Comrade Yetta*, a novel about Jewish radicalism, and speculated about Jewish "single-mindedness and consistency of purpose" in contrast to "Anglo-Saxon . . . compromise and confused issues."

In general, it may be said, Dr. Harap is fully and commendably alive to the documentary potential, the documentary implications, of fiction by non-Jewish writers. He is as much interested in Judeophobic writers like Frank Norris, Owen Wister, Edith Wharton, Jack London, and David Graham Phillips as he is in more sympathetic fictionists like Mark Twain, William Dean Howells, O. Henry, Thomas Nelson Page, and Dorothy Canfield Fisher. He understands that, "to achieve a comprehensive picture of the status of the Jew in our literature . . . it is not enough to study how the Jewish writer regarded his own Jewishness." He wants us also to "look at the way . . . non-Jewish writers depicted the Jew and met the challenge of anti-Semitism." As Dr. Harap points out, "the responses varied widely."

Readers may rely on Dr. Harap for formidable learning, and also, it is a pleasure to add, for a most accessible expository style. It is an honor to help bring these volumes to print; they will in time to come, I am confident, be recognized for the classics they are.

Jacob Rader Marcus
American Jewish Archives
Hebrew Union College-Jewish Institute of Religion
Cincinnati, Ohio

Preface

This work is conceived and organized around the concept of Jewish presence in American literature. The study of Jewish development as refracted in the nation's literature in the present century flows out of this concept. In this context literature is viewed as a social manifestation whose meaning extends beyond the "literary" in the specialized sense, essential as this literary aspect is to the total grasp of a work. Thus to trace the Jewish presence is to follow the rapid changes in the Jewish situation, in the material and social status of Jews, and in the conditions of their life as these form the generative basis for literary expression as well as the mode in which Jews make their appearance within that expression by both Jews and non-Jews. The content of the ensuing work is then the literary rendering of the acculturation process, the making of the texture of American-Jewish social life in the specific historic circumstances of this period of mass immigration and its aftermath.

The centuries-old history of the Jew as alien in Christian civilization and the strong inertial power of anti-Semitism and discrimination, the temptation to use the Jew as scapegoat in time of trouble, the traumatic effect of the necessary transition from the largely hermetic East European milieu to the contrasting mores and atmosphere and language of the "land of the free"—all these provided, willy-nilly, the ground of Jewish life in this country. Significantly, then, Jewish presence in the first half of the century and even beyond is a name for the acculturation of the main body of American Jews.

Jewish presence in literature is a complex phenomenon. Within it is the basic dichotomy of the Jew as writer and as subject or character. A Jew is no less Jewish when presented by a non-Jewish author than when included in work by a Jewish writer, regardless of the varying degrees of intimacy between author and subject. It is especially important to consider the release of the Jew in literature from the age-old stereotype, which prevailed in most writing of the past century. As the new century progressed, we find more sophisticated treatment of Jews as rounded individual characters. In such changes we can perceive the close connection between the strictly literary and the social, since the literary change from a cliché to a fresh creation reflects both more knowledge and, usually, a related new attitude. Throughout the century attitudes toward the Jew, as depicted in literature, are largely dependent on the status of the Jew in society. The non-Jewish author's attitude toward anti-Semitism is important in determining how he will present his Jewish characters. Hence, were one to omit examination of non-Jewish treatments of the Jew, the ensuing account of the Jewish presence in literature would be severely truncated.

The wider the arc of inclusion of elements of Jewish relevance in work by both Jewish and non-Jewish authors, the fuller the emergent picture of Jewish status at a given time will be. Our inquiry here is by no means strictly literary; one might best, perhaps, term it socioliterary. We have therefore given considerable attention to the development of the social situation during the century, and specifically to its anti-Semitic manifestations, whether those are presented by the story material alone or shared or condemned by the author. Our aim has been to achieve the most comprehensive view of the situation of the Jew in each period as adduced from the information available in the various components of presence. Indeed the entire work has been organized to bring out the various elements of presence. While all genres are subject to the same basic social conditions, out of which they all spring, each has its own special problems relating to its specific public and its internal formal requirements. In view of these differences, the variety of talents each calls upon, and the favorable or unfavorable social atmosphere for their evocation, the genres develop at different rates and with different qualities. These factors will be suggested in each case.

The evolving picture calls for a chronological periodization. It has seemed helpful to divide the first half century roughly into decades. The two decades from the opening of the century to the end of World War I form the first division; the 1920s, second; the Depression 1930s a third; the 1940s, the war decade, a fourth; the 1950s and beyond, a period of relatively full acceptance of the Jew in life and in the literary mainstream, the last. Within each period for the most part we examine separately the work of non-Jewish and Jewish writers. During the first three decades we find three important recurrent fictional themes: (1) the progress of acculturation fiction, (2) the radical novel, and (3) the manifestations of anti-Semitism in the work of non-Jewish authors as well as their own attitudes toward it. Within this third theme of anti-Semitism there are several striking phenomena which are discussed in separate chapters. First is the anti-Semitic attitudes in Jewish writers and in their Jewish characters, which illustrate what has been called "self-hate." Second, the war novels of World War II by both Jewish and non-Jewish writers are studied with a focus on the widespread anti-Semitism in the armed forces that they reveal.

Among the new developments in the nation after World War II we find, together with an increase in the number of important woman writers and the emergence of many impressive Black writers, the movement of Jewish authors into the central currents of American literature. The 1950s saw so many widely read novels, both popular and sophisticated, by Jewish writers and/or with central Jewish characters that it is no exaggeration to call this the "Jewish decade." We explore the genesis of this emergence in the 1920s and 1930s. A chapter is devoted to a number of Jewish literary critics who participated in these developments; Delmore Schwartz and Isaac Rosenfeld are discussed as harbingers of much postwar writing, and a chapter is devoted to each of four major Jewish novelists—Saul Bellow, Bernard Malamud, Philip Roth, and Norman Mailer. The return to religion in postwar writing is discussed, as well as the literary relations of Blacks and Jews.

Our study appears in three volumes. The first covers fiction from 1900 to the 1940s; the second resumes with the fiction in the 1950s, which we have designated "The Jewish Decade" for reasons there stated, until the 1980s; and the third takes up a survey of the drama from 1900 to the post–World War II period, as well as poetry and humor from 1900.

As any student of American literature must be aware, aspects of the Jew in literature as both author and subject, particularly in the latter half of the present century, are an area under increasing critical and historical scrutiny. There are already numerous studies of many themes and tendencies as well as of individual authors, groups of authors, and literary periods. However, of the present work, as of my earlier volume, it is, I think, true that no study so comprehensive has yet appeared. The abundance of material has, of course, made it necessary to be highly selective, and other scholars will inevitably differ in choices or in emphases as well as in general outlook. Yet they will, I hope, find their tasks easier for the broad survey here presented.

Acknowledgments

After publication of *The Image of the Jew in American Literature: From Early Republic to Mass Immigration* (1974), I turned to reading and writing on other, though related, topics. Toward the end of the Preface to that volume I had written, "We leave the proliferation of literature by and about Jews in our century to other, younger hands." But the respite proved brief. I was strongly encouraged by the late Oscar Cohen, by then retired program director of the Anti-Defamation League, to continue my research on Jews in American literature from the cut-off date of the earlier volume, 1900, to the present. I soon found myself committed to the second part of a comprehensive study of the Jew in American literature from the days of the early Republic to our own time. I am indebted to Oscar Cohen for his stimulus to continue on this project and for his many kindnesses.

My thanks also are due to several libraries and their helpful personnel: New York Public Library and its Library of the Performing Arts, the Bobst Library of New York University, the Harvard University Library, and the Hebrew Union College–Jewish Institute of Religion Library in New York City. The dedicated staff of the Southwest Regional Library of the Vermont State Library system responded most helpfully to my numerous requests for books on interlibrary loan, thus enabling me to work in my mountain home.

Some materials in this book have previously appeared in articles, some in different form, in publications which have granted permission to reprint: *Jewish Currents, Midstream* (October, 1984), *Judaism, Studies in American Jewish Literature,* and *American Jewish Archives* (November, 1984).

I wish to thank Jacob Sherman, of Rutland, Vermont, who devotedly typewrote the manuscript at various stages so accurately. Both Mr. Sherman and his wife Madeline helped with other kindnesses relating to the preparation of the manuscript, as also did a Jewish group in Rutland. My thanks are also due to Joan Wright, who typewrote the final draft for the press.

Morris U. Schappes kindly loaned me his valuable files on several current authors. Professor Ellen F. Schiff, of North Adams (Massachusetts) Community College, read the material on drama and made helpful suggestions.

Most particularly I wish to thank Dr. Annette Rubinstein for her careful, critical scrutiny of the entire manuscript, for her editorial suggestions, and for her copy-editing at several stages of the writing. We did not always agree, but she was ever sensitively aware of the distinction between difference of interpretation and indefensible error on my part. My debt to her is very great.

However, full responsibility for the entire work, mistakes and all, is of course mine alone.

Introduction

Participation in American literature by Jews before the twentieth century was meager. Ancient Hebrews were very much on the minds of Americans, and voluminous treatment of Jews who lived during the early Christian era did interest the reading public in the nineteenth century. But before our century the contemporary Jew found his way as character into current fiction only occasionally—though more frequently than one might suppose—and that almost always as money-obsessed or a stereotype of one kind or another. Until the end of the nineteenth century Jews were a minute part of the country's population although in the first third a few even wrote for the stage. After mid-century some German-Jewish immigrants, under the stimulus of the Reform leader Isaac M. Wise, took to writing novels, of which only one, *Differences* (1867), by Dr. Nathan Mayer, a Civil War novel of some interest, merits reading today. The poet Emma Lazarus was perhaps the most talented and most noted of pre–twentieth-century Jewish literary figures. At the century's end in San Francisco, Emma Wolf, the second-generation daughter of French-Jewish immigrants, published several readable novels about Jewish life in the United States. But the leading rabbis of the century, the Orthodox Rabbi Isaac Leeser and the Reform Rabbi Isaac M. Wise, were disquieted by the American Jews' lack of literary activity, which they attributed to the adoption of the prevailing American absorption with business. With some exceptions one may agree with Alfred Kazin's observation that "as late as 1910 there was no significant type of the Jewish writer in this century."[1]

But this restriction applies only to Jews writing in English, for the mass immigration from the 1880s onward produced a number of writers in Yiddish of fiction, poetry, criticism, and drama. However, the number and quality of Jewish writers in English increased and improved as the twentieth century wore on. They grew in numbers, influence, and competence, especially in fiction, literary criticism, and drama, though more slowly in poetry. In the 1930s their importance increased during the Great Depression. But it was only after World War II that Jewish writers came into their own. They then entered full tilt into the mainstream of American literature. They were accepted by the general American reading public as well as by the literary audience and achieved full literary citizenship. The story of this journey from the periphery to the center of American literary life and creation during the present century is attempted in the present study.

Because the range and quality of their literary work are so different from that recorded in my previous volume, *The Image of the Jew in American Literature: From Early Republic to Mass Immigration,* the problems to be dealt with are also considerably different. While anti-Semitism remains a constant in both parts of this study, the present work is far more concerned with the Jew as author, as well as subject matter. (The cut-off date of the first part was about 1900, except for the fiction of Abraham Cahan from the 1890s into the present century.) Before 1900 what passed for Jewish character in fiction was largely one or another stereotype, while later the Jew achieved more and more full status as a human being as knowledge of and personal acquaintance with Jews increased. The Jew then commanded respect as an individual and matured as a writer to achieve full literary status, ranging from successful popular authorship to a position of high literary quality and eminence. Our century has witnessed the transition of the Jew from an exotic to the symbol of modern man, from the Jewish writer as *rara avis* to a numerous and generally recognized species.

These developments implied acceptance of the Jew into American life in general to a degree hardly ever achieved before in the United States, despite periodic revivals of active anti-Semitism during several periods before World War II. The war against Nazism followed, and, after a few years the nation experienced a remission of anti-Semitism. This was attributable not only to shocked awareness of the Holocaust, but also respect for the Jews engendered by the establishment of Israel and by the sheer economic demands of postwar economic expansion, which made necessary the lowering of barriers in many areas of business and the professions previously almost closed to Jews. It would, however, be a grave error to assume from these developments that the sense of difference between Jew and non-Jew had disappeared or that anti-Semitism was gone. Postwar studies of anti-Semitism showed that active prejudice had declined, but that latent anti-Semitism was widespread and waiting to be called forth under crisis conditions, as began to become evident in the late 1970s and 1980s. Nevertheless, the high degree of acceptance of writing by Jewish authors during the postwar period was symptomatic of acceptance in society itself.

These various influences operating simultaneously indicate the complexity of the situation we face in this study. There is the social momentum of centuries-old attitudes that were changing under pressure of events, of advances and reverses in the relations of non-Jews and Jews. The picture was never simple, but in the twentieth century it was more complex than ever under the variegated influences of rapid social change throughout society. While in my earlier book I could without exaggeration suggest that the situation of the Jew in literature was a chapter in United States anti-Semitism, in the twentieth century the literary situation for the Jews is indeed far more than that, and more strictly a literary situation.

While we are here concerned with American Jewish literature, there is no consensus on the meaning of "American Jewish writer." Many such leading writers as Saul Bellow, Bernard Malamud, Philip Roth, and Arthur Miller disclaim such a designation. They assert that they are "American writers" and Jews who write. They affirm their Jewish identity but regard themselves as indistinguishable from non-Jewish writers in literary nationality. The addition of "Jewish" to their designation as writers seems to them to diminish their full citizenship in the American republic of letters: they regard it as bearing overtones of the parochial and as limiting their scope to the particularistic rather than to the American-ness that is taken for granted in the non-Jewish writer. They do not wish in any way to be separated from their non-Jewish colleagues. While all this is understandable, it seems to me based on an unnecessarily prescriptive notion of American-Jewish writing. The fact is that in some significant respects they are different from their colleagues, a difference that need carry no implication of narrowness or loss of universality, but is rather descriptive of the human locus and context from which they embark on their exploration.

An argument sometimes used against this designation is that one does not generally refer to "American-WASP" writers. Why then "American-Jewish" writers? But the recency of American-Jewish entry into accepted literary society and their recognition are indefeasible psychological phenomena. At the same time the differences in context from the non-Jewish writer by virtue of differences in origin, the presence of American-Jewish content, make their Jewishness an object of attention. The same is true of the group of postwar writers who stemmed from the South, and yet no one heard any objections offered to their designation as "Southern writers." Why should the distinctiveness of Southern writer—or writers of any other origin, geographic, or ethnic or regional—be less objectionable than that of American-Jewish? What is determinative is not the name but the content. To call Saul Bellow an American-Jewish writer no more diminishes him than to call William Faulkner a Southern writer.

But let us be clear as to just what we mean by American-Jewish. The simplest but least meaningful definition is: any writer who identifies himself or herself as Jewish irrespective of content. But literature written by a Jew which is indistinguishable in content from that written by a non-Jew, and which is related to Jewishness only by the denotative identity of a Jew gives little substance to the term in a literary sense. A more significant definition would differentiate the writer in some meaningful literary way from his colleagues, and that can be found only in some difference of content or approach.

Although there are some who believe that such content must be religious in order to be distinct, there are several reasons for rejecting this. Like the definition of a Jew as one who adheres to the Jewish religion, it is arbitrarily limiting and simply shuts out of Jewish identity the non-religious person. Correlatively, limiting the Jewish content of the writer to the Jewish religion is to cut out the large area of life that is ethnic though non-religious. This would, for instance, exclude novels like *The Old Bunch, Jews Without Money*, and *Herzog* from the roster of American-Jewish literature. All novels of acculturation that are not religiously centered would slip out of this category. Obviously such a restriction is impossibly narrow, and the definition on which it is based is parochial and narrow.

Jewishness is a many-faceted form of ethnicity with not only theological and traditional aspects, but also intellectual, environmental, familial, sociological, characterological, and generational ones. All these are of course interrelated, and many overlap. All, however, are one or another aspect of ethnicity. Whatever is descriptive of any aspect of the life of Jews pertains to its ethnicity. As such they are present in some way in any literature designated as American-Jewish. Before Emancipation religion was an integral part of Jewish life just as, for instance, Christianity was an integral part of medieval life among Christians of the time. Since Emancipation religion has become less and less necessary for Jewish identification. So long as Jewish identity endures, some degree of ethnicity persists.

The American-Jewish novel under such a concept includes the acculturation novel and any other which includes in its content some specifically Jewish aspect of Jewish life in the United States at any period, or even of the Jews in any part of the world, for that matter, since such a novel is written from the perspective of the American-Jewish author. It can include anything from *The Rise of David Levinsky* to *Call It Sleep* to the novels of Chaim Potok or Philip Roth or Bruce Jay Friedman. Our study will show that the range of American Jewish literature is limited only by the imaginative power of the author. Such fiction is American-Jewish, first by the Jewish identity of the author, and second by the ethnic character of its content. What is excluded is that writing by Jews that contains no Jewish ethnic element whatever, that is, is totally indistinguishable from the work of non-Jewish authors.

Not all fiction dealing with Jewish life is "American-Jewish" if it is not written by a Jew. Thus, among the earliest novels written about Jewish life in New York City several were published in the 1880s by Henry Harland under the "Jewish" pseudonym of Sidney Luska. One of the best of the East Side novels before 1910, *Joseph Zalmonah* (1892) was written by Edward

King, and one of the best socialist novels of the East Side before World War I was *Comrade Yetta* (1913) by Arthur Bullard. None of these was authored by a Jew, and therefore none can be designated "American-Jewish."

Despite the increasingly secular character of Jewish life in the United States, residues of religious practices are not excluded from the writing of Jews. The religious festivals of Passover and Purim or others may even survive in secularized form and be celebrated for their social and human rather than their religious significance. Also, ideas in the prophetic tradition of Judaism such as the passion for social justice may be carried over into secular significance devoid of religious conviction. Located within the context of life in America, such fiction is no less American than any other in our pluralistic society. Only such separatistic groups as extreme Orthodox sects can be said to be non-American enclaves minimally related to American society. Most Jews, however, especially in the second generation and beyond, by now live a highly integrated life within the larger American society, and large numbers can be said to be more American than Jewish. But what Jewishness remains is not incompatible with non-Jewish American life. It only introduces some cultural differences from other parts of the society, as is the case with regional literatures like the Southern or Black or any distinctly ethnic writing.

It is the rare novel of Jewish life that does not, despite the recession of anti-Semitism, contain allusions to, or incidents of, anti-Semitism. Only at their peril will Jews lower their guard against that even in favorable times like the postwar period. In the late 1970s and 1980s, for instance, there are signs that anti-Semitism is on the increase again under the influence of hard economic times and tensions arising from the Middle East crisis. In confronting the occurrence of anti-Semitism in fiction, prejudice felt by the fictional character must be distinguished from the attitude of the author. Sometimes, as among some leading writers in the 1920s, the author himself or herself is implicated in anti-Semitism; at others it is quite clear from the context that the author does not share the attitude of his prejudiced character. In any case, this unhappily ubiquitous aspect of the life of Jews in the larger non-Jewish society must never be lost sight of.

Because of such considerations any attempt to examine the Jewish aspect of a literature must also observe how non-Jewish authors deal with this phase of the problem. In our study of the twentieth-century treatment of the Jew in literature, we explore the attitudes of both Jewish *and* non-Jewish authors. However, since the number of Jewish authors in the twentieth century is so large, only a small sampling of non-Jewish authors—and even of Jewish authors—can be considered.

Clearly, a study like the present one, whose aim is to contribute to an awareness of the place of the Jew in American literature and in American society as reflected in that literature, cannot restrict itself to literary considerations alone. The values we find in writing are not only literary but also sociological and documentary. Thus, for instance, some pre–World War I novels may have minor literary value and yet reveal much about attitudes and conditions in relation to Jews of the period. Indeed a selection of passages culled from American Jewish novels in our century, chronologically or thematically juxtaposed, could form a vivid and fairly descriptive montage of American Jewish life during this century. Such a montage would draw upon the socialist novels early in the century, the acculturation novels at various stages in development of Jewish life, the novels of Abraham Cahan, Samuel Ornitz, Henry Roth, Daniel Fuchs, Meyer Levin, Mike Gold, and many others down to our own time.

One final caution. In the course of our century, and most particularly after World War II, literature has proliferated in number and variety of subject matter. Since the 1920s literally hundreds of novels have been published on one or another aspect of Jewish life, not to mention the critical observation and analysis of this work. Our study makes no pretense at exhaustiveness but is instead highly selective of what seem to be significant figures and trends from the several viewpoints, literary and sociological. If any important American literary figure or trend is not here represented, it is likely that the reason is absence of Jewish relevance. Obviously we do not have here a history of twentieth-century American literature as a whole, but only of one aspect of it. In this respect, at least, it is hoped that no significant figure or trend is omitted. I recognize that other scholars might make a different selection of works or features for extended treatment. It has been most important to trace the changes in the quantity and quality of Jewish writing over the century; to examine the writers' relation to Jewishness within the context of American culture; to locate the Jewish writer as American writer; and to pursue the vicissitudes of the Jewish literary character through the century.

1

The Apprentice Years: 1900–1919

Fiction writing in the first two decades of the new century was generally minor, except of course for the production of those major writers—Mark Twain, Henry James, William D. Howells—who survived into the twentieth century. The spurt of the new realism in significant writers like Stephen Crane and Frank Norris expired with their deaths by 1902. Theodore Dreiser's *Sister Carrie* was first published in 1900, but its circulation was literally aborted by his publisher for its "immorality" and did not substantially reenter the literary scene until 1912. But the seeds of the literary efflorescence of the 1920s and of modernism were planted in the 1910s with the work of Van Wyck Brooks, Ezra Pound, and others.

In those early decades the nation was absorbed in its new emergence as a major world power, with its heady quick victory over Spain and its entry into the world arena as an imperialist power controlling Cuba, acquiring Guam and Puerto Rico, conquering the Philippines, and annexing Hawaii. It was undergoing the greatest economic growth in its history, and in fact led the world in industrial production. The number of industrial workers doubled between 1900 and 1919; capital multiplied about five times. Virtual control of government was gained by Big Business, the Money Power; corruption in government was rife; and graft of politicians, soon to be mercilessly exposed by the muckrakers, scandalized the country. The safety valve of the Western frontier had been closed by the end of the century with the virtual end of homesteading. Alert farmers more and more applied scientific methods to agriculture.

Manpower for the unprecedented industrial development was supplied by mass emigration from Eastern and Southern Europe. Between 1881 and 1920 almost 23.8 million had immigrated, about 2.1 million of them Jews. During these decades the total population more than doubled, rising from

50 million in 1880 to 106 million in 1920. About three-quarters of the immigrants had settled in the cities and the work force of the nation was changed from predominantly Anglo-Saxon or Northern European to Eastern and Southern European foreign workers. This immense army of workers manned the burgeoning industrial development. Most Jews settled in the large cities, mainly places like New York, Boston, Philadelphia, and Chicago; the rest were scattered in small groups all over the country. They moved into light industry, most particularly the garment industry, both as workers and employers, and revolutionized clothing production, making it into an efficient, mass-produced sector of the economy. Fighting against sweatshops and intense exploitation, Jews organized unions and conducted militant strikes, gradually compelling improvements in pay and working conditions.

Dislocations in the heretofore unchallenged political and economic positions of the established Anglo-Saxon population fed deep resentment over this intrusion of foreigners, as is vividly exemplified in the obsessive anti-Semitism of Henry Adams. Racist theories of the superiority of the Anglo-Saxon and Teutonic peoples gained adherents among the established population. After 1900 a "scientific" eugenics claiming support from the Mendelian theory of genetic inheritance was made to support notions of racial superiority. Racism and eugenics acquired respectability and were commonly taught in colleges as "science." The Jews were a special target of the Anglo-Saxon supremacists, as is shown in the doctrines of Madison Grant's popular *The Passing of a Great Race* (1916). In the South the long-established subjection of Blacks as an inferior people meshed with the growing racist theory. The anti-Semitism that sometimes cropped up even in populist movements reappeared in Tom Watson's political efforts in Georgia, culminating in Leo Frank's lynching in 1915, when he was falsely accused of murdering a white Christian factory girl.

But the headlong advance of industry oblivious of human welfare, the dominance of government by moneyed interests, the civic corruption, the intense exploitation of labor, the spreading racism, and anti-Semitism were not unopposed. They called forth countervailing forces. Populist movements, which protested against real grievances but were marred by offers of dubious solutions and sometimes by scapegoating anti-Semitism, had risen and receded in the 1890s. In the new century a succession of reform movements arose, ranging from Theodore Roosevelt's Progressive party to Woodrow Wilson's New Freedom. Prominent Protestant clergymen, led by Walter Rauschenbusch, preached the Social Gospel, which urged economic and social amelioration as a Christian duty. Society's evils were sensationally exposed by many such muckrakers as Lincoln Steffens and Ida M. Tarbell, and Upton Sinclair's *The Jungle* (1906) actually prompted remedial legislation in the meat-packing industry. Yet the American Federation of Labor, founded in 1886, was largely an assembly of craft unions of skilled workers with patently opportunistic policies. Its growth, tripling between 1900 and 1914, was not as great an increase as might have been expected from the militancy and extreme exploitation of the period; by 1920 it still had had only 5 million members. The great mass basic industries remained largely unorganized. During this period, however, socialism became respectable under the leadership of Eugene Debs and was especially inspiring to writers and artists.

Jews in the United States participated in the phenomenal expansion of industry as well as in resistance to its abuses. Many German Jews of the mid-nineteenth-century immigration had, by the end of the century, achieved wealth in banking, retail trade, and other spheres of the economy in many parts of the country. But the incoming Eastern European Jews of the mass immigration were predominantly working class. By 1900 there were about 1 million Jews in the country, and by 1914 that number had grown to about 3 million through immigration and natural increase. Settled chiefly in the cities, they were packed into ghettos, and most were crowded into the East Side of New York. They were brutally exploited, largely by Jewish employers in the sweatshops and factories, and lived in miserable conditions. They resisted from time to time, forming militant unions, conducting strikes, and developing widespread socialist agitation.

Discrimination against Jews in employment increased as racist ideas spread and competition for jobs grew. Not only naturalized Jews but virtually all non-Anglo-Saxons, or Eastern and Southern Europeans, were regarded as foreigners and racially inferior. Pressure for restriction of immigration became more intense as the century wore on, but resistance was strong enough to ward it off until 1920 and, more decisively, 1924, when immigration of the "undesirable" Jews and Eastern and Southern Europeans was legally reduced to a trickle. At the same time prodigious efforts were launched to Americanize those immigrants already here. There were two tendencies in the Americanization movement: one wished to suppress immigrant ethnicity altogether and to impose complete Anglo-Saxon conformity; the other, exemplified by the generous-minded college settlement movement, set up clubhouses in slum districts to facilitate adaptation to American life while at the same time not discouraging, and even encouraging, cultivation of ethnic culture.

This adaptation occurred in many modes and degrees. The process was called variously assimilation or integration or acculturation. We need to define specifically what we mean by acculturation, which will be a key concept in our overview of the relevant literature in these early decades. Since Jews were part of a predominantly English-speaking society, even if they lived and worked in the largely Yiddish-speaking East Side, they needed to make some language accommodation to the world around them; this was compulsively true of the second and succeeding generations. They had to adapt not only to the language, but also to the customs and behavior of

the established American Anglo-Saxon culture, which had more than three
centuries of developed practice. While it was possible for the most rigid and
inflexible of Orthodox immigrants to live out their lives without learning
English or in any way altering their way of life from the earlier mode in
Europe, this was not possible for the younger generation. They were subject
to compulsory education in the English language and could scarcely survive
without considerable adaptation on several levels. Parental rigidity and mutual incomprehension were often the source of that bitter conflict between
the generations which was so common in the ghetto. Added to this was the
ghetto children's shame of their parents' lack of education and alien manner
of life, which reflected the constricted ghetto environment. The liberated,
secular American life was more appealing to most ghetto children than the
residual medievalism of their parents. Often the shame was mixed with
contempt for their parents' alien mentality. The second generation went on
to take advantage of access to the general American life with its free schools,
libraries, equality before the law, open avenues to some (not all) professions,
a free field in which to explore or develop new marginal and innovative
industries. The acculturation process was central to the lives of the Jewish
immigrants and to the succeeding generations while the persistence of racism
and anti-Semitism hindered unfettered accommodation to the new life.

In what, more particularly, did this acculturation consist? Language was
of course primary and elementary, and in practice many Jews became at
least bilingual, speaking Yiddish at home to their parents and other older
people and English in school and to their peers. They also tended to adopt
the manners and customs of the general population—in table manners, diet,
personal hygiene, modes of speech and dress, choice of entertainment as
well as in other aspects of American cultural life such as literature, music,
theater, newspaper and magazine reading, education, and professional aspirations—in short, all those attitudes and activities that we identify as
culture in the broader sense. As a result the life-style of those undergoing
acculturation was different from that of the tradition- and language-bound
older generation whose mode of life so closely resembled the life they had
left behind in Europe. Yet, acculturation does not of itself necessarily imply
abandonment, elimination, or limitation of ethnicity. The acculturating person may in some degree or other also maintain identity with his or her
original ethnic group and its culture.

If acculturation can coexist with one's original ethnicity, another term is
necessary to describe total elimination of ethnicity and total adoption of
the majority way of life. Acculturation can and often does occur without
acceptance by the dominant ethnic group. Jews may be excluded from the
personal lives of the majority through social discrimination in housing, social
clubs, and resorts. Nor does acculturation require acceptance by the majority
as marriage partners. Nor would prejudice or the sense of intergroup competition for jobs or economic power or cultural influence necessarily cease.

In short, acculturation may proceed without total assimilation, that is, without obliteration of the original ethnic character, that condition requiring the elimination of all forms of prejudice, discrimination, and competition.[1]

Obviously these conditions are not being met in America. There is no effective "melting pot." It is true, as Nathan Glazer and Patrick Moynihan have written, that "the melting pot did not happen."[2] There is no prospect in the foreseeable future for this to happen to the Jews, considering the persistence of prejudice on the one side and the tenacious sense of Jewish identification on the other. The sense of loyalty among the Jews to their membership in a people with a long and continuing history of persecution is too strong, the wound inflicted by society too deep, for Jewish identity to be surrendered. Yet Milton M. Gordon has noted in the case of the Jews (at least by 1964, when his book, on whose analysis our discussion draws, was published) that acculturation had been substantially achieved, as was absence of competition with the non-Jewish community in the economy. Still, social acceptance has only been partially gained. Discrimination and prejudice continue in some form, intermarriage is limited, and Jewish identification is still strong. Gordon correctly presents the phenomena entailed in assimilation, but its desirability or likelihood is a different problem. We shall proceed on the view that total assimilation is wholly unlikely in the foreseeable future. So long as ethnicity continues as a social fact owing to imperfect social arrangements and fallible human beings, the free exercise of ethnic expression remains a democratic right to be respected and provided for. Ethnic rights are equally the right of *all* ethnic groups and in practice today are lacking or seriously deficient for Blacks and Hispanics, among others. A truly democratic society actively encourages ethnic culture, bringing out the varied possibilities of human expression which enrich the life of all humanity.

What is sure is that a central problem of the immigrant and following generations during the first few decades of the century was the necessity to achieve some degree of acculturation. And one of the most frequent, striking, and sometimes traumatic aspects of the experience was the encounter with anti-Semitism. All these were registered in the literature of the period by and about Jews.

The prodigious struggles of the masses of immigrant Jews to establish a life for themselves and their families in a strange land provided a fertile subject for literary creation by both Jewish and non-Jewish writers. Indeed, the best known early effort to depict this immigrant life was by non-Jewish writers who were attracted by its exoticism or motivated by a sympathetic attempt at understanding. Some were unusually well informed about Yiddish cultural life, trade union activities, and radicalism of the ghetto Jews.

Sociological studies of East Side life were published by the well-intentioned Jacob A. Riis and others. And the best and most understanding delineations of everyday life on the East Side as well as of its culture was the now classic study by Hutchins Hapgood, *The Spirit of the Ghetto* (1902). Especially noteworthy of Hapgood's study was his informed awareness of the rich cultural life in Yiddish and on the East Side. There was the Yiddish fiction of Sholem Aleichem, I. L. Peretz, and others who remained in Russia as well as of some who had immigrated; there were the worker-poets like Morris Rosenfeld, playwrights like Jacob Gordin working for the remarkably popular Yiddish theater, and scholars of Yiddish and Hebrew.

In American literature the Jew had until this time most often been depicted as an unpleasant stereotype. As for Jewish authors, there were few before the twentieth century, and even fewer worth remembering; perhaps none except Emma Lazarus and a few others.

But Abraham Cahan, who began publishing short stories in the 1890s, was exceptional among the East Europeans. It was to take a little more time for writers of literature to emerge from the Eastern European immigration. Yet these Jews not only had a far larger reservoir of human Jewish material to draw upon than those of the earlier immigrations, but they also arrived at a time when the country was entering a new era of literary development, and they proved to have a vast diversity and abundance of literary and artistic talents waiting to be tapped. Free education and public libraries had nurtured and stimulated the intellectual, professional, and artistic aspirations of countless first- and second-generation poor young immigrants. These youths almost invariably had to endure anti-Semitism from their gentile neighbors and could not escape the rigors of the class struggle between Jewish workers and their Jewish employers. How could these vital issues escape treatment in the fiction they were later to write?

The air of those early decades was filled with discussions of the ethnic and class tensions with which the immigrant generations were beset. Americanization was sometimes interpreted as the effort to combat both ethnicity and radicalism because labor and socialist militancy were often identified with immigrant figures and groups. The problem of adaptation to the new life was put most dramatically in the very popular play, *The Melting Pot* (1908), which set the problem in vivid, not to say lurid, terms. Written by a great admirer of American democracy, the Anglo-Jewish Israel Zangwill, it was dedicated to Theodore Roosevelt and attracted large audiences all over the country, popularizing its title as the American nickname for the assimilation process.

The notion of the melting pot was not new in American society. In 1782 Hector St. Jean de Crèvecoeur wrote in his *Letters from an American Farmer,* "Here individuals of all nations are melted into a new race of men...that race now called American." And Ralph Waldo Emerson in his Journal of 1845 rejected the anti-foreignism of the current nativism. "I hate the narrowness of the Native American Party," he wrote. "This continental asylum of all nations—the energy of Irish, Germans, Swedes, Poles, and Cossacks—of the Africans, and of the Polynesians—will construct a new race, a new religion, a new state, a new literature, which will be as vigorous as the New Europe which came out of the melting-pot of the Dark Ages."[3]

These are benign conceptions of the melting pot concept, which left untouched the crucial questions of what would happen to the original cultural ingredients of the prospective culture and new people. To what extent, if any, would those cultures be expunged? Or retained? Separately retained or only as part of a new amalgam? But there were theorists of assimilation who wished to obliterate the ethnic cultures of the constituent groups. These were the protagonists of the Anglo-Saxon supremacy. Their view was put quite unequivocally by the benevolent Harvard historian of literature, Barrett Wendell, in a 1906 essay, "American Nationality." He wished that all those in America of foreign origin would become "Yankees." The teacher, he wrote, encounters students whose "names are uncouth to his Yankee ears." Yet he had a "growing certitude" that those students are "primarily, fundamentally, not Frenchmen or Italians, Irishmen or Germans, or Jews. They are Yankees like their Yankee teacher. . . . The power of assimilation in the national character of America proves still unbroken." Wendell categorically denied that "the national character of our modern America is composite" or contains any influence on American culture from the new immigrants' ethnic cultures. What is truly "American," he held, is "derived from pre-Revolutionary England."[4]

The message of the Zangwill play, not so limiting as Wendell's, did not exclude influences from non-Anglo-Saxon national cultures. We may dispense with the absurd plot of the play, but Zangwill's theme is contained in the hero's ecstatic exclamation:

America is God's Crucible, the great Melting Pot where all the races of Europe are melting and reforming! . . . Here you stand in your fifty groups, with your fifty languages, and histories, and your fifty blood hatreds and rivalries. But you won't be long like that, brothers, for these are the fires of God you've come to . . . Germans and Frenchmen, Irishmen and Englishmen, Jews and Russians—into the Crucible with all of you! God is making the American. . . . the real American has not yet arrived. He's only in the Crucible—he will be a fusion of all races, perhaps the coming superman![5]

Most critics treated the play as "claptrap." Opinion was divided among Jewish critics between the assimilationists and the pluralists as to the play's message. In *The American Hebrew* the banker-philanthropist Jacob H. Schiff disagreed with Zangwill's advocacy of intermarriage, asserting that "the Jew should not assimilate, should not cease to exist as a separate factor . . . until the brotherhood of men is realized."[6] Not unexpectedly the assimilationist Oscar S. Straus thought it "a great play."[7] *The American Hebrew* wrote that while the third act was "sentimental, hysterical, melodramatic clap-trap, what you will, the fact remains that the third act grips you, thrills you." The critic concluded that while the play was not a satisfactory contribution to the Jewish problem, it nevertheless raised many pertinent questions.[8]

Judah L. Magnes, liberal rabbi in this country and later in Palestine, did not mince words in condemnation of the play's message in a sermon at Temple Emanu-El on October 9, 1909. The play, he said, was

pernicious. [It preached] suicide for us. For that is what the play means for all the nationalities in this great Republic—... Americanization means what Mr. Zangwill has the courage to say it means: Dejudaisation.... The Jew is asked to give up his identity in the name of brotherhood and progress.... There may be Jews without Judaism, but there can be no Judaism without Jews. [Zangwill's idea of] Americanization is the old Know-Nothing view and is, in large part, outworn even in America.... The melting process glorifies disloyalty to one's own inheritance. [Zangwill was a] false prophet.[9]

Several years later, Dr. Abram Lipsky, in *The Maccabean,* emphatically rejected the play's doctrine. The play itself, he thought, was full of "crudities" and "hysterics" and "braggadocio about the Jewish race." The play is interesting not for itself, he said, but for its melting-pot theory. "Many a stubborn, stiff-necked Jew," wrote Lipsky, "will scorn the prophecy [of total amalgamation], and insist that he has no desire to become anything different. He will refuse to yield to the disintegrating and reforming heat of the crucible." In any case, concluded Lipsky, the prophecy of the final American as one homogeneous type is "extremely remote."[10]

When Zangwill published the play in England in 1914, he wrote an afterword responding to criticism. As to the technical defects charged against it, he cited the enormous continuing popularity of the play. It "has been universally acclaimed by Americans as a revelation of Americanism—.... Played through the length and breadth of the States since its original production in 1908, given, moreover, in Universities and Women's Colleges," it has had "edition after edition in book form, and was cited by preachers and journalists, politicians and Presidential candidates." He cited a favorable comment by Jane Addams, who said the play performs "a great service to America by reminding us of the high hope of the founders of the Republic." But Zangwill then tried to correct what he considered some people's misinterpretation of the play's meaning. "The process of American amalgamation," he wrote, "is not assimilation or simple surrender to the dominant type... but an all-round give and take by which the final type may be enriched or impoverished." The ultimate American language, he continued, will "bear traces of the fifty languages now being spoken side by side with it." He granted that internal "discords together with the prevalent anti-Semitism and his own ingrained persistence, tend to preserve the Jew even in the 'Melting Pot' so that dissolution must necessarily be slower than that of the similar aggregations of Germans, Italians, or Poles."[11]

Resurgence of ethnic awareness in recent years and the wide acceptance

of cultural pluralism—cultivation of minority cultures as well as participation in the concomitant majority culture—shows how erroneous Zangwill's viewpoint was. Later developments were foreshadowed more by
several of Zangwill's critics. In the 1909 sermon cited above, Magnes proposed that "the America of the future is to be not a Republic of individuals
and religions alone, but a Republic of nationalities as well." America, he
said, was a "refining pot," where nationalities would lose their national Old
World hatreds and jealousies. "To be a man, he need not cease being a
Jew."[12] In somewhat similar terms Lipsky proposed that "America can show
the world a nation living at peace with nations upon the same domain. . . .
Not a community of blood, but a community of purpose binds these millions
together. Here national respect and tolerance reign between men of most
diverse origins."[13]

Whatever Zangwill may have believed, clearly the concept of the melting
pot did not mean that the Jews, or any other minority people, would retain
their minority culture in any form, except possibly that of religion. It certainly did not contemplate cultivation of minority cultures in addition to
participation in the majority culture. Two attitudes toward the minority
ethnic group were current in those early decades, as is illustrated in a book
of short stories by Myra Kelly, a kindly Irish school teacher on the East
Side. In *Little Citizens* (1904), she tries to help her little charges to achieve
acculturation without interfering with their ethnic character. She "delivered
daily lectures on nail brushes, hair ribbons, shoe polish, pins, buttons, elastic,
and other means to grace. Her talks . . . on soap and water became almost
personal. . . . And yet the First Reader Class, in all other branches of learning,
so receptive and responsive, made but halting and uncertain progress toward
that state of virtue that is next to godliness." One day her superintendent,
Tom O'Shea, comes to inspect her teaching, and exhibits the coercive assimilative attitude. He snappishly enjoins her, "I hope you realize that it is
part of your duty to stamp out dialect."[14] Now, many years of experience
with the acculturation problem for a variety of minority groups have shown
that the ethnic culture of those being acculturated cannot simply be ignored
by the educational system. While numerous ethnic minorities do leave their
imprint on the majority culture and do effect changes in its language, arts,
and even manners, this does not mean that the minority culture passes out
of existence. It survives in some form as a secondary culture. The "new
American person" does not necessarily abandon the culture of his or her
ethnic origins.

As we saw, contemporary criticism of the melting-pot idea was not long
in appearing during the discussion of Zangwill's play. The most important
argument was offered by Horace M. Kallen. While Barrett Wendell's Anglo-
Saxonism is different from the melting-pot notion, both envisaged the vanishing of ethnicity: both were polar opposites of Kallen's idea of cultural
pluralism, which envisages the survival of ethnicity. It is therefore ironic

that Kallen was a student and friend of Wendell and was encouraged by
him. The irony becomes even more stringent when one learns that on grad-
uating from Harvard in 1903, Kallen was recommended by Wendell for a
teaching post in English at Princeton. Kallen was appointed, but when his
Jewish identity became known, he was rejected for reappointment. Kallen
was committed not only to his Jewishness but to democracy in its fullest
implications. Thus it was that perhaps more than any other single person
Kallen changed the thinking of the country on ethnicity. In an essay, "Democracy *versus* the Melting Pot" published in *The Nation,* February 18 and
25, 1915, he drew out the implications of basic democracy for the problem
of ethnicity, formulating the theory that came to be known as "cultural pluralism." Kallen contrasted the virtual homogeneity of the eighteenth-century
American (which Wendell was convinced had remained an unchanged Anglo-Saxon down to his own day), with the variety of ethnic strains acquired
from immigration since the last century—French, German, Irish, Scandi-
navian, Italian, Slavic, East European, Jewish, and even Oriental. Americanization and external conditions might seem to have fused these into a
new Anglo-Saxon cultural homogeneity, but in fact, as Kallen showed, the
self-conscious effort to assimilate was not without tensions caused by ethnic
influences. These tensions were already quite marked when Kallen wrote.
To the native American, that is, the Anglo-Saxon, the ethnic "is merely a
Dutchman, a Mick, a frog, a wop, a dago, or hunkey, or a sheeny and no
more." Furthermore these various ethnic stocks had a hierarchy of status
both within their own group and in Anglo-Saxon eyes. The languages and
religions of the different ethnic groups were an important vehicle for cultural
expression for each, and formed a barrier against assimilation.[15]

Kallen's description of the course of ethnic awareness, though written
more than sixty-five years ago, forecasts what has taken place in the past
few decades among the country's ethnic groups. They

develop their own literature or become conscious of that of the mother country. As
they grow more prosperous and "Americanized," as they become freed from the
stigma of "foreigner," they develop group self-respect: the wop changes into a proud
Italian, the hunky into an intensely nationalist Slav. They learn, or recall, the spiritual
heritage of their nationality. Their cultural abjectness gives way to their cultural
pride and the public schools, the libraries and the clubs become beset with demands
for texts in the national language and literature.

Because the Jews more often than the others came here to escape persecution,
they were the most eager to become Americans. But at the same time, Kallen
points out, "the most eagerly American of the immigrant groups are also
the most autonomous and self-conscious in spirit and culture." The democratic objective, Kallen holds, is then "a cooperation of cultural diversities,
as a federation or commonwealth of national cultures." What America
needs, he affirmed, is not "unison" but "harmony." He looked forward to

a "truly democratic commonwealth...its form...a federal republic; its substance a democracy of nationalities, cooperating voluntarily and autonomously through common institutions in the enterprise of self-realization through the perfection of men according to their kind." English would be the common language, but each group would cultivate its own speech and aesthetic and cultural expression as well.[16]

Kallen's case for cultural pluralism was strengthened in 1916 by Randolph Bourne, who had read Kallen's article. In the *Atlantic* for July, 1916, Bourne published his own "Transnational America." He opened this essay by proclaiming the "failure of the melting pot" and offered "a higher ideal than the melting pot." Like Kallen, he denounced "the Anglo-Saxon element" for "the imposition of its own culture on the minority peoples," even though the "imposition" was "mild" and "semiconscious." "The foreign cultures," he asserted, "have not been melted down or run together, made into some homogeneous 'Americanism,' but have remained distinct but cooperating to the greater glory and benefit, not only to themselves but of all the native 'Americanism' around them." As if in reply to the anti-Semites, Bourne said that the Jews who were "dangerous" to the country were not those proud of their past and "venerable culture" but rather the ones who had "lost the Jewish fire and become a mere elementary, grasping animal." The immigrant groups, Bourne affirmed, were "threads of living and potent cultures, blindly stirring to weave themselves into a novel world international nation, the first the world has seen.... America is coming to be, not a nationality, but a trans-nationality."[17] Today the strong movement toward ethnic pluralism, reinforced by events like the creation of the State of Israel and the upsurge of Black, Hispanic, and Indian assertions of nationality rights, confirms the critique of the melting pot by the early Jewish critics and by Kallen and Bourne.

Later in 1916 Bourne applied his views specifically to Jews in the *Menorah Journal*. In "The Jews and Trans-National America," he acknowledged Kallen's leadership. Although he was not at home with much of the material in this essay, his statement of the two opposing theories is succinct:

two ideals of American nationalism.... One is that of the traditional melting-pot, the other is that of a co-operation of cultures.... The idealism of the melting-pot would assimilate all Europeans, as they are received into the American social and economic scheme, to a very definite type, that of the prevailing Anglo-Saxon.... What the Anglicized American prophets of the melting-pot really mean shall happen to the immigrant is that he shall acquire, along with the new common English language, the whole stock of English political and social ideals.... The effect of the melting-pot ideal is...to obliterate the distinctive racial and cultural qualities, and work the American population into a colorless, tasteless, homogeneous mass.[18]

The case for full assimilation, that is, obliteration of Jewish ethnicity of American Jews was set forth in Mary Antin's *The Promised Land* (1912), the classical account of this process. So pervasive was the interest in the question that her book was the first by an American Jew to become a best seller. How complete the journey to assimilation was in her case is implied in an observation by an acute contemporary Jewish woman. Visiting Mary Antin's home and seeing Mary Antin's child, she asked if the child understood any Yiddish. Mary Antin "seemed shocked that I should intimate such a thing. 'Oh! no—not a word!' "[19] She was the ideal Jewish immigrant for the era of Americanization, and the popularity of her book, as is so often the case, signified that her work exemplified at high tide an idea that has since receded. About half the book recounts life in her native Polotzk in the Russian Pale of Settlement. She came to this country in 1893 at the age of twelve and settled in Boston. An obviously bright child, eager for education, she was befriended by New Englanders of old families, Barrett Wendell among them, and received a thorough education. Her faith in and devotion to Americanization and assimilation are totally uncritical, though she's fully aware of the passion for education among Jews. But she has no conception of a possibly viable Jewish cultural existence alongside the American.

She sees the problem in terms of the conflict of generations, "in every immigrant household where the first generation clings to the traditions of the Old World, while the second generation leads the life of the New." This experience was common enough, as the novels of the period amply demonstrate. "This sad process of disintegration of home life may be observed in about any immigrant family of our class and with our tradition and aspirations. It is part of the process of Americanization, an upheaval preceding the state of repose. It is a cross that the first and second generations must bear, an involuntary sacrifice for the sake of future generations."[20] The "repose" she contemplates is total assimilation. Randolph Bourne appropriately commented that Mary Antin was right to see the foreign-born "as the people who missed the Mayflower and came over in the first boat they could find." What she does not remember, he adds, is that they did come in ships named *Maiblume, Fleur de Mai, Fior di Maggio, Majblomist*.[21]

This clash of ethnicities was as much at the core of the social life of Jews of the mass immigration as was their struggle to make a living. So basic, ubiquitous, and all-absorbing were these problems, so essential were they to the texture of Jewish immigrant lives, that it is not surprising to find them also becoming the primary themes in many novels by and about Jews in the first few decades of the century. The earlier German-Jewish and Sephardic immigrations had been much smaller and produced few writers, almost none of consequence, if we except Emma Lazarus. This is not to say that Jews did not publish fiction in these early years of the century. A bibliography of "The Jew in American Fiction" printed in 1906 in *The American Hebrew*, a journal dominated by the German Jews, included the names of some eighteen American-Jewish authors who had published fiction between 1900 and 1906.[22] Some of these had begun to write in the 1890s, and most were probably of German-Jewish origin. Aside from Abraham Cahan, few of the immigrant generations were yet writing in English. Time had to elapse before those brought here as children could learn American life and language well enough to write fiction.

In a fuller, more professional bibliography ten years later some forty-one American-Jewish writers are named who had published fiction between 1900 and 1916, many of them still of German-Jewish origin. In addition, a number of non-Jewish writers included Jewish characters in their fiction.[23] Dominating all these works, aside from religious, that is, biblical or Christological stories and historical novels—and even these betray signs of attitudes toward contemporary Jews—were themes of acculturation and labor struggles.

The early fiction of acculturation generally opened with the travails of Jews under Tsarist persecution in primitive *shtetl* living conditions. Motives for emigration are presented—escape from political police, flight from persecution, or simply aspiration for a better life, which the stories about the "Golden Land" promised. The plots follow the struggles of the first generation to claw themselves out of poverty and, in some cases, to rise in affluence. The earliest novels of the century are of so little literary value as to be negligible, except for their interest as social documentation. One of the earliest, *Children of the Light* (1903) by Bruno Lessing (pen name of Rudolph Edgar Block) is a collection of short stories about ghetto life. Selig Brudno's *The Fugitive: Being Memoirs of a Wanderer in Search of a Home* (1904) is a florid and melodramatic account in which the author takes the reader through virtually every problem facing the Jew in both Europe and in America. His "wandering" is geographical and spiritual, personal, religious, and political. The central character runs the gamut of ordeals, youth rebellion against Orthodoxy, pogroms, a ritual murder case, radicalism, intermarriage, emigration, the sweatshop (but no unions or strikes), struggle for education, antagonism between German and Eastern Jews, and Christian missionary activities. The novel winds mechanically through coincidence and is short on motivation.

Unusual for this early period—or any period until much later in the century—is Herman Bernstein's defense of Orthodoxy, not easily then compatible with acculturation, in *Contrite Hearts* (1915). Born in Russia in 1876, Bernstein immigrated in 1893 and became a journalist. He founded and edited the Yiddish daily *The Day* in 1914 and was editor of *The American Hebrew* from 1915 to 1919. In his story two sisters are followed to the United States by their lovers, one an apostate, a violinist, the other a nihilist. The young women undergo a life-draining existence with their pagan, irresponsible lovers, who soon abandon them. But the sisters are saved by the immigration of their two rejected, but still devoted, Orthodox suitors, are reunited with them, marry, and live happily ever after. The novel is exceptional in its obscurantist ideas.

The acculturation novel of John Cournos, *The Mask* (1919), deals with an emancipated Russian family. The style is self-conscious, pseudo-sophisticated, and pretentious in its symbolism of "the mask," the outward manner of an individual, which conceals a turbulent interior. Its main characters are a boy growing up in Philadelphia and his father, who squanders the family resources in futile, frustrating efforts at invention. The boy encounters prejudice. Although the family is "emancipated," they cling to their Jewishness, which they are, indeed, not allowed to forget by their neighbors. Cournos went on to become a well-known writer, was later converted to Christianity, and in 1938 urged his fellow Jews to acknowledge Jesus and be baptized.

The complete absence of any East European women among fiction writers in these decades is probably a consequence of the domestic position of women in the Orthodox culture, which was not conducive to their creative or intellectual development. The first woman author of the East European immigration, so far as I am aware (except for Mary Antin, who was a non-fiction writer), was Anzia Yezierska, who began to publish fiction in 1905. On the other hand, women of the Western European immigration did produce story writers. At the end of the century there were at least two, Adelina Cohnfelt Lust and Emma Wolf. Two more, much better known, emerged in the 1910s: Fannie Hurst, a third-generation German Jew, and Edna Ferber, second-generation. Both were middle class, and their early stories told of aspirations toward the middle class. In Fannie Hurst's collection of short stories, *Just Around the Corner* (1914), three stories are set in a petty bourgeois Jewish milieu with undisguised striving for gentility and small business success. They represent the second stage of acculturation, the movement out of the ghetto. Her 1919 volume of short stories, the highly successful *Humoresque,* carries the process forward. The German-Jewish aspirants are now in a second generation of successful business; Jewishness is taken for granted as an accepted part of life together with American identity. Awareness of anti-Semitism is totally absent, with a strong suggestion of a complacent *alrightnik* attitude. The title story exemplifies clichés of artistic aspiration in the third generation: the son becomes a world-famous violinist who patriotically enlists in the army at the outbreak of World War I. Another story, "Heads," follows the progress of a poor Jewish worker to affluence as a movie tycoon, while his thoughtless daughter is persuaded to postpone her marriage to an empty-headed movie star until she returns from Europe, and the parents see her off on the ill-fated *Lusitania.*

Edna Ferber was far more popular and versatile than Fannie Hurst. While the detective story writer E. Phillips Oppenheim was in 1920 the first American Jew to achieve a fiction best seller, *The Great Impersonation* (if one does not count Bret Harte, one-quarter Jewish, with his best-selling *Luck of Roaring Camp* in 1870–1871). Edna Ferber's serious novel *So Big* became a best seller in 1924, and she was often on the list thereafter. In 1925 her *So Big* made her the first Jewish writer to receive a Pulitzer Prize. She also collaborated on successful plays with George S. Kaufman and a few others. She had been born in 1887 in the Middle West of a Hungarian father and a third-generation German-Jewish mother, the dominant force in her non-religious family. In her early years her family owned a store in Ottumwa, Iowa, where she was subjected to anti-Semitic taunts until, after five years, her family could endure no more and moved to Appleton, Wisconsin, where they established another store. Edna's father's poor health compelled her competent mother to manage the store. On completing high school Edna Ferber became a reporter on an Appleton daily paper, and after her father's death, when she was twenty-four, she moved on to Chicago, more newspaper work, and finally fiction writing.

"All my life," she wrote in her autobiography, "I have been inordinately proud of being a Jew, . . . something to wear with becoming modesty."[24] She is reputed never to have allowed an anti-Semitic slur to pass without response. Vehemently anti-Zionist, even after the founding of the State of Israel, she returned from a visit there with an unfavorable impression—she thought it "a kind of Jewish Texas." She noted in her journal her growing "suspicion that the Jew himself is responsible" for his persecution, and that he "expects" and "even invites it."[25]

However, her sense of Jewish identity was not expressed in her fiction, for only her second novel, *Fanny Herself* (1917), is concerned with Jewish characters. This novel has added interest today for its assertion of female independence. The story is in part autobiographical: it traces the growing up of a Jewish girl in the Middle West and her mother's able management of the family store. In the story, after the mother's death (Ferber's actual mother survived), her daughter gives promise of carrying the store on successfully, but decides to launch her own business in Chicago. The story thus projects two independent women, her mother and herself, who succeeded in careers then unusual for women. The milieu of the novel is Jewish, with its problems of coexistence with Gentile children (mild anti-Semitism is encountered), and a description of a Yom Kippur service. When Fanny applies for a job in a mail order house in Chicago, she hopes to evade discrimination by concealing her Jewish origin, but the personnel manager is not deceived. "You've decided to lop off the excrescences, eh?" In Chicago she renews her friendship with her non-Jewish schoolmate, Clarence Heyl. There she also develops her talent for drawing as she wanders over the city sketching, and for catching the feeling of deep trouble and sorrow in city folk. When she shows her sketches to Heyl, he tells her, "It's in your blood. It's the Jew in you." Of her drawings of the Chicago ghetto he says, "It took a thousand years of suffering and persecution and faith to stamp that look in his face, and it took a thousand years to breed in you the genius to see it and put it down on paper."[26] In the end she quits business, marries Heyl, and turns to art.

With this novel Ferber ended her fictional treatment of Jews, and, except for the casual inclusion of Jewish characters in a few plays, did not return to them until her autobiographies. Her first autobiography, *A Peculiar Treasure* (1939), was dedicated "To Adolf Hitler, who made of me a better Jew and a more understanding and tolerant human being, as he has of millions of other Jews, this books is dedicated in loathing and contempt."[27]

The classic acculturation novel, the finest of the genre in English, and a permanent contribution to American Literature is Abraham Cahan's *The Rise of David Levinsky* (1917). (I have devoted a long chapter in my *Image of the Jew in American Literature* [pp. 485–524] to a discussion of all of Cahan's fiction in English, and especially of *David Levinsky*. See also the perceptive study of Cahan's fiction in both English and Yiddish, and its relation to Cahan's life and society in Jules Chametzky's *From the Ghetto*.) In its original, shorter version, the novel first appeared serially in *McClure's Magazine* in 1912–1913. Cahan richly documents many aspects of life on the Lower East Side as he spins out the story of how a penniless young immigrant developed from a shopworker to affluence as a garment manufacturer. John Higham calls the book "the unrivalled record of a great historical experience," that is, the acculturation of a large part of the Jewish segment of the mass immigration, and particularly the part they played in the rationalization of the mass production garment industry. Higham adds that the story is "among the best novels of American business . . . [and] a critically important chapter in American social history."[28]

With clarity Cahan demonstrates how ownership of garment shops passed from German Jews to Russian Jews of the mass immigration. In the 1880s and early 1890s, Cahan wrote, "the American cloak business, hitherto in control of German Jews . . . was now beginning to pass into the hands of their Russian co-religionists. . . . If the average American woman is today dressed infinitely better than she was a quarter of a century ago, and if she is now easily the best-dressed average woman in the world, the fact is due, in large measure, to the change I refer to." Cahan has Levinsky explain to a gentile businessman how this happened: "the Russian cloak-manufacturer operated on a basis of much lower profits and figured down expenses to a point never dreamed of before: . . . the German-American cloak-manufacturer was primarily a merchant, not a tailor; . . . he was compelled to leave things to his designer and a foreman, whereas the Russian was a tailor or a cloak operator himself, and was, therefore, able to economize in ways that never occurred to the heads of the old houses."[29] This process is worked out in the novel with clarifying fulness and detail.

At the same time Cahan deeply rendered the several phases of immigrant cultural and religious life. The immigrant's path to financial success, pursued in the manner of the business entrepreneur without moral scruple, finally ends in a poverty of human relationships. A conflict of values is opened up by the opportunity which the new country offers to pursue a life of integrity on the one hand, or capitulation to seduction by the reigning American Bitch Goddess, Success. The conflict is announced in the first paragraph:

I was born and reared in the lowest depths of poverty and I arrived in America in 1885—with four cents in my pocket. I am now worth more than two million dollars and recognized as one of the two or three leading men in the cloak-and-suit trade in the United States. And yet when I take a look at my inner identity it impresses me as being precisely the same as it was thirty or forty years ago. My present station, power, the amount of worldly happiness at my command, and the rest of it, seem to be devoid of significance.[30]

At the end, now that he has accompanied the reader through the experiences leading to his "success," Levinsky takes stock of his life. "I am lonely"; he has failed in love and friendship. "There are cases," he says, to himself, "when success is a tragedy." For in the process he has frustrated his real nature. "I think," he ruminates,

that I was born for a life of intellectual interest. . . . I think that I should be much happier as a scientist or writer, perhaps, I should then be in my natural element. . . . I have helped build up one of the great industries of the United States, and thus something to be proud of. But I should really like to change places with the Russian Jew, a former Talmud student like myself, who is the greatest physiologist in the New World, or the Russian Jew who holds the foremost place among American song-writers . . . David, the poor lad swinging over a Talmud volume at the Preacher's Synagogue, seems to have more in common with my inner identity than David Levinsky, the well-known cloak manufacturer.[31]

Thus, in terms of the conflicts aroused in Levinsky's struggle within himself does Cahan set forth the qualities and tribulations of life on the old East Side, the conflicts within the sensitive Jew on the way to acculturation. At the same time, as Isaac Rosenfeld showed in his famous essay, "America Land of the Sad Millionaire," originally published in *Commentary* (Vol. 14) in 1954, the novel is no less American than Jewish as the story of an American business success in which the businessman ends in disillusionment, loneliness, and a sense of spiritual failure, not unlike Sinclair Lewis' *Babbitt*.

ECHOES OF THE TIME

Beginning with the new century, Jewish writers existed at the periphery of the nation's literary scene. As the century advanced, they participated more and more actively in literary life. But this process was not accompanied by universal social or personal acceptance of the Jew. Some non-Jewish writers were not immune to prevailing prejudices that other non-Jewish writers consciously resisted. In their fiction the latter exposed and condemned anti-Semitism, decisively if not implicitly. In order, then, to achieve a comprehensive picture of the status of the Jew in our literature in those years it is not enough to study how the Jewish writer regarded his own Jewishness, or how he treated Jewish characters. One must also look at the way in which non-Jewish writers depicted the Jew and met the challenge of anti-Semitism. And we find that the response varied widely.

Anti-Semitism is an apparently simple term which, on further scrutiny, reveals considerable complexity. It turns out to be grab-bag that embraces many forms and degrees of intensity and overtness from latent or mild dislike of Jews as a whole to hatred. Over the centuries it has accumulated a variety of religious, economic, and social rationales, and it pervades the consciousness of the non-Jew in Western society. In individuals it is at least latent, deposited and transmitted by folk belief in Jewish responsibility for the crucifixion and by the ensuing images of the Shylock stereotype that lie quiescent until awakened during crisis situations; it largely accounts for social and economic discrimination, for hostile feeling verbally expressed, and finally for the ultimate, total expression of hatred in genocide. In any given individual it may be virtually absent, suppressed, repressed, or expressed and overt. It is essential to note that a preconceived conception of the Jew is entertained irrespective of the individual Jewish character; invidious traits are often attached to this preconceived notion and are indiscriminately applied to individual Jews. The reduction of the individual to a stereotype is not of course limited to the Jew; the Irish or the Italians or the Slavs were also subjected to this indignity and prejudiced treatment, as are, most severely, Blacks and Hispanics. To the anti-Semite the Jew is not an individual but a generalized type, usually regarded unfavorably. Because anti-Semitism occurs in such a range and variety of forms from the residual, largely innocuous, to the vicious and murderous, one must not lose sight of the variety of possible attitudes. Where any instance belongs within this range can be ascertained not only by its expressed form but also by its context.

Anti-Semitism can be religious (Jew as Christ-killer), economic (Jew as banker, usurer, money-obsessed), social (Jew as social inferior, "pushy," vulgar, therefore excluded from personal contact), racist (Jews as an inferior "race"), ideological (Jew regarded as subversive or revolutionary), or cultural (or as undermining the moral and structural fiber of civilization). It can be an inchoate feeling, a mindless repetition of anti-Jewish verbal clichés and locutions, which we might call "folk anti-Semitism," or it may be an articulated system of ideas that rationalizes the particular variety of anti-Semitism entertained. Nor is an anti-Semite restricted to any single variety of the above types. Very often one resorts to several contradictory types at once (an extreme example is the Bolshevik-Capitalist). What all have in common, what is inexorably present in all of them, is derogation of "the Jew," ignoring the individual in the Jew. Added to these potentialities were the racist and nativistic attitudes generated by American history.

From the 1870s into the 1890s anti-Semitism in the United States was building up to a level never before experienced in this country. This development coincided with the flow of mass immigration, and the connection was not fortuitous. The Anglo-Saxon patriciate was beginning to feel control of the country's political, economic, and social life slipping to foreigners; desperately bad labor conditions and pitifully low wages generated labor unrest; and depressions in 1873 and 1893 especially caused economic dislocation. The country was moving from an agrarian to a predominantly industrial society; it was gripped in chauvinism stimulated by the Spanish-American War and imperialist successes. Race theories were flourishing in this country; the effect of such views in Europe was also being felt here.

Anti-foreign feeling was reinforced by the mass immigration, and the Jews were among those targeted for hostility. As John Higham observed, "Anti-Semitism has ebbed and flowed on an international level," and at this time "developments ... repeatedly inflamed or dampened anti-Semitism on both sides of the Atlantic at roughly the same time."[32]

Signs of the new stage became manifest in the late 1870s. By this time a number of the German-Jewish immigrants of the mid-century immigration had become successful businessmen or bankers, and some wielded considerable financial influence. Many of them took on the traits of the nouveau riche displaying ostentatious and tasteless opulence, and some aspired to recognition of their class status by their non-Jewish peers. The established non-Jewish middle and upper middle classes tended to resist such attempts of Jews to associate socially in resorts and social clubs. The critical event which brought wide public notice to this attempt to exclude Jews from resorts and social clubs was the famous case of the German-Jewish banker Joseph Seligman. In 1877 he was turned away from a Saratoga Springs resort hotel.

The pattern of social discrimination had advanced so far by 1881 that Nina Morais, of an old Sephardic family, could set it forth completely in the *North American Review* in an article, "Jewish Ostracism in America." "In the popular mind," she wrote, "the Jew is never judged as an individual, but as a specimen of a whole race whose members are identically of the same kind." She then describes the features of the imputed "kind": he is "an objectionable character," conducts trade with "shrewdness" and "questionable dealings," and wears "large diamonds and flashy clothes." His language is "execrable"; he has no regard for "the proprieties and amenities of cultured life"; his conversation "rings upon the keynote of the dollar"; his "literature" is market quotations; he spends with "ostentation"; and he has "no higher sympathies." She does not altogether absolve the Jew of this reputation. Yes, she adds, "the body of rich Jews in America fails to display the culture that wealth demands," and "the Hebrew mounted too rapidly to the top of the commercial ladder." But not all Jews are like this, she stresses, yet "American Christianity" has been inculcated from the nursery with the notion that the Jew is a "God-murderer" and even the cultured see "the type of the Hebraic spirit in the usurer." She finally urges upon America that "there lie in the Jewish blood the mental and moral possibilities which give rise to prophets and thinkers."[33] She might have added, creative artists.

Ten years after Morais' article the same journal published an article by an aristocrat, Professor Goldwin Smith, "New Light on the Jewish Question," in which he blamed Tsarist persecution of the Jews on the Jews themselves because they are a "parasitic race" who "insert themselves for the purpose of gain into the homes of other nations." Like his fellow patricians he deplored the growing power of the lower economic orders, of labor, and of socialism, as well as of the Jews. By 1905 he was writing that if anti-Semitism "means simply fear of political, social, and financial influence, without the slightest shadow of religious antipathy," he readily granted that the term could be applied to him. It is interesting that his 1891 article was refuted editorially by the *Journal of the Knights of Labor*. "Unfortunately," said the editorial, "the laws of every civilized country, made and enforced by Christians, permit and encourage usury, profit mongering, land monopoly, and every form of injustice under which the working masses are exploited for the benefit of the privileged classes, only a small proportion of whom belong to the Hebrew race."[34].

The late nineteenth- and early twentieth-century mind was insensitive to the crude and open Jew-baiting that not only appeared in the press, as in the Smith article, but also in what passed for "humor" in such popular humor magazines as *Life* and *Puck*. Most generally these magazines exploited the economic stereotype of money-obsessed Jew. A few examples will suffice. The current canard of the Jew as arsonist for insurance money, as well as uneducated, is fuel for jokes. In 1895 *Life* ran a cartoon showing an obviously Jewish figure reading an oculist's chart. The oculist asks him to read the lines, and the Jew replies, "I can see noddings but the one at the bottom," which is, not surprisingly, simply a dollar sign. In a *Puck* cartoon for 1908, "At the Pawnbrokers Ball," a "Miss Sparkelstein" says, "It is a very striking gostume, Misder," to which Mr. Loanitski replies, "Dis suit vos a little idea of my own. I represent Ready Money."[35]

The denigrating stereotype was prevalent in fiction as well, and thoughtful Jews were not amused. In *The American Hebrew* in 1892, the Rev. Rudolph Grossman complained in "The Jew in Novels" that "It has been the fate of the Jew to be misunderstood and misrepresented, not only in the world of reality, but in the world of literature as well. . . . So long as playwrights and authors will insist on inserting falsities, misrepresentations and calumnies of the Jew in their portrayal of his life and character, so long will it be impossible to eradicate the deep-seated prejudices that rear a wall of separation between the Jew and the Gentile world."[36] And a decade later, Bernard G. Richards, a sophisticated Jewish publicist, noted the prevalence of anti-Semitism in the current media. "We have read about him [the Jew]," he wrote, "have seen him delineated in popular works of fiction, have observed him caricatured in various publications, have beheld him portrayed on the vaudeville stage."[37]

In the early decades of the twentieth century the unfavorable image of the Jew was conveyed by non-Jewish fiction writers, and some of these were among the leading writers of the time. The economic stereotype, with a tincture of racism, was manifested in Frank Norris; patrician anti-Semitism in Owen Wister and Edith Wharton; and racism in Jack London. Besides Mark Twain and William Dean Howells, there were also a number of unprejudiced minor writers who even defended the Jews, as in the instances of O. Henry, Thomas Nelson Page, and Dorothy Canfield Fisher.

Frank Norris quite explicitly advanced a racist view of man as I showed in my earlier volume (*Image*, pp. 391–95). There I also demonstrated how his Zerkow, a Jewish character in *McTeague* (1899), was one of the ugliest caricatures of the Jew in all of American literature. In *The Octopus* (1901), Norris offers a repellent example of the economic stereotype, the money-obsessed Jew, in S. Behrman, who, though nowhere mentioned as a Jew, plainly exhibits the stigmata of the stereotype. In his study of the novel Robert Forrey has shown that Behrman is described with the characteristics of the type, the porcine Jew made familiar in current cartoons of the Jewish banker.[38]

Behrman is an unofficial agent for the rapacious railroads in their western land foreclosures and thus the visible symbol of the railroad tycoons' ruthless repossession of farms. As Behrman gloatingly watches an immense shipment of wheat being loaded, he accidentally falls into it and is smothered to death. The hatred of the railroads because of their responsibility for the rape of farmland and cattle ranches is deflected to Behrman, the Jew, classic scapegoat for economic ills. The Jew as the visible executor for predatory superiors was thus a diversion from the real source of oppression. The Jew played a similar role in contemporary Tsarist Russia where the peasants were incited to make pogroms because the Jewish agents for the landowners were as rent collectors visible and immediate targets of oppressed peasants. Apologetic articles appeared in the United States, like that by Goldwin Smith mentioned earlier, blaming the Jews for anti-Semitic outbursts and justifying the peasants' venting their wrath on the Jews.

Patrician anti-Semitism is illustrated in *Philosophy Four* (1901), a widely read novella by the popular novelist Owen Wister, author of *The Virginian*. A poor, aspiring Jewish Harvard student Maironi is made the object of ridicule by both the author and his two Harvard upper-class student playboys, carefree and bibulous. The two engage Maironi, who is working his way through Harvard, to tutor them in philosophy for the approaching examination, since they have neglected their studies for the pleasures of drink. Wister cannot resist alluding to the current insurance-arsonist stereotype in a strained allusion. When the playboys ask Maironi to lend them his notes, he refuses for fear, he says, that the notes might be destroyed in a fire. "At this racial suggestion," Wister observes, "both boys made the room joyous with mirth." The boys discuss their feeling about Maironi. He is not, they think, motivated by love of knowledge but by love of himself, and he uses this knowledge to "show that self off." They reassure themselves that this feeling about Maironi does not mean they do not love poor college boys, since not all poor boys are like him. For Maironi's "young days have been dedicated to getting the better of his neighbor because otherwise his neighbor would get the better of him."[39] It turns out that these easy-going aristocrats get 86 and 90 in their examination while the alien Jew Maironi gets a mere 75. And twenty years later, Wister adds, they are successful in business and finance while Maironi scratches away as the author of a work on a minor Renaissance poet and is a book reviewer for the *Evening Post*.

A more serious example of patrician anti-Semitism is Edith Wharton's portrait of Simon Rosedale, modeled on August Belmont, in her masterpiece, *The House of Mirth* (1905). Rosedale is dominated by two aims, money making, for which he has great talent, and his determination to climb to the top of the social ladder. Inasmuch as these objectives also figured in the life of the model, a case might be made against anti-Semitism on the ground that these invidious traits had their counterpart in actuality. The anti-Semitism consists rather in the author's identification of Rosedale's character traits with his "race" and "blood," as well as the palpable contempt with which she treats him. "In appearance," she writes, "he was a plump rosy man of *the Jewish type*"; "he has his *race's* accuracy in the appraisal of values"; he has "that mixture of artistic sensibility and business astuteness which characterized his *race*." To the impoverished aristocrat Lily Bart, whom Rosedale is courting because he can offer her an affluent life in exchange for her easing his social acceptance by the aristocracy, he is repellent. "Sim Rosedale! the *name,* made more odious by its diminutive, obtruded itself in Lily's thoughts like a leer." Wharton clearly shares her heroine's revulsion from the Jew in Rosedale. At a later stage of Rosedale's social climbing, after he had made a killing in the market and bought a house on Fifth Avenue from a victim of the market crash, "Rosedale knew he should have to go slowly, and the *instincts of his race* fitted him to suffer rebuffs and put up with delays." When Rosedale courts Lily, he tells her crudely, "I've got the money and what I want is the woman—and I mean to have her too." Late in the novel, when Lily is driven by a desperate need of money, she holds out some hope of yielding to him, whereupon he is "a little flushed with his unhoped for success, and disciplined by the *traditions of his blood* to accept what was conceded, without undue haste to press for more"[40] (all emphases added). Throughout the novel the reader is never for an instant allowed to forget that Rosedale is a Jew and therefore a strangely repugnant object ipso facto to be held in contempt.

Racist anti-Semitism can be detected in that curiously mixed figure, Jack London. According to his racist evolutionism the "weaker races" are condemned to be dominated by the stronger. He returned from his reporting of the Russo-Japanese War in Manchuria to warn of "The Yellow Peril" from the Japanese. They imitated the material achievements of the West but were immune from its spiritual nature, from "our soul stuff."[41] The Far East, that is, China, he said, "is a menace to the Western World."[42] He clung to an impossible mixture of racist evolutionism and revolutionary socialism.

This dualism emerges in *Martin Eden* (1914), in which the Jewish people are subsumed under the inferior races. At a socialist meeting

a clever Jew won Martin's admiration at the same time that he aroused his antagonism. The man's stooped and narrow shoulders and weazened chest proclaimed him the true child of the crowded ghetto, and strong in Martin was the agelong struggle of the feeble, wretched slaves against the lordly handful of men who had ruled them and would rule over them to the end of time. To Martin this withered wisp of a creature was a symbol...of the whole miserable mass of weaklings and inefficients who perished according to biological law in the ragged confines of life. They were the unfit.

London never shook off his association of the "weak races" with the "ghetto." After he had resigned from the Socialist party, because it was too "refined, quietistic," he remarked that he still believed in public ownership of the means of production, but, "Mention confiscation in the ghetto of New York and the leaders will throw up their hands in holy horror"—as if the socialist Jews were of a single, quietistic persuasion.[43]

It would be a disservice to American letters to assume that all non-Jewish authors of the period were unfriendly to the Jews. The surviving major writers, Mark Twain and William D. Howells, as I showed in my earlier volume, were friendly to the Jews, and Howells helped Abraham Cahan develop as a writer of English fiction. Several minor writers also aligned themselves against the current anti-Semitism. No prejudice is apparent in the eight Jewish characters in O. Henry's short stories. These are ordinary people like his others: the Jewish store clerk, pawnbroker, second-hand dealer, women's garment buyer, policeman, jeweler. Though the range is limited—as it still was for Jews in those early days of the mass immigration—O. Henry treats these characters with the same quiet sympathy as his non-Jewish characters. One story, "The Door of Unrest," is an ingenious variation of the Wandering Jew legend.

The Virginian novelist Thomas Nelson Page militantly defended the Jew in a "philo-Semitic" vein in his *John Marvel, Assistant* (1909). Page was a leading propagator of the false cavalier legend of the early South and of nostalgia for the slave South when, he thought, the slaves were on balance quite happy. Without modifying these views he moved into the reform and muckraking tendency, of which this novel is an example. *Marvel* contains a leading Jewish character who is not only favorably seen but is even idealized and who also felt kindness and contempt for the Blacks in accord with white mores of the period.

At a liberal arts college Leo Wolffert, son of a rich merchant, rooms with John Marvel after Wolffert's previous roommate had fled when Wolffert "proclaimed himself a Jew." The student body subjects Wolffert "to a species of persecution which only the young Anglo-Saxon, the most brutal of animals, would have devised." Fellow students joke about "this incongruous pairing . . . of the light haired, moon-faced, slow-witted Anglo-Saxon, and the dark, keen Jew with his intellectual face and deep-burning eyes in which glared the misery and mystery of the ages." There are frequent discussions about the Jews throughout the novel. Wolffert delivers a "burning defense" of the Jews: "they have civilized the world, and what have they gotten from it but brutal barbarism. They gave you your laws and your literature, your morality and your religion—even your Christ; and you have violated every law human and divine in their oppression," and more. Wolffert becomes a writer-champion of the poor in the city (New York City?) and is reviled as a Jew as well as a socialist and anarchist. He becomes associated in this work with the wealthy girl, Eleanor Leigh, and Marvel, now a preacher. They find Wolffert "different from the typical Jew," but question if there is a typical Jew. There are frequent, not very enlightening, discussions of socialism, with which they charge Wolffert. Eleanor endows him with her highest praise—he is a Christian: "I wish I were only half as good a one. I do not care what he calls himself, he is!"[44]

All become involved in a streetcar strike that turns violent, with responsibility laid on the strikers, and an anti-union tone enters the author's exposition. Current racist thinking is echoed by a visiting old classmate. Among the strikers, he says, he "could not descry one Saxon countenance or even one Teuton. They were all dark, sallow, dingy, and sombre. . . . Could this . . . be the element we are importing? and what effect would this strange confluence have on the current of our life in the future?" Wolffert defends the strikers, who are apparently Jewish, but admitting that "the Jew is often an element of ignorance and superstition, though he is not alone in this," and the second generation will be "useful American citizens." The strike climaxes in a riot—blamed on the strikers—and Wolffert is killed while trying to restrain the rioters. His friend then sees him as "one of the Prophets . . . inspired by a passion for his own people to extend his ministrations to all mankind . . . denying that he was a Christian, and yet dying a Christian death in the act of supplicating those who slew him. . . . He opened my eyes." His death is also a convenient solution to the problem of intermarriage, for Wolffert had loved Eleanor, but never proposed "because I am a Jew!...I could not allow myself—I could never—never allow myself—It is impossible—for me."[45]

The Vermont novelist Dorothy Canfield Fisher had a more relaxed attitude toward Jews than most. Her acceptance of Jews is apparent throughout her career. She wrote in an early sketch how, while a student at the Sorbonne, she attended the lectures of Professor Paul Meyer, who had testified as a handwriting expert at the second trial of Dreyfus. Meyer, she writes, was thereafter "attacked in the streets, insulted, boycotted, his classes filled with jeering young men who yelled him down when he tried to speak." In class she admired his stoical response to one Jew-baiter—he was "not scornful, not actively courageous, not resentful, not defiant; rather the quiet, unexcited, waiting look of a man in ordinary talk who waits to go on with what he has to say until a pounding truck of iron rails has time to pass the windows."[46]

Jews appear in several of her short stories. In "The Artist" (1915) she depicts a Jewish art dealer with dignity and respect, unlike those presented with invidious overtones in the writing of Henry Adams and Henry James. In another story, "The City of Refuge" (1916), she reveals a rare sensitivity toward the immigrant by her description of a Jewish actor famous for his dignified rendering of the immigrant, in contrast to the ridicule and "humor" to which the immigrant is usually subjected. This actor, she wrote through a playwright in the story, "took that figure that has been treated jocularly, sentimentally, melodramatically, every cheap and obvious way our cheap and obvious dramatists could treat it, and he made a figure of such moving pathos and power that to see it was a revelation of one's own capacity for emotion."[47]

Many years later she returned to her resistance against anti-Semitism as it threatened in the small Vermont town of "Clifford" in the novel *Seasoned Timber* (1939). The basic theme is the corrupting power of money as in Mark Twain's "The Man That Corrupted Hadleyburg" and Durrenmatt's play *The Visit*—only in this case the outcome is different. The liberal principal of the local academy, T. C. Hulme, admits a musically talented Jewish boy from New York to the school despite the disapproval of a Wall Street trustee, Mr. Wheaton, who warns Hulme, "let in Jews...and the ghetto pushes in after him. We old Americans must stand solidly against the flood of them that is pouring in from Europe." Hulme is indignant at the bigotry of Wheaton with his "terrible and awful power for evil," with his "mountains of dollars from which he ruled people, institutions, human endeavors he was proud of not being able to understand," and adds, "*that* man to talk about the harm Jews do to his America."[48]

Wheaton offers the academy $1 million on condition that the name be changed to "Wheaton Preparatory School" and that no Jew be admitted, "Jew" being defined as a "person with any relative of Hebrew blood."

Controversy rocks the town. Acceptance or not is to be determined by the town's election of a school trustee whose vote will decide the issue. Hulme tells the town, "This isn't a question of Jews, or no Jews. It really hasn't anything to do with Jews, except that they happen to be the people Mr. Wheaton didn't like." At the town discussion meeting Hulme asserts that the million-dollar offer "is an attempt to bribe us to betray the principles on which our country was founded," and he threatens to resign if the offer is accepted.[49] The discussion in the town is hot, and sentiment for approval is associated with reactionary and backward views on other issues. The bribe is refused by a great majority. If only "Clifford, Vermont" were more representative of American towns than "Hadleyburg"!

SOCIALIST FICTION

Fiction of these early decades of the century touched more or less fully on the several basic problems facing the Jews. All Jews had in some manner to adjust to the necessity for acculturation. Anti-Semitism was an important formative influence, whether through direct impact or a pervasive sense of differentiation and lesser social eligibility. The necessity of earning a livelihood was of course primary. Since the overwhelming mass of immigrants came with little or no money, all activity had to be adjusted to the needs arising from this poverty. But this need did not exclude the urgency of the ethnic issues emerging from the process of acculturation and from anti-Semitism. Together with this ethnic factor, the relations of employee and employer loomed very large in the ghetto. In addition, then, to the ethnic there was also the basic class aspect to immigrant life.

The labor question differed in several important respects from that of acculturation and anti-Semitism. In the process of acculturation an *accommodation* had to be made to the host culture, at the least as much change in the manner of living as would facilitate and advance life in the new country. As for anti-Semitism, it had to be *resisted* if possible or at least its damage had to be minimized. After all, this was nothing new for Jews, and anti-Semitism in American society was in any case far less severe than the institutional reality they had faced in the old country. It was a disturbing intrusion in the process of acculturation and in some cases was a strong motivation for obliterating the original ethnic identity by total assimilation.

But the labor question involved a qualitatively different type of relationship to the society. Its aim was at the least to *modify* existing economic relations, to improve the workers' economic position on wages and working conditions. At the most, in its socialist or radical form, it aimed to *change* the basic economic structure. Anarchist and socialist politics in those decades were strong enough in the Jewish immigrant communities to make radical aims a power for the Establishment to reckon with. Indeed, so formidable was this element in the community that a literary genre of the radical novel, in terms of the labor and socialist movements, was developed during the first decades. Unfortunately no major works of literature emerged from this tendency before the 1930s.

As the pace of industrialization quickened after the Civil War, trade unionism continued to grow by fits and starts. With mass immigration exploitation of the rapidly multiplying foreign-born work force became more intense, and the labor movement gained strength. Jewish immigration was heavy from Eastern Europe. The inflow of about 200,000 in the 1880s was doubled in the 1890s, and, among these immigrants were revolutionaries fleeing from Tsarist persecution and police. Abraham Cahan was one of these, arriving in 1882 to evade Tsarist arrest. Many of these immigrant radicals became organizers for the Jewish trade unions that took form in the 1880s, and anarchists and socialists were numerous among their leaders. Although the Socialist Labor party advocated assimilation for the Jews, it learned that it could not reach these masses except through the Yiddish language, and was forced to give some attention to their special problems. A group of Yiddish-speaking Jewish socialists in 1887 formed the famous "Branch 8" of the party; its prime task was to organize the Yiddish-speaking Jews. One of its earliest activities was the foundation in 1888 of the United Hebrew Trades. Beginning with affiliation of eight unions which totaled 1,200 members, it had grown by 1890 to twenty-two unions with 6,000 members, and continued to increase and play an important role in Jewish trade union activity. The largest percentage by far were engaged in the garment industry—a survey conducted on the East Side in 1890 and reaching one-third of its Jews showed that 78 percent of the Jewish workers surveyed worked in the garment trade. Union leadership was to a large extent in the hands of socialists and anarchists, many of whom had received their baptism in radicalism in Tsarist Russia; they gave their unions a socialist coloration.

Nor did they limit their organizing to unions. Lacking in those days any but the most primitive social services, they tried to fill this need through fraternal organizations. They also created a considerable press and cultural groups. The *Jewish Daily Forward (Forverts),* which began publication in 1897, became after a few decades the largest Yiddish newspaper in the world, and each socialist or anarchist or Labor Zionist faction published its separate propaganda and theoretical journals. There was a flourishing Jewish culture in Yiddish with fiction, poetry, essays, scholarship, and an immensely popular theater, beloved of the mass Yiddish-speaking audience, with its gifted actors and dramatists, as Irving Howe has vividly presented in *The World of Our Fathers.* In short, there was created in the Yiddish-speaking ghetto in the first few decades of mass immigration what Arthur Liebman in *Jews and the Left* has called "a radical subculture," with its flowering of a literary, intellectual, and social life, which touched a large part of the immigrant population. So great was the radical influence that by 1914 the East Side elected to Congress the Socialist Meyer London by almost half the votes in a three-candidate field.

At first the union movement grew falteringly. It demanded a shorter work day, a rise in the pathetically low wages, and improvements in working conditions. But what success a union might have was only too often dissipated by the drastic weakening of their bargaining power during the frequent devastating economic depressions—in 1883, 1893, 1903, and 1907. The great International Ladies Garment Workers was founded in 1890, but the Amalgamated Clothing Workers had to wait until 1914, when the militant workers organized it as a breakaway union from the non-Jewish, anti-Socialist, reactionary-led United Garment Workers. The cap, hat, and millinery workers were also organized in these decades, as were the furriers. Organizations of Jewish workers were among the most advanced, active, and militant in the entire labor movement of the nation.

In the five years from 1909 to 1914 the Jewish unions really took wing, years often called the "heroic period." The crisis of 1907 had taken a terrible toll of employment and had depressed wages and worsened inhuman working conditions in the sweatshops of New York and other large cities. The leading attack of this labor offensive was mounted by young women—70 to 80 percent of them Jewish and 20 to 30 percent Italian—in the shirtwaist shops. Late in 1909 there was a general strike in the shirtwaist industry, which was called the Uprising of the 20,000. It was conducted by the young women with unabated, heroic militancy in the face of police violence and mass arrests at picketing sites. Their heroism aroused the city, including a number of wealthy patrician women who materially aided the strikers. The Women's Trade Union League, for example, helped the strike substantially by fund raising. After two and a half months the employers' front was broken and gains were made by the strikers. Their union had grown from about 100 in 1909 to about 10,000 by the time the strike ended in victory. The fire ignited by these young women swept through the immigrant Jewish communities in several parts of the country. The next year about 50,000 cloakmakers in New York and about 40,000 in Chicago went out on strike. In 1912 about 9,500 fur workers also struck and formed a national union. In 1911 a general strike of men's garment workers in New York was followed by the organization of the Amalgamated Clothing Workers. All these strikes and the gains they won gave inspiration to the entire American labor movement and fostered a period of socialist growth. Yiddish-speaking Socialists formed the Jewish Socialist Federation, which affiliated with the Socialist party a few years later. The United Hebrew Trades had grown from 69 unions with 65,000 members in 1909 to 104 unions with 250,000 workers in 1914.

Considering how large a part these labor struggles played in the lives of ordinary Jews on the East Side, it is no wonder that union and socialist movements made their way into fiction. Many intellectuals were radicals, as were many writers. So callous was the exploitation of the workers, so appalling were the working and living conditions, so compelling the heroism of common workers that these subjects won inclusion in fiction by gentile as well as by Jewish writers. Nor did the situation escape the attention of muckrakers and social reformers, most of them non-Jews, who were active in those decades, though virtually none was socialist. They were especially interested in describing and exposing the harsh living conditions in the ghetto. In a study of the writing on the ghetto, Rudolf Glanz observed, "The Jewish group was conceived by the muckrakers as a completely outsider group that still had to be integrated into the total picture of the country," and he added with heavy documentation that for these writers the Jewish ghetto became "the great social theme."[50] Upton Sinclair, who was a socialist, suggests something of the role played by radical Jews in the radical movement. In *The Jungle,* his searing exposé of the horrible working conditions in the Chicago stockyards and of the dangerously unsanitary processing of meat, he relates how the Polish protagonist is introduced to radicalism by one Ostrinski, a Polish-Jewish socialist. With the customary "delicacy" of the time, Sinclair does not mention the word "Jew." Instead, Ostrinski is "a member of a despised and persecuted race" who "lived in the Ghetto district" and was a "pants presser."[51] Jewish labor and socialist leaders were active not only among Jewish workers but in the general community. (Morris U. Schappes has observed that in the 1890s Jews in the largely non-Jewish labor locals were in leadership positions in various parts of the country, citing a number of examples from large and small cities.)[52]

What was emerging in the radical sector of American-Jewish life was a new Jew, and this called forth a change in the image of the Jew in literature. Already in 1892 the non-Jewish novelist and journalist, Edward King, had produced in *Joseph Zalmonah* a richly documented portrait of some of these new figures in American life (see my *Image,* pp. 479–84), in stark contrast to the prevailing stereotypes which had endured for centuries in the literatures of Europe and had come down in our own, with only occasional lapses into reality. In the radical fiction this new Jew was depicted in work whose theme was centered on the labor and socialist movements or on some radical criticism of society.

There is a certain symbolic significance to the fact that the first work in this new genre in the new century was by a Jewish writer, Isaac Kahn Friedman.[53] Friedman based his *By Bread Alone* (1901) on the Homestead steel strike of 1892. It was written from the viewpoint of the vague current notion of the "Cooperative Commonwealth" and vehemently opposed any use of violence. Friedman was born in Chicago in 1870 of a well-to-do German-Jewish family and, one must assume from his writing, was an assimilationist. Several Jews in his earlier fiction are treated no differently from the stereotyped Jews in the current popular fiction (see *Image,* p. 452).

In his short story, "Aaron Pavansky's Picture" (1896), the father Solomon Pavansky is a pawnbroker straight out of the stereotype: "His face was mean enough ordinarily, literally, as well as figuratively, without a redeeming feature—a harsh, hard, cunning, repulsive face, a face that made it useless for the owner to deny sordidness and avarice and tyranny, a face that bore the marks of thirty years of Russian persecution, and a face that bespoke a sullen waiting for vengeance."[54] In his radical novel the only significant Jew depicted is one Sophie Goldstein, an anarchist leader obviously modeled on Emma Goldman, though she is nowhere identified as a Jew except by name. As an implacable enemy of anarchism Friedman's portrait of Goldman is more nearly a caricature. She is identified as a Russian woman, and variously as conveying "a suggestion of cruelty, hardness, of fanaticism"; she "did all the good in her power for the sake of evil"; her harangues were an "appeal for blood and blood and vengeance.... The woman seemed transformed into a wild animal."[55] Friedman's proposal for achieving his ideal commonwealth was by influencing legislation through public office.

While Friedman's novel takes us into the heat of the labor conflict, Henry Berman's *The Worshippers* (1906) concerns what one might call "parlor radicalism" among pseudo-intellectual professional and artistic Jewish circles in Philadelphia. The novel has a certain Jewish cultural content, albeit on an elementary level, and includes a Yiddish poet as an important character. He is involved with a wealthy married middle-class Jewish woman who lives with him in New York while attempting to make a career as an actress. She fails, leaves her poet-lover, and returns to her husband in Philadelphia. Berman probably intended to compose a satire on the pseudo-intellectual, pretentious radicals whose socialism is only talk. They spurn Yiddish as a language that "cramps because of narrowness of vocabulary, and makes hideous with uncouthness of sound [sic]." Their knowledge of Yiddish seems as poor as that of English. "A poet in Yiddish," says one, is an "incongruity."[56] The extent to which the author shares the views of his characters is unclear, but in any case the novel is not good.

Other Jewish writers of the radical novel between 1900 and 1919 were better literary craftsmen. Walter B. Rideout has noted that six of the thirty-five authors he identified as writing radical novels in those years were Jewish.[57] In addition to Friedman and Berman, there were James Oppenheim, Elias Tobenkin, and Abraham Cahan who wrote about Jewish characters. Considering that the Jewish population in 1900 was about 1 million out of a total population of about 76 million and about 3 million out of 106 million in 1920, the percentage of Jewish writers in this genre is high. This number is consistent with the disproportion of radicals in the Jewish population. Of these writers the most important and best, from the general cultural as well as the literary point of view, was Abraham Cahan. In my view his *The Rise of David Levinsky* cannot be counted a radical novel in the strict sense, but is rather the richest of the acculturation novels. However, his much less known *The White Terror and the Red* (1905) is obviously radical. I have already discussed this novel in detail (see my *Image,* pp. 508–13). More than any other novel I know, it conveys with fullness and insight the life of intellectual and radical Jews in the Pale of Settlement in the 1880s, and is significant for our own radical history because many of the Jewish-American radicals of those years had fled Tsarist police and, after immigration to the United States, exerted influence on American-Jewish and general life. Though not so successful a novel as *Levinsky,* this earlier novel has been unduly neglected. Its wealth of documentation illuminates the lives of several types of Jewish intellectual: the bourgeois intellectual assimilationist, the brilliant medical student and erstwhile Talmudist turned revolutionary, the revolutionary become a Jewish nationalist after disillusionment because of insensitivity to anti-Semitism in the Russian populist movement.

The central female Jewish character, Clara Yavner, is among the distinctly new figures in radical American fiction and indeed in all American fiction. She is a member of the People's Will party. Her faith in her party is unshaken through all the consternation caused by that party's temporary belief that pogroms were a sign of a revolutionary mood among the peasant masses. Their intention was to join the peasants in the pogroms, so that they could persuade the peasants to deflect their fury from the Jews and turn it against their real enemy, the Tsarist regime. The populists were disillusioned when the peasants turned on them instead as "Jew-lovers." But Clara Yavner is of special interest because she anticipates the new place of the Jewish woman in radical fiction of the first few decades of the century—the courageous, effective, able Jewish woman labor organizer and socialist.

The immigrant novel of conversion to socialism can also be interpreted as a story of acculturation as instanced in Elias Tobenkin's *Witte Arrives* (1916). Immigrating as a child of seven, Emil Witte undergoes poverty and suffering to gain an education amid loving home relations. In time he becomes famous as a writer and marries into an old New England family. He has left Judaism behind but retains his Jewish awareness. This is contrasted with the attitude of his brother-in-law Alex Stein, who deliberately minimizes his Jewishness. The author's observation here is precisely descriptive of many young acculturated Jews of that decade. In Stein's "circle it was considered a sign of good breeding to have got away from the ancestral language no less than from the customs." But Witte's relations with his non-Jewish colleagues end at the door of social acceptance: "going back to college days the conviction had been forced upon him that the anti-social attitude which Christians were taking toward Jews in the old world had not entirely been overcome in the new. And friendship with a Gentile had best not be pushed too far." In newspaper days in Chicago he noticed Jews and non-Jews might be friends in the office, but "after office hours their ways parted," and newspapers made a "subtle distinction . . . between 'society news' and 'news of Jewish society.' " In the end, despite Emil's total assimilation of the American tradition in his writing, a rift grew up between him and his New England wife Barbara. "What stood between . . . was race," even though neither was especially religious.[58] Despite the intellectual harmony, his awareness of persecution of the Jews in other parts of the world seemed to separate him from her. Midway in his career, however, Emil meets his Uncle Simon, who had left his Talmudic studies to become an effective Bundist (Jewish Workers' Socialist party) and who has just escaped from Siberia. Simon completes Emil's education by inducting him to socialism. While this conversion is the thematic aim of the story, in its totality the story exemplifies one type of acculturation process, which at the end leaves Jewish identity intact while the protagonist has acquired socialist convictions to guide his life.

More nearly the type of man of letters is James Oppenheim, who was prominent in literary circles of his time as an editor as well as a poet and novelist. He was born in St. Louis in 1882 of German-Jewish parents, attended Columbia University for a few years, and became a social worker on the Jewish East Side. From 1905 to 1907 he was head of the Hebrew Technical School for Girls. Together with Waldo Frank and Paul Rosenfeld he helped found *The Seven Arts* in 1916, but the magazine soon had to close because the editors refused to support World War I.

Oppenheim's *Dr. Rast* (1909) portrays incidents in the life of a German-Jewish doctor practicing on the East Side among the Eastern European Jews who needed doctors so badly. The poverty and the desperately bad living conditions of the area, which Oppenheim knew from his social work, are described vividly. Dr. Rast espouses a socialism that means to him love of family and others and renunciation of hate. Generational problems are set forth in extreme form when a neighborhood girl, Jane Grabo, is able to attend medical school only through great sacrifices by her family, whom she nevertheless scorns and ignores while she is the intellectual center of a group of bright minds uptown. When she callously tells Dr. Rast that she "cannot bother with these people," that is her family, he replies, "It can't be that you are one of those vulgar second generation . . . girls who are ashamed of their parents." "Why shouldn't I be ashamed of them," she answers, "—kikes, Yiddish, you hear their broken English, see how they live in a pigsty—and their manners—their ignorance." But she does open her mind and conscience under his influence. Typical of Dr. Rast's conception of socialism as a form of benevolence is his reply to an ardent, irrational socialist woman who preaches love of the poor and hatred of the rich. "And that," he says, " . . . is your Brotherhood of Man? . . . First be a woman, *just a woman,* and then be a real Socialist. You will lead, and not mislead."[59] Dr. Rast's medical practice is one expression of his socialism. Similar renunciation of lucrative practice among the middle class, though not in the name of a species of socialism, is also central to the later Dr. Abelson of

Gerald Green's best-selling *The Last Angry Man* (1957), who practices among the Brooklyn poor.

Dr. Rast was written before the Great Revolt, as the great union organizing period between 1901 and 1914 has been called. Under the inspiration of the first few years of these events Oppenheim published *The Nine-Tenths* in 1911. In this novel his non-Jewish hero Joe Blaine, editor of a pro-labor journal, takes an ameliorative position toward social problems as he learns from the great strikes. These strikes, he says, "end in a little betterment,... hardly a dent....how slow!...*Patience*!...It will take worlds of time... unnumbered forces—education, health—work, eugenics[!], town-planning, the rise of woman, philanthropy, law—a thousand thousand dawning powers." He denies that he is a socialist, but he does have deep empathy for the workers and concern about the wretched conditions under which they live, "especially the women [who] had to add the burden of earning a living to the overwhelming burden of child-bearing and homemaking, and still worse, millions of children...drafted into the service of industrialism." With his journal and actions he devotes himself to the cause of the strikers in the Revolt of the 20,000, the heroic rising of the young shirtwaist makers, and the strikes that followed. Addressing the strikers, he declares, "You belong to a race that has been persecuted through the ages, a great race, a race that has triumphed through hunger and cold and massacres." "I'm not," he says, "any kind of *ist*...I stand for human beings."[60] The novel is full of dramatic events based on the feverish union activity of the time, and the author is concerned with the life and work of "the nine-tenths," the working class.

The sheer human drama of the Jewish labor struggles during this heroic period yielded fruitful material for novelistic treatment by labor-inclined writers. It is unfortunate that none was of great distinction, for here was indeed material for a great novel. One event in particular had a traumatic effect on the entire city and especially its Jewish people. Seven hundred young women worked in the Triangle Waist Company factory, a ten-story building off Washington Square. On March 25, 1911, fire broke out in the structure. There were no fire escapes; the women worked behind illegally locked doors; a panic quickly ensued; women were trapped in the inferno; women jumped out of windows, and many were trampled to death or burned to death inside. The dead numbered 143 young women, Jews and a small number of Italians. The Jewish community was benumbed with horror and grief. When the union organized a commemorative march ten days later, 50,000 joined the procession through the East Side. This event provided dramatic material for a number of novels, plays, and poems. Oppenheim was perhaps the first to incorporate this event into fiction in English in one of the episodes of a factory fire in *The Nine-Tenths*. The fire is a turning point in the hero's development from labor agitator to advocate of a non-socialist transformation of society. Blaine comes to the full realization that "literally millions were living in abject poverty, slaves to their pay envelopes."[61] These are the "nine-tenths" of society, and he founds a magazine with that title to advance their welfare and helps promote a great woman's garment strike. However fuzzy Oppenheim's socialism was, he was a principled man and refused to support World War I.

As socially important as his protagonist, however, was Oppenheim's recognition that the waistmakers' strike in 1911 had brought forward perhaps for the first time in the United States the "New Woman," the active and heroic participant in labor struggles and the struggle for a better world. She emerged from both the working class and from more privileged strata. Oppenheim writes about Sally Heffer in *The Nine-Tenths*, "A new kind of woman!... Sally was of the new breed; she represented the new emancipation; the exodus of woman from the home to the battle-fields of the world; the willingness to fight in the open, shoulder to shoulder with men; the advance of a sex that now demanded a broader freer life, a new health, a home built on comradeship and economic freedom."[62] At least three other novels of the period were centered about the militant labor organizing and strikes of Jewish women. Interestingly enough, these three were all written by non-Jews. What is especially interesting is the image of the new Jewish woman that is central to them and that is so different from the idealized, domestic model of a Rebecca which many non-Jewish authors had heretofore employed. The new woman is a militant, radical, independent, intelligent, able organizer who has emerged from the labor and radical movements. She is really a sequential development from the Clara Yavner of Cahan's novel into the later American industrial milieu.

This new Jewish woman stands out in the novels of Florence Converse, Zoe Beckley, and Arthur Bullard who had real-life originals to draw upon. The teen-aged Clara Lemlich, in one of the great moments of the Jewish and American labor movements, rose in November, 1909, to electrify a mass meeting of cruelly exploited shirtwaist makers by calling eloquently for a general strike. Her call released the floodgates of militancy in the industry and began the Uprising of the 20,000. She was a strike leader, beaten by police on the picket line; she raised money from sympathetic wealthy women and spoke everywhere on behalf of the union. Hers is the most dramatic figure, but there were others. There was Rose Schneiderman, for instance, who emerged early as the leading woman in the American Labor movement. She immigrated in 1890 at age six, became a militant unionist early as a worker in the shops and a leader of her union before she was twenty, and held leadership positions until her death in 1972. The strike that Clara Lemlich's eloquent speech had detonated seized the imagination of the country and helped change the image of woman into a significant force in the labor movement. The contemporary liberal weekly *Outlook* wrote on July 2, 1910, "These young, inexperienced girls have proved that women can strike, and strike successfully."[63] Clara Lemlich continued her radical activities as a union organizer for the patrician Women's Trade Union League and in the suffrage movement and indeed remained a radical throughout her life.

Two of the three novels about Jewish women labor organizers and socialists and their inspiring, courageous union pioneering are unfortunately quite inferior. Elizabeth Converse's *The Children of Light* (1912) gives the story of a general strike of women in the garment industry led by Bertha Aarons, who tells the workers that neither the foremen nor the bosses are personally responsible for low pay and bad conditions. "No," she says, "I blame the system—that keeps the means of production in the hands of capital and chains the worker in slavery."[64] The story shows the cooperation of the Women's Trade Union League with the strikers, the support of the strike by *The Torch (The Call)*, and the help given by wealthy Socialists. The second, Zoe Beckley's *A Chance to Live* (1918), delineates the friendship of a Jewish and non-Jewish girl at the "Circle Waist Shop," which has a fire obviously based on the Triangle fire. At the shop Yetta Kaplan "tries to organize the girls into a union. She talked of 'sweating' and 'exploitation' and 'strikes.' She talked 'socialism' which Annie began to think must mean deliverance for the poor since the rich opposed it." Annie is later introduced to socialism by a soap box speaker and other Jewish girls and they finally together join the Socialist party and "help toward the cooperative commonwealth and brotherhood of democracy."[65]

Far better than these two, and arguably the best novel about the Jewish radical movement in those early years, is *Comrade Yetta* (1913) by Arthur Bullard, published under the pen name of Albert Edwards. He reveals considerable knowledge of East Side life. Bullard was from an old New England family and was an active Socialist, a radical social worker and journalist who joined other patrician Socialists in building the daily *Call* and later wrote for *The Masses*. As a newspaper correspondent in Russia in 1900 and during the 1905 Revolution he became acquainted with Russian revolutionaries. He was also in Russia from 1917 to 1919 as the representative for a committee of public information and ended his career in the 1920s as an ardent advocate of the League of Nations and a Democrat. Bullard's knowledge of the East Side was acquired as a social worker. His heroine, Yetta Raevsky, accepts her Jewish identity but feels little special relation to the Jews; as a typical socialist of the time she lives a minimally Jewish life. She is the talented organizer and journalist whose "People," she says, whatever their "trade or nationality," are "my People—the People in Bondage who are striking out for the promised land."[66] She uses biblical imagery to express the universality of her allegiance. A perceptive contemporary review of the novel in *The Bookman* notes that the first half of the book, which deals with Yetta's adolescence and her experience as a sweatshop worker and strike leader, forms "a graphic and unforgettable picture of a section of life only beginning to yield its materials to the American novelist."[67]

The reviewer was also aware of the new image of the female character. "What is mainly important," he wrote, "is that the author has taken a fresh new figure in fiction and traced her evolution through work and contact with a sad segment of our society into a dominating figure."[68] He nowhere mentions the Jewish aspect of the novel or of Yetta's life, but it is strongly implied and perhaps omitted out of a curious sense of delicacy or hesitancy about just how to handle a sensitive subject in an anti-Semitic society. Bullard traces Yetta's development as the daughter of an East Side bookseller who immigrated in 1870 and despises Yiddish because he is a dogmatic Hebraist. "Yiddish," wrote Bullard, "was to him the language of the Kovno ghetto, the language of persecution and pogroms. The pure Hebrew of the Scriptures—Yes!—he would have every child of the Race know that.... It was the reservoir of all the rich traditions and richer promises. But Yiddish was a bastard jargon which his people learned in captivity. It held no treasures of the past, no future hope. Let his people supplement the language of their forefathers by one of freedom. Let them learn the speech of the land of Refuge." And Bullard perceptively adds, "His contempt of Yiddish, of course, isolated him from everything vital in the life of the East Side." Her father teaches Yetta Hebrew, but she shows no sign of any enduring interest in the language after his death. After she has proven herself as an organizer and strike leader, a patrician friend offers to see her through college, but she declines. Her place, she says, is with her people, like a Moses abandoning the ease and prestige of life with the Egyptians. "Her people" are not only Jews but all working people, whatever their nationality— "whether it's Eyetalians or Polacks or Jews or Americans."[69] For her the strike was the "Blazing Bush," which revealed to her that her place was with the poor.

Bullard cannot refrain from speculating about the Jewish psychology of the East Side. He found the "refugees from the Russian and Galician ghettoes hard to understand." The Jew, he thought, "is marked by single-mindedness and consistency of purpose," in contrast to the "Anglo-Saxon tradition of compromise and confused issues." Because of their "abject poverty," it is "small wonder that many a Jewish lad decides that the Holy Grail is made of American dollars." But the self-denial of the "money-grubber" is no different in the Jewish character from that of the "East Side poet" who "will stick to rhymes in Yiddish, although it never gave him a decent living, and the Jewish Socialist who will hold fast to his principles through starvation and persecution."[70]

Yetta's father dies when she is thirteen, and she is driven to working in the sweatshops. Vivid pictures of working conditions are presented. Apt at learning, Yetta becomes a "speeder" in the waist-making shop. She is intended to set harsh production standards for the other girls by her example. But she soon becomes aware of her exploitative role and quits. At a union dance she meets Mabel Train, a patrician official of the Women's Trade

Union League and becomes her friend and an organizer for the league. She successfully organizes strikes at women's garment shops and becomes famous when arrested during a strike. The second half of the novel is taken up with her love story and career as a journalist, but, as the *Bookman* reviewer suggested, the first half is the most significant. Yetta has an unrequited love for a Columbia instructor who is a labor sympathizer and rejects the proposal of Isadore Braun, editor of the Socialist paper, *The Clarion*. (Bullard was a founder of the actual Socialist paper *The Call*.) She writes a labor column for a "yellow" newspaper, *The Star,* until they refuse to print her exposure of the labor conditions in a department store owned by one of the paper's big advertisers. She then resigns and writes for *The Clarion*. When Braun becomes ill, she takes care of him and finally falls in love with him and is married to him by a Christian Socialist minister.

Although *Susan Lenox: Her Fall and Rise* by the muckraker David Graham Phillips is by no means a socialist novel, it may be considered "radical" in the sense that it is severely critical of its society's mores, although labor does not figure in it anywhere. It may also be described as "naturalistic." Its treatment of sex and prostitution caused it to be called "obscene" by John S. Summer, the Boston guardian of morals. Completed in 1911, the novel was not published as a book until a two-volume edition appeared in 1915. It can be considered feminist, since it is centrally concerned with the "liberated" Susan's struggle to sustain existence as an independent person. The second part of the book paints an extraordinary picture of slum life and prostitution in New York and shows the terrible pressures upon unemployed girls to resort to prostitution for survival. This is what happened to the heroine, Susan Lenox, and the second volume is in part devoted to her life as a prostitute.

Since Susan lives in the East Side slums, Jews briefly enter the story in the second part. Phillips' description of Jews and his attitude to them is at best ambivalent. He describes the nephew of her Jewish employer at a factory: "The young Jew with the nose so impossible that it elevated his countenance from commonplace ugliness to weird distinction." A girl friend is called a "pretty near straight Jew." When Susan tries to get a job at a cafe, she meets a man

at least partly of Jewish blood, enough to elevate his face above the rather dull type which predominates among clerks and merchants of the Christian races....He clearly belonged to those more intelligent children of upper class tenement people, the children who are too bright and well-educated to become workingmen and working women like their parents...so the cleverer children of the working class develop into shyster lawyers, politicians, sports, prostitutes, unless chance throws their way some respectable way of getting money.

The particular one he is describing, however, is a recruiter for white slavery. He gives Susan a drugged drink, but she evades capture. Other unsavory

Jews are the "little Jew-girl who's [the] side partner" of a prostitute, Dr. Einstein in Grand Street who demands his five-dollar fee in advance of examination, a "kike" who shot a hoodlum "all to pieces in a joint on Seventh Avenue." Not until Susan gets to Paris toward the end does she meet a favorably presented Jew in the playwright Gourdain, "an architect on the way to celebrity."[71] He falls in love with her, but she does not respond. With all Phillips' noncomformity and feeling for the oppressed, he seems to have uncritically reflected popular prejudiced attitudes toward the Jew. He is another of a long line of persons of good will in whom anti-Jewish feeling stubbornly survived.

The prosperous 1920s was a virtual hiatus in the radical novel. Walter B. Rideout lists only ten radical novels published in the 1920s, half of them written by Upton Sinclair. Why this recession in radical fiction? Once the adjustment to a peace-time economy was made after the war, an era of apparently unending prosperity seemed to open up, even though labor was active and there were important strikes like those in mining, railroads, and garments and textiles. The flush times were not conducive to a popular response to radical talk, which fell strangely on ears infatuated with "Normalcy." The mirage of unending prosperity made it easy for a disillusioned people to look on radicalism as a bizarre irrelevancy. This was the decade, it will be recalled, when many forms of reaction, from racism to the Ku Klux Klan to anti-labor dominated the public mind. It was the decade in which the best-known intellectuals, who considered themselves radical, hailed Henry L. Mencken, apostle of cynicism, elitism, and anti-democratism. This is not to say there was no activity on the Left. Such movements existed, but they were disorganized, disunified, weak, and generally disdained. There were even left-wing currents among writers and intellectuals, especially in the later years of the decade, but they scarcely received expression in fiction.

2

Fiction of the 1920s

THE SECOND GENERATION LOOKS BACK

By the 1920s young Jewish writers of the second generation were exploring the immigrant experience and that of their own generation. No longer as in the prewar period was American literature only "for the native Americans, about native Americans, and by native Americans."[1] Jewish writers demanded more and more of the attention of the literary public just as the non-Anglo-Saxon sections of the population gained power and helped to change the face of America itself. There were some Jews among the "lost generation"—literary aspirants like Harold Loeb, Matthew Josephson, and, for a while, Joseph Freeman, soon to become a Communist literary leader—and there were such accepted mainstream literary figures as Waldo Frank and Lewis Mumford (half Jewish) and Paul Rosenfeld. That these Jewish literary figures to whom expatriate Gertrude Stein must be added, were among the avant-garde, signified the emergence of Jewish writers with a literary sophistication equal to that of the Anglo-Saxons. In the 1920s Ludwig Lewisohn also became influential for his work in dramatic and literary criticism. He was perhaps the first Jewish critic to exert literary influence on American cultural history, flawed though his work was by idiosyncratic emotionalism. Alfred Kazin noted his importance: "Lewisohn was never a 'simple' figure, and his worst qualities represented the exaggerations of a mind in itself indispensable to the growth of modern criticism in America."[2] Such Jewish writers as these in this "last Anglo-Saxon decade," as Digby Baltzell has called it, were harbingers of the end of Anglo-Saxon dominance which was now to be shared with oncoming multi-ethnic forces in the intellectual, literary, and artistic, as well as in the economic and social spheres.

The decade saw not only a rise in the general level of fiction among Jewish writers, but among authors generally, and also a great increase in their sheer numbers. We noted earlier that a 1916 bibliography of Jewish fiction writers since 1900 named about forty-eight Jewish writers. An intimation of the increase by 1922 can be gathered from "a list of Jews in the United States who gained recognition" in literature and drama, among other arts and professions, published in the *American Jewish Yearbook* for 1922–1923. These names were drawn from standard "Who's Who" listings in various fields. There were "275 names of men who were writers, authors, novelists or critics" (no women?) and twenty-seven dramatists and playwrights.[3] However, we may safely conjecture that there were some who did not introduce their Jewish experience into their writing, in view of the strong assimilative tendencies among intellectuals at the time.

Among these were some who had come here with their parents as young children and who were reaching maturity in the 1920s. Those who joined the avant-garde scarcely noted the Jew as such in their writing, and most did not attempt to recapitulate their immigrant experiences or the tensions within the ghetto environment. But there were those who did look back on their immigrant past and the conflicts that arose between immigrant parents and the non-Jewish world they were entering. They were second-generation despite their foreign birth, since their formative years had been lived in this country. Of the few good acculturation novels in the decade, none approached in quality Abraham Cahan's *The Rise of David Levinsky*. Although Cahan's fiction was far from polished and was even awkward at times, he displayed an insight into the immigrant reality in which he himself was so deeply immersed. As with Dreiser, if on a lower level, the penetration of his writing raised it above the work of many of his contemporaries.

Second-generation writers on the acculturation theme were generally too deeply absorbed in coming to terms with their special ethnic problems to write explicitly in the mode of the prevailing postwar disillusionment, although they were generally tough-minded in their approach to their material and did exhibit the tendency of the period to cynicism and even naturalism. These writers were concerned with the desperate, sometimes unscrupulous, ascent of the second generation from poverty and slum living, the conflict between generations in the process, intermarriage, confrontation with anti-Semitism, and submission to or resistance against the corrupting temptations offered by American political and business life, and finally, as in the case of Ludwig Lewisohn, confrontation with the problems of assimilation and Jewish identity.

A transitional figure in the twentieth-century novel of acculturation, and the first woman of the East European immigration to achieve prominence in fiction, was Anzia Yezierska. She was "transitional" because her efforts to adjust to the larger American life were in the end a failure, largely because she had not immigrated until sixteen, without education, already formed, and hence less adaptable. Perhaps she can be regarded as a martyr to the acculturation process; yet, we may also look on her as best exemplifying a transition that never reached its goal of self-realization in the American milieu, painful as the process was to her. She was able to convey genuine compassion for the poverty, suffering, and aspiration that she experienced and observed on the East Side of New York City. Except for a few unhappy interludes in Hollywood and New Hampshire she spent most of her life there among her people, and she could write with authority, "I stand on solid ground when I write of the poor, the homeless, and the hungry."[4] But both as a person and as a writer this talented woman remained unfulfilled. She lived in poverty nearly all her life. Her hunger for education, for love, and for a tranquil life for herself and her people in the ghetto left her always unsatisfied.

Although the subjects of her writing were not new, her voice was fresh, unsophisticated, and passionately compassionate, her longings for love and culture indubitably genuine. Her first short story was published in 1915 when she was thirty, and she was given the O'Brien Award in 1919 for the best short story. Her first book, *Hungry Hearts,* a collection of short stories, appeared in 1920, and the title was symbolic of her feeling throughout her lifetime. She greeted with incredulity Hollywood's purchase of this book for $10,000 and the contract she received to write for the movies. Her brief stay in Hollywood was a failure artistically as well as personally. Despite the disappointment and material loss, she never regretted abandoning artificiality and falsity in the Hollywood mode of life. Its wasteful luxury appalled her, and Hollywood writing was altogether alien to her scrupulous devotion to depicting with utter honesty the life about her. By 1932 she had published six somewhat similar books and apparently wrote no more books until her autobiography, *Red Ribbon on a White Horse,* which created a stir when it appeared in 1950. She died on the East Side in 1970.

From her autobiography we can confirm how faithful her stories were to her experience and to the life around her under the oppressive East Side tenement conditions. Indeed, her stories and autobiography are practically interchangeable. The same tone is sustained, and similar events occur in both. Despite the occasional sentimentality and the sometimes strange word usage and grammar, the stories are so charged with honest emotion and aspiration for individual emancipation and social justice that they rise above mere documentation. Their value in revealing the real conditions of East Side poverty is also great.

In order to grasp fully the nuances of feeling in her short stories, one must have a lively sense of just how alien to the immigrant experience American life was, how remote it was from the customs, manners, and approaches to everyday life (as I am personally aware from my own boyhood on the East Side in those years). The ghetto habits of thought bred in Jews for centuries were not quickly transcended in the New World, even for those born here. Thousands of adult immigrants, especially if they were Orthodox, never outgrew that older mentality. And it was in this milieu that most of her stories are placed.

Four themes stand out in them. First, the yearning for culture and love are intertwined as she longed for the love of a man with whom she could share a common striving toward "the life higher." Second, the deprivations suffered by her neighbors and the injustice they revealed; third, generational conflict; and fourth, merciless exposure of male supremacism in the Orthodox home. Several stories illustrate these themes.

In "Hunger," a young woman is frustrated in her love for John Barnes, a college teacher and investigator of East Side life, whom she ecstatically regards as a "prince" who "opened the wings of your soul."[5] Despite her unrequited love, she has hope. "But only—there is something—a hope—a help out—it lifts me on top of my hungry body—the hunger to make myself a person that can't be crushed by nothing nor nobody—the life higher!"[6] Yezierska's dream love and culture are realized in a wish-fulfilling tale, "The Miracle." An immigrant girl falls in love with her teacher who goes away, but finds he must return—"the miracle"—because he loves her.

The sympathy with which she observed parents rejected by their nouveau riche second-generation children is apparent in a story of successful children living on Riverside Drive. They are ashamed of their mother's ghetto manners while they ply her with rich things, but she prefers to live among her East Side neighbors. She tells them, "What have I got from all my fine furs and feathers when my children are strange to me? . . . The grandest feathers can't hide the bitter shame in my face when my children shame themselves from me."[7]

Yezierska's sensitivity to the suffering and hardship of her neighbors is movingly expressed in another story of a woman who painted her kitchen white in honor of her son's prospective return from World War I, only to have the landlord raise the rent because of the improvements she had made and paid for. She can't afford the higher rent and is evicted. "Is this already America?" she asks. "What for was my Aby fighting? . . . Did I wake myself from my dreaming to see myself back in times of Russia under the czar?"[8] Another story gives a bitter picture of the snobbish and callous treatment of immigrants by the "Social Betterment Society." The vacation resort to which the society sends the immigrants "free" is more like a prison.

Yezierska's own effort to lead an independent life is suggested in "My Own People," in which the girl Sophie, obviously Yezierska herself, moves away from her family to a room of her own in order to write. In her imperfect immigrant's English she exclaims, "Ach, at last it writes itself in me! . . . It's not me—it's their cries—my own people—crying in me!—They will not be stilled in me, till all America stops to listen."[9] A part of America did stop, at least for a time, and read, especially after this book was made into a movie. Added to her assertion of independence was her uncompromising exposure of her father's male supremacism exercised under cover of religion. In her patently autobiographical novel, *Bread Givers* (1925), she describes her struggles with poverty and her father's exploitation of his daughters and their traditionally inferior status. In the 1970s feminists recognized the strong assertion of women's rights in this novel and have reissued it as a feminist document. Living at the edge of poverty on Hester Street with her mother, father, and three sisters, Sara and her sisters support the family, for the father does not work but spends all his time studying Talmud. An obsessive egotist, the father justifies the utter slavery of his wife and daughters with sanctions from the Torah. He demands that his daughters turn over all their wages to him. He drives away any suitors who are not rich and will not tolerate the loss of his daughters' wages by their marriage. He forces them into unhappy marriages with supposedly moneyed men who turn out to be frauds, but Sara finally leaves home, goes to school and college, and becomes a teacher. The author's account of the father's male supremacism is chilling:

Always Father was throwing up to Mother that she had borne him no son to be an honour to his days and to say prayers for him when he died. The prayers of his daughters didn't count because God didn't listen to women. Heaven and the next world were only for men. Women could get into Heaven only because they were wives and daughters of men. Women had no brains for the study of God's Torah, but they could be servants of the men who studied the Torah. Only if they worked for men, and washed for the men, and didn't nag or curse the men out of their homes, only if they let the men study the Torah in peace, then, maybe, they could pull themselves into Heaven with the men, to wait on them there.[10]

Writing out of bitter immediate experience, the immigrant life rendered by Yezierska was a harsh, unyielding form of existence whose only saving grace was its opportunity for education and the acquisition of culture. Even this avenue of escape was closed to many who had no conception of a cultured life. However, in later years her attitude toward her father was softened by nostalgia. In her autobiography she recalls her father's values with retrospective approval. "Now," she wrote, "all these years since his death, the old ideas he tried to foist on me revealed their meaning. Again and again, at crucial turning points in my life, his words flared out of the darkness. He who separates himself from people buries himself in death. . . . Can fire and water be together? Neither can godliness and the fleshpots of Mammon. . . . Poverty becomes Jews."[11]

If Yezierska was a transitional figure in acculturation, Thyra Samter Winslow exhibits in her clever short story, "The Cycle of Manhattan" (1923), completion of the process in sharpest contrast. She follows the progress of immigrants from their primitive beginnings in Greenwich Village at the turn of the century to their youngest sons' return to a bohemian life in the Village, with the stages in between illustrating affluence and homogenization with the American environment. The story is a paradigm of the Americanization of one type of immigrant family.

At each stage of ascent there is a change in dress, in name, in residence, in furnishings, in class status. Each of the children represents a different variant of second-generation middle-class life, culminating in the bohemianism of the youngest. The Rosenheimers, with their four children and their cousin Abramson, arrive by steerage in the 1890s. They live in the then slum area of MacDougal Street. By 1897 a new child named Dorothy is born; the family moves to East 77th Street and buys new furniture. Cousin Abramson gives his son the first name MacDougal after their street, and shortens the family name to Abrams; the Rosenheimers become Rosenheim; Ike changes his name to Irving. The partnership factory of Rosenheim and Abrams prospers, and the Rosenheims move to the Bronx, buy new furniture, shorten their name to Rosen; Yetta gets a new piano and changes her name to Yvette. With greater prosperity, they move to 116th Street in Harlem, get new furniture; the name now becomes Abraham Lincoln Rose, Abrams becomes Adams, and Yvette marries MacDougal Adams. Business expands, the family moves to Riverside Drive, again new furniture. The youngest, Maurice, becomes Manning Ross, and the whole family changes its name to Ross. Irving, now a lawyer, becomes Irwin. The family moves to a great house off Fifth Avenue on East 65th Street. It is furnished by an interior decorator. Finally Manning leaves school, becomes an art connoisseur, moves to Greenwich Village and invites the family to visit him—coincidentally in the same apartment on MacDougal Street in which they lived on their first arrival in America. Cycle of Americanization completed.[12]

Sharply contrasted with this schematic and typological overview of the acculturation odyssey of one upwardly mobile immigrant family is the naturalistic, detailed, articulated account of the variety of acculturation experiences of a group of East Siders in Samuel Ornitz's *Haunch, Paunch and Jowl* (1923). This is one of the five radical novels of the 1920s not written by Upton Sinclair and the only one concerned with the Jew. It was radical in the sense that the author ruthlessly exposed the seamy side of the acculturation process in the second generation on the East Side. Trade unionism enters Ornitz's story at only one point and does not form the center of the novel, as it often does in the later radical novels. In fact, it is primarily an acculturation fiction written from an anti-capitalist viewpoint, since it harshly documents the anti-social possibilities opened up by the incentives of money and political power. Realities are honestly depicted and the many facets of life on the East Side in the second generation—vocational, artistic, and political—are exemplified in the lives of the book's characters, with all their anti-social and countervailing aspects touched upon.

Ornitz published his novel anonymously as the purported autobiography of a successful Tammany politician, Meyer Hirsch, the pivot of the story, beginning his life as an immigrant boy in the 1880s at nine and ending with his success as a superior court judge. But while Meyer is the central figure, a remarkable, closely documented picture of the surrounding East Side life is shown. Emphasis is placed on the movement from poverty to a great variety of careers by a gang of boys originally organized around the young Hirsch. The author was a sharp observer and could articulate his critique of capitalist society as it impinged on the East Side, as well as the careers of the gang in business, the arts, and politics. Leadership in various fields of American life stemmed from the original boys' gang and from their girls. What Ornitz did was to exemplify the gang developments on the East Side as they actually occurred. Because he did not stop with the positive aspects of these developments but probed the underside of ghetto life, Ornitz's book disturbed some monitors of Jewish life who thought that such exposure was bad for the Jews.

Most of the boys lived in a quite separate world from that of their parents, whom they ignored as much as possible. The boys were "transient, impatient aliens in our parents' homes," which was in sharp contrast with the "strict, rarified public school world. The manners and clothes, speech and point of view of our teachers extorted our respect and reflected upon the shabbiness, foreignness and crudities of our folks and homes." As for the *heder,* the primitive locus of Hebrew instruction, it was "harsh and cruel" and breathed an "atmosphere of superstition, dread and punishment." And there was the street life, "sweet, lawless, and high-colored," in which the restraints of the other aspects of the boys' lives were released. As the gang's "brain of operations," Meyer credits himself with originating many practices later used by organized crime, such as extortion of "protection money." The adult Meyer used the expertise he had gained as a gang leader in the interest of his factory owner uncle, Philip, a merchant and an innovator in the employment of goons to break strikes. Street warfare with Irish gangs is described, and Meyer takes credit for originating use of steam boiler covers as shields, as indeed they are still used in Harlem. (I myself remember from my East Side boyhood seeing ash-can covers similarly used as shields in street gang warfare.) Ornitz adds that closer acquaintance between Jews and Irish later made them "amicable neighbors" and "the most powerful local gangs were made up of an admixture of Irish, Jews, and Italians."[13]

This novel differs in one important respect from its most distinguished predecessor, Cahan's *Levinsky.* While the titular character of the latter is the focus of the action throughout, and all events and characters are centered upon him, Ornitz's novel is more pluralistic in that it follows the lives and careers of nearly all the members of the original gang. The variety of careers makes the novel a microcosm of East Side life in the first few decades of mass immigration, for these careers run the gamut of the younger immigrant generation life-work, all beginning with nothing but their brains and ending variously, politically and occupationally. There is the lawyer, Meyer Hirsch himself, who rises to affluence and respectability by ruthless aggrandizement

and corruption. Another starts life as a fence for boy thieves and ends up
a rich merchant. One becomes a manufacturer who innovates the practice
of giving out work to be done at home by women and children. One of the
girls, writes Ornitz, "grew up to help make women suffrage history and
lead the girl waistmakers' union to victory."[14]

Other gang members became entrepreneurs in the arts. One becomes a
leading popular song writer. Several others begin as cafe singers and vaudeville agents and finally develop the biggest music publishing house in the
country. Another is a theatrical producer largely of musical comedies. Still
another blossoms into a poet under Walt Whitman's inspiration. In contrast
to the strike-breaking employers and corrupt politicians are the variegated
radicals of the period, one a "cross between a philosophical anarchist and
a single-taxing Socialist," a Tolstoyan, a Socialist, an anarchist. There were
doctors among them as well. There is Dr. Lionel Crane, born Lazarus Cohen,
who is a "race psychopathologist" for whom the Jewish problem is a mental
sickness. This anticipates Lewisohn's view of self-hatred as a form of insanity, but Crane's theory is exactly the opposite to Lewisohn's. Crane
attributes the problem to the Jews' "bizarre Jewishness." For Lewisohn the
cure is embrace of Jewishness in all its aspects; for Crane it is intermarriage
and total assimilation. Says Crane, "I will take the sick ego of my people
to the clinic."[15]

Many characteristic features of East Side life are also vividly described.
There is the dreadful "shop sickness," as tuberculosis was then called, which
ravaged the slums. Antagonisms of the wealthy, established German Jews
of the earlier immigration toward the new Eastern European immigrants is
reciprocated. The notorious Yom Kippur feast—the blatant violation by
radicals and younger Jews of the sensibilities of the older religious Jews of
the most sacred of their holidays—is recalled. The intellectual life of the
ghetto is suggested by the description of the "Talker's Cafe, . . . a rendezvous
for free thinkers."[16]

The plenitude and variety of aspects of East Side life contained in this
book should not mislead one into suspecting superficiality or overcrowding.
The work is vital and vividly documented; the writing is muscular and taut.
The work is dominated by the implied condemnation of the corrupting
alternatives held out by capitalist society. It proved popular, going into
thirteen printings in its first two years. Although its penetration into its
society or its literary importance is not as great as that of Cahan's *Levinsky*,
it is the high point of the acculturation novel of the 1920s.

Novels of acculturation were by no means limited to life on the East Side
of New York. Although the country's Jews were largely concentrated in
New York, they were also thinly dispersed over many parts of the country,
and writers growing up in other cities and towns depicted life in their areas.
While the general outlines of their social life and development basically
resembled the pattern in New York, since the acculturation process was

essentially similar for all Jews, local differences did exist and appeared in fiction. There had been novels of Jewish life on the West Coast and in the Middle West in the 1890s, and we have already seen how Edna Ferber situated her *Fanny Herself* in Wisconsin and Chicago. In the 1920s and 1930s Myron Brinig pictured a Jewish family through several generations in Minneapolis and "Silver Bow" (Butte), Montana. Brinig's novel *Singermann* (1929), together with its sequel, *This Man Is My Brother* (1932), is a three-generation story of one middle-class family. These novels are competent and indicative of the rise in the general level of fiction written by Jews in the 1920s. Though Brinig was no radical, his work takes a tough-minded look at fallible human beings. The Singermann family emigrates from Rumania, and the father is shown to be a family tyrant. "He was the Lord of the household, and in European Jewry there is no debating with the Lord. A woman is a chattel, her purpose is to raise children and to keep house. The husband does not look to her for intelligent advice, and he resents her meddling in his affairs."[17] When Moses finally settles his whole family in Minneapolis, he is a wagon peddlar. Eight years later they move to Silver Bow, where the family sets up a store. Moses is an extreme reactionary, a minority phenomenon among Jews in that respect. The varied careers of the second generation are pursued, each enmeshed in unhappiness; businessman, daughter married to a bigamist, a frustrated artist, a son in an unsuccessful mixed marriage, a prize fighter, a suppressed homosexual, and an aspiring journalist.

The sequel, *This Man Is My Brother* (1932), literally takes up the story where the first leaves off and carries it into the third generation. An added theme is the trauma of the acculturated Jew in an alien Christian society, a trauma which has become acute in a third generation poised between the Jewish world of their family and the general American society in those areas where Jews were not numerous. Then follow problems of intermarriage, dilution of the sense of Jewish identity in the second generation while encounters with anti-Semitism exacerbate the problem of Jewishness, especially for the third generation. The author's own conclusion would seem to be, "If assimilation is the only answer to the problem of persecution and intolerance then the world has failed and there is no nobility in man and God."[18]

Brinig's writing adds scope to the documentation of Jewish life in the 1920s. His technique throughout, devoting one chapter to each character in turn, tends toward a certain monotony in the story's progress, but the narrative pace within each chapter is strong enough to offset the recurring sense of mechanical structure.

A few novels written by sons of the earlier, established, middle-class German-Jewish immigration in the 1920s are quite different in character from the Eastern European immigration. Their preoccupation is not with East Side life, but with life in a comfortable, even affluent milieu. Both groups had in common the encounter with anti-Semitism, which afflicted Jews regardless of class. Three 1920s novelists of German-Jewish origin are Emanie Sachs, the distinguished musical critic Paul Rosenfeld, and Ludwig Lewisohn. The German-Jewish middle class was wealthy, aristocratic, and contemptuous of their Eastern European fellow Jews. But when they gained wealth in the last third of the nineteenth century, their attempts to associate themselves with the non-Jewish Americans of their class were rebuffed by social discrimination. By the twentieth century they had built up their own social institutions; their families largely restricted their social lives within an orbit of their Jewish social peers and a strict social code.

A member of this clan, Emanie Sachs (Mrs. Augustus Philips), published a revealing and critical novel dealing with the social life of this social stratum. *Red Damask* (1927) opens in the early years of our century with the heroine, Abbey Hahl, resenting the restrictions on her life imposed by their code. She is prevented from studying architecture, from going to college, and from moving to Texas with her husband, a move she attempts in order to escape the stranglehold of the family. While anti-Semitic exclusion from gentile clubs and social affairs is also shown, this book emphasizes a devastating picture of the suffocating mores of this wealthy group by one whose life was lived among them. The novel is not outstanding, but it provides an acute self-criticism of what was an important sector of Jewish life more than a half-century ago.

Another novel of German-Jewish life was Paul Rosenfeld's *The Boy in the Sun* (1928). Rosenfeld was a music critic, a prominent intellectual associated with the avant-garde movements of his time, and a friend and colleague of notable literary figures. His family was well off and, like so many German Jews of the time, joined the Ethical Culture movement, which provided an escape from or an alternative to Judaism in a non-theistic, non-denominational humanist view of life. Rosenfeld had a private school education like the young protagonist of his story. The central theme of the novel is the encounter of an adolescent boy and his family with assimilationism in the face of anti-Semitism in the outside world.

Divvy, as the boy is called, is not told at home that he is Jewish, so that he replies to Jew-baiting in school, when he is eight, with, "I'm not a Jew!" His mother tells him to dismiss the whole episode—of course he's a Jew. "But, Mamma, what does it mean to be a Jew?" His father tries to explain, "I thought that since you were not what might be called a typically Jewish looking child, and had none of the unattractive mannerisms, the whole thing would never come up at all, especially as there are so few Jewish people in this portion of Harlem." "Of course," he adds, "if there were, I could understand anti-Semitic feeling, particularly if they were Pollacks. I'd be the first one to object to the presence of Pollacks, particularly a whole neighborhood of them." He further assures the boy that he has nothing to be ashamed of, since the only difference between Jews and others is religious.

"The Christians believe that God's son, Jesus Christ, came to them and the Jews believe he has not."[19]

At prep school Divvy is exposed to Jew-baiting from his principal and others. Despite his indifference to Jewishness he refuses to conceal his Jewish origin by changing his name, to surrender his Jewish identity, or to submit to anti-Semitism. He accepts his being Jewish but goes no further than bare acquiescence. This attitude would seem consistent with that of many young Jewish intellectuals of the 1920s, who largely turned their backs on Jewishness. The novel also illustrates the evasion of Jewishness by one sector of the well-to-do assimilationist German-Jewish group. Unfortunately Rosenfeld's apparent effort to model his writing on Henry James' late style has the result that meanings are sometimes indirect and obscure. This in fact accounts for the failure of the novel to attract readers. Lionel Trilling reviewed the novel on its first appearance and pronounced it "a rather complete failure." The prose, he said, had a "disagreeable pulpiness and dulness." Trilling in the end attributed the novel's failure to a misapplication of a musical cast of mind to prose.[20]

Quite different is the case of Ludwig Lewisohn, who published his vehemently anti-assimilationist novel, *The Island Within* (1928), in the same year. The novel had a successful career with thirty printings and has recently been reissued. It is a landmark in American-Jewish writing and history, not only because Lewisohn was one of the earliest literary advocates of a return to active Jewish self-awareness, Zionism, and the practice of Jewish religion, but also because he was the first Jewish intellectual to achieve national literary and cultural influence. Not until the post–World War II period would Jewish literary figures again occupy themselves with problems of identification and religion, though not with his highly charged idiosyncratic emotionalism.

Born in Berlin in 1883, Lewisohn came to this country with his parents in 1890, lived and was educated in Charleston, South Carolina, and attended Columbia University in 1902. His parents were thorough assimilationists. Young Lewisohn thought of himself as a Methodist. Despite recommendations from the distinguished Professor Trent, he was denied a teaching post in English at Columbia because of his Jewish origin and returned to Charleston in 1906. He had become interested in German literature at Columbia, and since a Jew could not get an appointment to teach English literature—not until the 1930s would Columbia appoint its first tenured Jew, Lionel Trilling, in the English department—Lewisohn succeeded, through the intercession of his friend William Ellery Leonard, in securing an appointment in 1910 in the German Department at the University of Wisconsin. From there he went to Ohio State University in 1911, still in German language and literature. Because of his ardent pacifism during World War I, as well as his German cultural interests, he was uncomfortable in the chauvinistic, anti-German atmosphere of the period, and left in 1917.

In 1919 he was called to New York as drama editor of *The Nation,* where he served until 1924. From then until he became professor of English at Brandeis University at its founding in 1948, he poured out a continual stream of books, fiction and, later, propagandistic works on Zionism and Judaism.

Before the 1920s, his traumatic treatment in academia left no impression on his work as an influential and prolific critic and historian of drama, and of German and French literature. This hardly alluded to the Jews. His selected drama reviews from *The Nation,* republished in a book, was, according to Alfred Kazin, an "exciting contribution to the postwar renaissance at its best." In the immediate post–World War I years, Kazin continues, "Lewisohn was more than a working critic, he was a force for progress." Yet here, as in his later espousal of Jewish identity, Lewisohn apparently had an irresistible tendency toward emotional excess which threw his historical and critical work off balance, and, as Kazin continued, "he began more and more to write the history of literature as the history of Ludwig Lewisohn."[21] Whatever he did, whether it was literary history and criticism or a discussion of the Jewish Question, he was finally carried away by Freudianism and by Jewish nationalism, all in terms of his idiosyncratic emotional perspective.

By 1924 the significance of his experience as a Jew had borne down on him with full force and changed his life. He studied Martin Buber's writing and immersed himself in Jewish history and culture. Thereafter he completed a stream of books, both fiction and non-fiction, in which he agitated against assimilationism and for Jewish identification with an intensity that verged on obsession. In his autobiographical *Mid-Channel* (1929) he recounted the story of his transition to Jewish affirmation after decades of unconsciousness as an assimilated Jew. His "living experience drew me irresistibly toward" Jewish identification. He

discovered first that my true self is a Jewish self, even as the true self of one friend that I have is American, and of another German and another French. But that Jewish consciousness of mine had little or no Jewish interest. And so, without abandoning or for one moment misprizing the American and Jewish content of my mind, I went in search of a Jewish content to satisfy my Jewish instincts and also to quicken and enrich with what is mine by birth and blood that which is mine by study and love.[22]

The culminating work of this first phase of his return to Jewish identity is the novel, *The Island Within.* Its first quarter is taken up with the European origins of the central figure, Arthur Levy, patterned after Lewisohn's own family history. Levy's grandfather Efraim, son of a Vilna rabbi, was married to the daughter of a wealthy Polish Jew who set his new son-in-law up in the German branch of his business. Efraim's son Jacob immigrated to the United States in 1879, was taken into a department store, and married Gertrude, a girl with a dowry which helped make him a partner in an

innovative furniture business where he prospers. Arthur Levy and his sister
Hazel are born of this marriage. They are brought up without explicit Jewish
awareness, but somehow they have a sense of their identity, ascribed to
"ancestral memories, to instinct, to the voice of the blood." The notion of
"blood," which recurs in Lewisohn's writing of this period, probably derives
from his reading of the early Martin Buber. Arthur's sister Hazel, who
pathologically detests her Jewish origin, wants to marry the brother of
Arthur's non-Jewish friend, Georgie Fleming, but the family succeeds in
preventing this intermarriage. She protests to Arthur, "I've never liked a
Jewish boy in my life." Later, after Arthur has become a psychiatrist, and
Hazel is unhappily married to a Boston Jewish businessman, Arthur concludes simplistically that "the mechanism of the Jewish anti-Jewish complex
was precisely analogous to the mechanism of insanity."[23]

Like Lewisohn in actual life, Arthur goes to Columbia and becomes a
pacifist and internationalist during World War I. He finds that even his
good, tolerant, Scotch-Presbyterian friend Dawson is not altogether free
from prejudice. Arthur's deep interest in Freud then leads to his becoming
a psychiatrist. As such he observes Jewish self-hatred in some young Jews
and radicalism in others as alike in fleeing from "a disagreeable reality,"[24]
like that of his own sister Hazel. Arthur falls in love with a non-Jew,
journalist Elizabeth Knight, daughter of a minister. They marry in spite of
their parents' grief. Elizabeth cannot fully accept Arthur's parents, and,
despite the birth of a son, the couple draw apart. Finally their increasing
separateness leads to its inexorable conclusion in divorce.

While the failure of the marriage need not necessarily explain Arthur's
return to Jewishness, it is thus intended by Lewisohn, and the novel seems
to me essentially to fail at this point. To be sure, Arthur's experiences with
his non-Jewish friends, as well as his psychiatric experience with Jews,
contribute to his return to Jewishness, and the troubles of his Jewish patients
resemble his sister's problem of Jewish self-hatred. But the breakdown of
his marriage is the decisive factor. Lewisohn maintains that the final incompatibility of the couple is somehow "racial." When their son is born, Elizabeth offers no objection to his circumcision. "I didn't know you were so
Jewish," she says. When he asks if she minds, she smiles and says, "I have
atavistic attacks myself when I hear Gospel hymns." Their further estrange-
ment is not necessarily an extension of difference in feelings about background. While critical opinion may differ on this, it seems to me more
plausible that their differences arise from incompatible temperaments—a
quite different matter from what the author is trying to prove, although the
author believes these temperaments are based on "race." Elizabeth enjoys
parties, light company, the independence of the "modern woman." But
Lewisohn sees these as gentile traits, rather than pertaining to the times,
gentile or Jewish. "All he knew," says Lewisohn of Arthur, "was . . . that,
except in imitation of their Gentile sisters and more or less from lips out

ward, Jewish women were not dissatisfied with their position and did not protest against the dominance of the male." However, could it not also be argued that most *non*-Jewish women of the time did not protest against male dominance? Non-Jewish as well as Jewish feminists advocated women's rights and protested such attitudes equally. Their incompatibility can be explained otherwise. The one was a gregarious, free person, the other a solemn, seclusive one. Arthur later admits, "Maybe I'm wrong...because Elizabeth is a very modern woman and I am...an old-fashioned man."[25] By the author's own account of their incompatibility, this seems to me their basic problem, and not their difference in origin. Even if Arthur does not believe this to be the real reason for their separateness, it is at least as good an explanation for their diverse lives, which could not find a common path, as are Arthur's assumptions about "instinct" and "blood." They agree to separate. Arthur then undertakes an intense study of Jews. He does part-time volunteer work at a Jewish hospital and finally accedes to the request of a rabbi at the hospital to join a delegation to investigate anti-Semitism in Rumania. The book ends with his full commitment to Jewishness.

In one of his authorial prefaces to a chapter in the novel Lewisohn expanded his theory of assimilation as "protective mimicry" and renounces the Emancipation. When medieval restrictions upon Jews were dropped,

the badges of shame were removed, the ghettoes were opened; the Jews flooded the desert of the world.... The nations said: Be like us and we shall be brothers and at peace! Then began the Jewish practice of protective mimicry; and it was practiced then and has been practiced since,...not consciously to escape differences, conspicuousness, and hence danger, but in a spirit of devotion, love, loyalty, fellowship. The Jews wanted profoundly to be Americans, Englishmen, Germans, even Poles.

Out of this condition grew the "modern Jewish soul," which Lewisohn regards, for all its other qualities, as subtly tormented and as rarely creative. Lewisohn generalized this analysis of the assimilated Jew to universality. Assimilated Jewish intellectuals, he held, were so "drained of anything of their own." They were "poorer than the poorest Gentile," who could resort to his native earth.[26] Instead of granting the complex effect of the Enlightenment on Jewish life, intellectual and political liberation on the one hand, and the problematic nature of the consequent Jewishness on the other, he ignored the former and dilated the latter as if it were the whole. This sharply contrasts with such a development as that of Horace M. Kallen, who reconciled the two in cultural pluralism.

Lewisohn carries his theses forward in his autobiographical *Mid-Channel* (1929), in which he elaborates on his condemnation of assimilationism. The more assimilated a Jew is, he held, the less human. "It is grotesque and less than human to live by mimicking another's tradition." He makes the excessive assertion that "The Jewish problem is the decisive one of Western civilization. By its solution this world of the West will stand or fall, choose life or death."[27] Certainly the Jewish problem has clearly been demonstrated in the past century to be a major issue on the world scene, but it cannot be regarded as the decisive one. Its solution is, in Aristotelian terms, necessary but not sufficient for the decent survival of civilization. Solution of problems of poverty, equality, color prejudice, and social justice in its widest sense is decisive. Consequent upon the intensification of his Jewish Orthodoxy and nationalism and his intemperate condemnation of Jewish Emancipation, Lewisohn ended his years as a reactionary.

"THE LAST ANGLO-SAXON DECADE"

If the 1840s and 1850s are regarded as an American literary renaissance, with its quintet of major writers—Emerson, Thoreau, Hawthorne, Melville, Whitman—we shall not be far off the mark in considering the 1920s a second American literary renaissance, with T. S. Eliot, O'Neill, Fitzgerald, Hemingway, Faulkner, and some others. The 1920s received from these writers a series of masterpieces from *The Waste Land* in 1922 to *The Sound and the Fury* in 1929. Of course, other major artists came along between the appearance of these two clusters, but the nature of a renaissance is that it brings forth a contemporary *group* of major artists rather than an individual great one here and there. These two periods had in common that they both emerged during the decline of a hitherto dominant stratum or class. "The 1920s," wrote E. Digby Baltzell, "marked the last decade in American history in which the members of the WASP establishment, protected by countless caste barriers from the rest of the people, had everything more or less their own way."[28] There was a sense of impending loss of dominance, and one effect was an unthinking indulgence in the prevailing anti-Semitism or ambivalence toward the Jews, which spilled into the work of Anglo-Saxon writers.

The literary 1920s had their roots in the pre–World War I period. The vigor of the New England tradition was spent and degenerated into a "genteel tradition," as Santayana put it. In 1911 he contrasted the incredible speed and intensity of economic life with the timid, quiescent life of the mind. "The truth is," said Santayana in 1911, "that one-half of the American mind, that not occupied intensely in practical affairs, has remained, I will not say high-and-dry, but slightly becalmed; it has floated gently in the back-water, while, alongside, in invention and industry and social organization, the other half of the mind was leaping down a sort of Niagara Rapids."[29]

But there was movement, of which Santayana himself was a sign, in that becalmed air. In literature, Van Wyck Brooks was articulating discontent with the debilitated New England spirit. He argued the need for American culture to confront the wider class, geographic, ethnic, and economic realities of the day. In *America's Coming-of-Age* in 1915 he deplored the condition of Puritan culture, which was attenuated by an artificial distinction between an approved and sanitized "Highbrow" literature and a rejected lower-class, more earthy "Lowbrow" sort. Brooks urged that we revitalize our culture by transcending this artificial distinction and coming to terms with the new reality in a cultural fusion of the usable past with the democratic and new in the present. It was Whitman, Brooks thought, who had achieved such a synthesis. Brooks also argued that this new vitality could not be indifferent to, and independent of, the social scene, but needed to be compatible with socialism, which was for him, as for so many of his contemporaries, a vaguely conceived state of social benevolence. Around Brooks gathered a group of advanced intellectuals who included some Jewish figures—Alfred Stieglitz, Waldo Frank, Lewis Mumford, Paul Rosenfeld—as well as non-Jews like Sherwood Anderson.

These new modern currents stirred in all the arts. In 1912 Harriet Monroe founded *Poetry Magazine* in which the new vigor of poetry was embodied; the Armory Show in 1913 marked the public entrance of modern art on the American scene. A new maturation of drama was initiated with the founding of the Provincetown Playhouse in 1915 and the emergence of Eugene O'Neill in that group; Randolph Bourne was promoting a "Young America" movement, which, with Brooks, crusaded against a complacent status quo in literature and social life. One sign of the new atmosphere was the fact that Dreiser's *Sister Carrie*, whose publication was aborted in 1900, could see the light in 1912. In a sense World War I put an end to an exhausted genteel tradition. The assault on that tradition finally ended it, after the demagogic slogans of "a war for democracy" and a "war to end all war" were revealed as deceptions. The realization that the carnage of that war was futile and that it was finally perceived to be a clash of national aggrandizements, and the disillusionment which followed the war also swept over literary artists. They fled what they saw as a philistine beehive of money-grubbing and business to the more congenial atmosphere for art in Paris.

The expatriates were the "lost generation," suspended between the culture that had died of irrelevance and the cultural waste land that they conceived a commercial America to be. Out of that tension was created one of the great literary decades of our history. Eliot drew on the French symbolists; Hemingway saw in the spare, direct prose of Mark Twain and Sherwood Anderson the living style of American writing. After Joyce's *Ulysses* became known in the 1920s, his influence proved pervasive, especially in the work of Faulkner. They became modern writers, adopting the detachment that is the earmark of modernism, manifested in its purest form in Flaubert, as well as its social sophistication in the sense of a style of manners. Among intellectuals generally the reigning cultural critic was H. L. Mencken, who set the tone of cynicism and contempt for the bourgeoisie.

While the lost generation seldom alluded to social problems directly in their fiction, the characters in their stories were most significant as exemplars of postwar disillusionment, who largely ignored political happenings in the world around them: most concentrated more on exemplifying their sophisticated life-style and were indifferent to prevailing social problems, at least the first half of the decade. They were therefore passive vehicles of the effects that a ruthless, aggrandizing world was having on the value system of society. A few contributed to the literary activities of the political left at home in such journals as *The Liberator* (1918 to 1924) and *The New Masses,* which succeeded it in 1926. They were scarcely aware of, much less able to resist, the anti-Semitic tendencies of that decade, but were rather its passive reflectors. Some were distinctly and explicitly anti-Semitic; some were ambivalent, exhibiting a hostile attitude at one time, a neutral attitude at others, and a friendly attitude at still another; and a few were consciously opponents of anti-Semitism.

Those who care about American literature are confronted with the unpalatable fact that this cluster of great writers was generally passive before pervasive anti-Semitism, and nearly all at times manifested hostility to Jews in their work. In this respect most of them not only acquiesced in but were hardly critical of the prejudiced social atmosphere. Certainly there were differences among them in this regard. But it is striking that there were few exceptions among the leading writers of the 1920s, who each indulged, for longer or shorter periods, and in varying degrees of intensity, in anti-Semitism.

The reasons why anti-Semitism was so widespread can be found in the economic and ideological pressures of the decade. The bickering of nationalistic peace negotiations followed by the economic depression of 1920–1923 brought disillusionment to an American people previously raised to a pitch of enthusiasm and idealism over the "war for democracy." The Bolshevik Revolution provided additional stimulus to an already existing Jew hatred and was exploited by a know-nothing red scare with a wholesale round-up of radicals, especially the foreign-born, in the Palmer Raids of 1920. "The Jew," wrote John Higham, "offered the most concrete symbol of foreign radicalism.... A Methodist clergyman testified before a Senate Committee that Bolshevism in Russia was drawing much of its inspiration and support from the Yiddish sections of New York. The same doctrine that Bolshevism was a Jewish movement echoed from the pulpits of many churches."[30] And when a flood of Jews fled to the United States from a war-torn Europe at the war's end, the agitation for immigration restriction at last succeeded. Unemployment brought on by depression helped create the atmosphere in which, in 1920, restriction was enacted; in 1924 the quota was reduced even more drastically. A contemporary publicist, Burton J. Hendrick, wrote in 1923 that the immigration law was "chiefly intended—it is just as well to be frank about the matter—to restrict the entrance of Jews from eastern Europe."[31]

The depression of 1920 also fertilized the soil in which the Ku Klux Klan, revived in 1915, quickened its activity. Its targets were Blacks, Catholics, and Jews. In 1920, a financially straitened Henry Ford, who had been compelled to borrow from the Wall Street he excoriated, was persuaded that the Jews were responsible for his and the nation's troubles. His *Dearborn Independent*, which circulated through Ford dealers, reprinted serially the Tsarist forgery, *The Protocols of the Elders of Zion*. For years Ford promoted this ignorant calumny until the threat of a boycott caused him to issue a public apology to the Jewish people in 1927 and to end his campaign.

Although anti-Semitism abated somewhat with prosperity in the latter years of the decade, it did not by any means go away. The general atmosphere of intolerance and conformity fortified discrimination against the Jews as the overt anti-Semitism of the Klan and of Henry Ford's campaign receded. But Jews were subjected to drastic discrimination not only in housing, social clubs, and resorts, but in jobs as well. A *numerus clausus* was imposed in colleges and medical schools, and Jews found it difficult to obtain teaching jobs in higher education. So widespread was exclusion from clerical jobs in New York that Jews would be employed, in great majority, only by fellow Jews.

Racist doctrines had been seeping into the United States from Europe for decades, and in the 1920s they reached their zenith here, reinforced by residual nativism and the chauvinistic "100 percent Americanism" generated by World War I. By 1923 Madison Grant's racist *The Passing of a Great Race*, first published in 1915, went into several editions; his disciple Lothrop Stoddard in 1920 published *The Rising Tide of Color*. The popularity of this book was such that we find a central character of Fitzgerald's *The Great Gatsby* (1925), Tom Buchanan, remarking that he is reading "Goddard's *The Rising of the Colored Empires*," that is, Stoddard's book. Tom goes on, "the idea is if we don't look out the white race will be—will be utterly submerged. It's all scientific stuff. It's all been proved."[32] It is not obvious that Fitzgerald disagrees. There were editorial soundings of racist ideas in such journals as the *New York Times* and the *Saturday Evening Post*. The eugenics movement was advancing the pseudo-scientific theory that the "superior" races should remain pure and unsullied by contamination from the "inferior." There were even highly placed academic scholars and literary critics like Brander Matthews and Stuart P. Sherman who propounded such theories.

Further evidence of the respectability of such general theories, and of anti-Semitism in particular, can be found in the *Harvard Lampoon* of the decade. This student "humor" magazine in 1920 mercilessly red-baited Harold Laski when that distinguished political thinker was invited to lecture at Harvard. The "Laski" character in a one-page dramatic sketch is referred to as the

"Senator from Semitia."[33] By 1922 the *Lampoon* felt no need to soften its anti-Semitism. Again a one-page sketch, "A Divine Comedy," centers on the efforts of "Simmie, the spirit of a prominent Boston ex-banker," explicitly Jewish, to enter Heaven by trying to bribe St. Peter, beating St. Peter down from a $3 million to a $1 million payment, with much stupid anti-Semitic, stereotyped "humor."[34]

A writer very often fluctuates in his attitude, is ambivalent, or changes over time. Such changes are usually the effect of external events in society as a whole, as was the case with some of the authors studied here when the horror of Nazism bore down on them. The importance of prevailing attitudes is apparent in the mood of the 1920s, in giving rise to such attitudes in many writers of that decade.

How were the major writers of the 1920s affected by the prevailing anti-Semitic influences and moods? Much as we revere this group, to ignore this problem would leave a void in our account of how the Jews fared in the literature of this century.

When Sherwood Anderson was twenty-four in 1900, he delivered a speech on Zionism at an Ohio college that a local paper called "a plea for the Jew."[35] When his literary life was well under way, he came to know Jews intimately, for he notes in his memoirs how many he associated with, and he expresses his appreciation of them. "What a debt of gratitude," he wrote, "I owe to men like Paul Rosenfeld, Stark Young, Alfred Stieglitz, Waldo Frank.... I did not believe I was too much prejudiced."[36] In 1939 he noted that "anti-Jewish feeling is apparently growing stronger—often, I have noticed, in places where there are no Jews and among men who know personally no Jews."[37]

Yet there is evidence that he did not escape ambivalence toward Jews in his creative work. In *Dark Laughter* (1925), a negative character, Fred Gray, is sitting at a roadside in France after a battle during World War I. A man sitting near him "was evidently a Jew. You can almost always tell," Fred ruminates: "Odd notion, eh, a Jew going to war and fighting for his country. I guess they made him go. What would have happened if he protested, 'But I'm a Jew. I haven't any country.' " He then remembers how, in his youth, there was one family of Jews in his town. The father owned a store, and "Once Fred joined several other boys who were ragging one of the Jewish boys. They followed him along a street shouting, 'Christ-killer! Christ-killer!' " Fred repeated the words to himself, not wishing to hurt the Jew, and he had "thoughts that burn and sting like bullets without saying them aloud."[38] Implicit in this account is the author's disapproval.

The evidence, then, points to ambivalence. Irving Howe is accurate, I think, in ascribing the negative aspect of Anderson's treatment of Jewish characters to a "preconscious remnant of that folk stereotype which regards Jews as the archetypal 'other,' alien, unknowable, and perhaps suspect."

Consistent with Anderson's ambivalence, I think Howe is further correct in holding that the balance would go in Anderson's favor if one set his favorable against his "disturbing" passages about Jews.[39]

There was hardly anything ambivalent about Ezra Pound's attitude, his well-known virulent, persistent, vocal anti-Semitism over a period of about a half century. It was the crude, vulgar kind—ending in defense of Mussolini's and Hitler's fascism—of know-nothing American nativists. It is true that he did not exclude Jews on a personal or artistic basis, as was evidenced in his high praise for his disciple, the poet Louis Zukofsky. It is also true that in 1967, during a visit which Allen Ginsberg had with him in Venice, he made the unsolicited admission that "My writing—stupidity and ignorance all the way through stupidity and ignorance. . . . But the worst mistake I made was that stupid, suburban prejudice of anti-Semitism. All along, that spoiled everything."[40] Such an admission at eighty-two, however, does not go far to cancel a half-century of venomous anti-Jewish vituperation, which penetrated deeply into his thought.

Not even the Holocaust or World War II could shake his admiration for fascism, and his treasonous broadcasts from Italy during World War II are well known, as is his trial for treason after the war and his confinement to a mental hospital to avoid jail. After his release in 1958 he returned to Italy, where he died in 1972.

As Allen Tate suggested, anti-Semitism "was in the middle of his poetry"[41] as in the *Cantos,* his central poetical work, on which he was engaged for four decades. In Canto 35, published in 1934, this master of language resorts to Yiddish "dialect," in which Pound abandons his respect for languages. In Canto 48, published in 1937, he writes in presumed confirmation that Bismarck laid blame for the American Civil War on the Jews, especially on the Rothschilds. Canto 50 goes farther back for Jewish power. He charges Wellington with being "a jew's pimp," a creature of the manipulating House of Rothschild. Canto 52 gives the Pound scholar Hugh Kenner an opportunity to attempt to condone Pound's anti-Semitism. From this Canto, which happens to be one of the densest with anti-Semitism, Kenner extracts two lines to show Pound tried to distinguish financiers from other Jews. "It was a pity," asserts Kenner, that emphasis was not allowed to be placed on this distinction "while he was still in the habit of making it." Kenner even goes so far as to conclude that Pound here "attempted a diagnosis" which "tended to decrease rather than to encourage anti-Semitism" when in 1937 Pound called "race prejudice" "a red herring."[42] What seems to escape Kenner is that the Rothschild-baiting in this Canto is a classic anti-Semitic device, that the attack on the financier-banker *as the Jew, rather than as banker,* has proved one of the most potent forms of anti-Semitic propaganda, and Pound used this device to the hilt, to say nothing of the deliberately ugly use of pseudo-Yiddish in this very passage.

Nor does Kenner note that in the same Canto, in addition to other Jew-baiting passages, is one of Pound's most egregious. Pound regurgitates in Canto 52 the ignorant forgery foisted on the country in the 1930s by the fascist Silver Shirt leader William Dudley Pelley that Benjamin Franklin was an anti-Semite who urged the country to exclude Jews, exposed as a forgery in 1934 by Miriam Beard and Carl Van Doren. Pound did not refrain from anti-Semitism in the Cantos even after the war. In the *Pisan Cantos,* published in 1948, he went right on with standard Rothschild-baiting. And in Canto 80 he praised Pétain with insults to Léon Blum in contrast.

After the war, controversy repeatedly arose around Pound and his works. Award to Pound of the Bollingen Prize for Poetry in 1949 aroused lively literary controversy and divided the literary world. In 1972, the Academy Council of Art and Sciences voted against award to him of its Emerson-Thoreau Medal by a vote of thirteen to nine with two abstentions. It would be inappropriate, it seems to me, to award him the medal bearing the names of two great American humanists.

Literary talent can coexist with reactionary political views, deficiencies in moral quality, dehumanized opinions, and insensitivity. For centuries, most of the greatest literary figures were anti-Semitic in one degree or another. But Ezra Pound's anti-Semitism was only one aspect of his crude fascistic social views. He is a tragic figure of American literature.

The predominant satiric vein of E. E. Cummings' writing offered an irresistible temptation to Jew-baiting in the anti-Semitic 1920s, and he succumbed. At a time when Jew-baiting in literature was a widespread practice, the line between satire and stereotyped folk ridicule was not drawn, and this was the case with Cummings.

The instance of the Jew in his World War I novel, *The Enormous Room* (1922), is not too clear. One presumes that much of this bitter, searing account of Cummings' unjustified imprisonment in La Ferté internment camp in France during the war was closely based on actuality. Among his many bizarre fellow inmates was a Jew, who was a valet-bodyguard of a wealthy Rumanian internee. Cummings described this Jew as "one of the most utterly repulsive personages whom I have met in my life—perhaps (and on second thought I think certainly) the most utterly repulsive.... I refer to The Fighting Sheeny." He is further described as "a creature whom ugly does not even slightly describe. There are some specimens of humanity in whose presence one instantly and instinctively feels a profound revulsion. ... The Fighting Sheeny was one of these specimens.... This face was most hideous when it grinned." It is quite possible that this horrendous description applies to an actual inmate at La Ferté, but one can't be sure. The descriptions of Jews as the ugliest creatures ever encountered occurs several times in other authors in definitely anti-Semitic contexts and makes one wonder if this element was entirely absent in the writer's characterization of "The Fighting Sheeny."[43]

However, the poems leave little room for doubt. In *is 5* (1926), poem

XV contains familiar Jew-baiting through Jewish names. The clichéd association of Jews as nouveaux riches and socially pretentious is clear in the verse. Questionable passages crop up in subsequent volumes, and some are unequivocally anti-Semitic. In *No Thanks* (1935), a satirical passage on passive entertainment gadgetry, Cummings concludes Poem 54 with insulting lines on a Jewish radio performer. Is the Jew to blame for mindless, mechanical diversions? After World War II and the Holocaust Cummings allowed these passages in his 1950 volume *Xaire*. Poem 46 charges the "kike" with financial manipulation.[44] The 1950 volume seems to reflect Cummings' disillusionment with post–World War II America. Justin Kaplan remarks, "Following a familiar, even grassroots pattern, the broken liberal turned reactionary and became a fan of Senator Joseph McCarthy." Cummings' refusal to attend a White House dinner became "The 'Kennedy-Kulchur (Mick-kike) tie-up' was an Abie's Irish Rosary."[45] The appearance of *Xaire* in 1950 and the bestowal on Cummings of a $5,000 Academy of American Poets Award once again precipitated as heated a discussion of anti-Semitism in his work as Pound did a few years earlier.

No major writer emerging in the 1920s included Jews more frequently in his stories than William Faulkner. And, like several other writers of the period, he passed from slighting, stereotypical, and sometimes severely negative allusions to Jews in the first few decades of his career to a more tolerant and an even friendly view in the 1950s.

A Jewish salesman named Schuss makes a brief, strictly stereotyped appearance in Faulkner's first novel, *Soldier's Pay* (1926), reflecting the old stereotype of the Jew's presumed evasion of fighting in wars in a World War I incident. More extensive treatment is given to two Jewish characters, brother and sister, in his next novel, *Mosquitoes* (1927), which is based on the writer's own New Orleans experience. The two are members of a weekend party on a boat, and this indicates that Jews were accepted in the bohemian society of the city. If there is any differentiation between the Jewish man and the others, it is only on the part of the author, who calls him "the Semitic man" from beginning to end of the 350–page book.[46] Only from conversation do we gather that his name is Julius, and that not until page 44. In another place, Julius tells the company, "You can't ignore money. . . . It took my people to teach the world that," and the subject of money is ever with him.[47] Julius' sister, Mrs. Eva Weisman, is very favorably portrayed by the author, even to assigning to her authorship several of his own poems. Both Jews are based on an actual Jewish man and woman with whom Faulkner associated in New Orleans.

Even when Faulkner's talent reached maturity a few years later in *The Sound and the Fury* (1929), the uncritical use of Jew-baiting continued. In the 1910 section, Quentin explored lower New York, "Land of the kike and home of the wop." In a later section, Quentin's father, Jason Compson, discusses speculation on the cotton market. "You boys," he says, "follow your own judgment. Those rich New York jews have got to live like every-body else." Small-town investors, he adds, are "suckers" for the "New Yorkers"—that is, Jews—who "produce nothing." "Well, I'm done with them. They've sucked me for the last time. Any fool except a fellow that hasn't got any more sense than to take a jew's word for anything could tell the market was going up all the time. . . . And just let me have twenty-four hours without any damn New York jew to advise me what it's going to do."[48]

Several stories about stunt flying bring out at least Faulkner's ambivalence toward Jews. His interest in stunt flying no doubt derives from his own service with the Canadian Air Force during World War I. In later fiction he would use his own frustration in completing his training as the war ended in time for him to miss the heroics of combat flying. The stunt flyer cycle of stories projects the Jew as so money-obsessed that he would risk death—his own and others'—for it. In the short story, "Death Drag" (1930), a Jewish stunt flyer, Ginsfarb, and his Jewish partner, Jake, together with a non-Jewish stunt pilot, Jock, barnstorm with the "death drag" stunt. Jock's hair has turned white because Ginsfarb insisted on making "the minimum of some specified manoeuvre in order to save gasoline." Ginsfarb speaks "in a dead voice, in the diction of Weber and Fields in vaudeville, making his *wh*'s into *v*'s and his *th*'s into *d*'s." He had "the jaw of a shark" and had "the most tragic face we had ever seen; an expression of outraged and convinced and indomitable despair." Jake was "handsome in a dull quiet way," and everyone knew "at once that the two strangers [Ginsfarb and Jake] were of a different race from themselves." Once again, Faulkner recalls the cliché about Jews' evasion of war service by Ginsfarb's reply to a question, "Were you a flyer in the war, Mister?" "The war?" Ginsfarb answers. "Why should I be a flyer in the war?"[49]

When Faulkner first submitted this story to *Scribner's Magazine*, the editor rejected it because "the character of Ginsfarb seemed too close to carica-ture."[50] In the "revised" version, however, published in January, 1932, Ginsfarb's character and description remained unchanged. Is the story anti-Semitic? Irving Howe believes it is not. He notes that in picturing Ginsfarb as "a Jewish merchant whom bankruptcy had driven to the extreme resort of stunt jumping," Faulkner showed his "indifference to the plausible." The "incongruity" of the story, says Howe, gave the story "a certain weird power." Howe then finds Ginsfarb "a large aching figure of modern lone-liness."[51] Ginsfarb then has a doubly alien figure, both as Faulkner says, as a "stranger of a different race" and as a daredevil with "the most tragic face he had ever seen."[52] This dual alienness intensifies the effect of loneliness.

Is the story therefore not anti-Semitic? Howe has surely probed an es-sential aspect of the story's meaning. But we cannot overlook the fact that Ginsfarb nevertheless has features of the stereotype: his negative attitude toward participation in any war, his physical appearance, and his evaluation of money above everything else, even life itself. But Faulkner here makes use of the stereotype to advance a striking technical effect.

Another vehicle for Faulkner's disparagement of the Jew is the figure of the Jewish lawyer in *Sanctuary* (1931). Early in the story, Ruby, the Black cook at the whorehouse to which Popeye has taken Temple Drake, tells about the Black woman's unsavory experience with a lawyer, who, it later turned out, was Jewish. Ruby's soldier brother had killed another soldier over a woman, and the lawyer she hired took cohabitation with her as payment. When she is later unjustly charged with the murder of Temple's child, she is defended by Horace, and offers to repay him with sex. "Good God," exclaims the shocked lawyer, "...what kind of men have you known?"[53] Intimidated by the lynch atmosphere at the trial, "the Jew lawyer from Memphis" said not one word at the trial and quickly left afterward. He was "sitting on his spine, gazing dreamily out of the window," says Horace.[54] Payment in sexual favors exacted by a Jew, as in *Sanctuary*, is again used in the short story, "There Was a Queen" (1934).

During World War II, Faulkner's attitude shows change. When the son of one of Faulkner's publishers, Robert J. Haas, was killed in 1943, the writer wrote about this in a letter to a friend. "During the times when I would be broke," he wrote, "year after year sometimes, I had only to write to him [Robert Haas] and he would send me money—no hope to get it back, unless I wrote another book. He's a Jew." The son was killed flying planes from factories to air bases. "All Jews. I just hope I don't run into some hundred percent American Legionnaire until I feel better."[55] Again, in 1950, Faulkner wrote a script for Abe Chasanov, who was asked for a "loyalty" affadavit, and the next day the victim of McCarthyism committed suicide. Faulkner's biographer Joseph Blotner, who details the incident, adds that "Neither Faulkner's hatred of anti-Semitism nor his detestation of Senator McCarthy had been enough to fuse life into the script."[56]

It is strange to read Blotner refer, without more documentation, to the author's "hatred of anti-Semitism." Faulkner's fiction after 1951 did indeed show a drastic change in his treatment of Jews. Perhaps the example of Haas' son accounts for several heroic flyers in the post–1951 fiction, in sharp contrast to the anti-Semitic depiction of Jewish airmen who displayed courage and daring. *A Fable* (1954), set in the final days of World War I, is an intricately symbolic anti-war fiction. One of three central symbolic figures is the young English Lieutenant Levine, late of Oxford, who dreams of glory in combat flight, unlike Faulkner's earlier Jewish flyers. But Levine's Jewish identity is actually solely that of a name. The quixotic Levine echoed the sophomoric sentiment that Faulkner, who enlisted in the Canadian Air Force in World War I, had noted in his story, "Honor," in the thirties: "the college campuses full of British and French uniforms, and us all scared to death it would be over before we could get in and swank a pair of pilot's wings ourselves."[57]

Proof of the positive trend in the writer's attitude toward Jews is confirmed in *The Mansion* (1959). The Jewish character in *The Mansion*, Barton Kohl, is, once again, a flyer, this time shot down in combat in the Spanish Civil War. He had married Linda Snopes; they had lived in Greenwich Village where he was a communist and a sculptor. He had volunteered "to fight Hitler" in Spain.[58] The departure from the stereotype of the Jewish evader of combat leads an incredulous man in town to say: "What? A Greenwich Village sculptor named K-O-H-L actually in an aeroplane where it could get shot down by an enemy." The favorable character, lawyer Gavin Stevens, remarks what sounds like Faulkner's own tribute to those who fought against Franco. "Kohl's airplane," says Stevens, "was a worn-out civilian passenger carrier, armed with 1918 infantry machine guns, with home-made bomb bays through which the amateurs dumped by hand the home-made bombs; that's what they fought Hitler's Luftwaffe with."[59]

In an article that is the only attempt I know to examine Faulkner's relation to the Jews, Alfred J. Kutzik offers insight into Faulkner's earlier anti-Semitism. He notes that, although the Southern aristocracy was probably more tolerant of Jews than any other stratum in the United States, this actually applied to the older South, and not to the part settled later of rural northern Mississippi from which Faulkner came. This rural area was also subject to some anti-Jewish feeling in the populism of the late nineteenth century, "in a town which never had a union local until 1946." Kutzik further suggests that "Faulkner like many writers before him, used the Jew as a symbol of the rapacity and inhumanity of modern industrial society," as well as a symbol of the foreigner.[60] He recalls that, at a time when Faulkner's reputation was at a low point in this country, the racist aspects of his writings appealed greatly to the Nazis and Italian fascists. However, Faulkner's last years witness a mitigation of his anti-Semitic bias.

Thomas Wolfe published his first novel in 1929, and was essentially a 1920s writer. His mind and sensorium were insatiable absorbers of impressions of sense and persons about him. Coming first, as a youth, to Harvard for a few years and then to New York, he was perforce in close touch with Jews. His biographer, Elizabeth Nowell, writes that "he was still in some ways a small-town southern boy," and "had the villager's dread and dislike of urban Jews," as well as "the traditional Southern feeling about Negroes."[61] In his everyday life, as in his novels, which so intimately reflected that life, his relations with Jews in his later years in New York had a love-hate character more complex, perhaps, than those of any of his contemporary writers. *Look Homeward, Angel* (1929) relates his boyhood experiences with Jewish boys in his home town, how he and his friends "make war upon the negroes and Jews ... [and] spat joyously on the Jews."[62]

But when he comes to delineate his New York experience while teaching at New York University in *Of Time and the River* (1939), Jews begin to figure prominently in his life and writing. The complexity of his own relation to Jews is illustrated by the close friendship he developed with one of his Jewish students, Abe Jones, whose father had been endowed with this surname by an immigration official exasperated by an unpronounceable Russian-Jewish name. Wolfe described Abe as "at this time an obscure and dreary chrysalis, and yet a dogged, loyal, and faithful friend, the salt of the earth, a wonderfully good, rare, and high person."[63] Wolfe meets all of Abe's family and expressed his feelings about them and what they symbolized to him in a lyrical stream of emotional hyperbole.

Wolfe had a love-hate relationship with his mistress of six years (1925 to 1931), Aline Bernstein, who was actually a half-Jew but was identified as a Jew. This relationship is extensively treated in *The Web and the Rock*, published posthumously in 1940. George (Wolfe's name in the book) meets Esther (Aline Bernstein) at the Neighborhood Playhouse and becomes acquainted with the East Side, which he describes in vivid detail, for him "the essential New York; by all odds the richest, the most exciting, the most colorful New York that he had known." Second Avenue is known as "the Broadway of the East Side." But he thought it a "better Broadway... with the warmth of life, ... of a richer and more secure humanity."[64] Esther is a theater designer, as indeed Aline Bernstein was, and through her he meets many people of the theater.

George moves into Esther's apartment and has visions of "a dark regiment of Jewish women in their lavish beauty," the erotic dream of the non-Jew based on his conception of Jewish women as exotic. And there was a male side to this fantasy: "the dark faces of great, beak-nosed Jews, filled with insolence and scorn, with dark pride and unutterable patience, with endurance and humility and an ancient and unspeakable irony as they saw their daughters and their wives yield their bodies into the embraces of Gentile lovers."[65] Life with Esther, although passionate and rewarding, finally turns ugly. He is the aggressor. They exchange insults—on his side, a resort to Jew-baiting.

Esther defends herself. "Wench! Hussy! Jew! These are some of the vile names you have called me, and I have been decent and faithful all my life!" She then turns to criticizing his family for turning him loose in the world when he was sixteen. "You Christians are a charming lot!" she cries. "You talk about the Jews.... Just try to find a Jew that would treat his sister's children that way!"[66] On another occasion they give way to mutual recrimination. Esther charges, "You're acting like a Christian," and he retorts, "And you're acting like a Jew. A damned crafty, Jezebel of a Jew!" "That's all right about the Jews," she replies, "...We're too good for you, that's all. You know nothing about us, and you never will be able in your vile, low soul to understand what we are like as long as you live!"[67] And George then realizes that she was speaking the truth, and he thinks to himself that he had not really intended to say the wounding words he used. Yet, in one of their last quarrels, George shouts, "God! You people make me sick!" Her reply points to the essence of a prejudice that ignores the individual and assigns him or her to an invidious category. "You people!" she replies, "... What people are you talking about? I'm no people!... You don't know what you're talking about!"[68] Soon afterward they part.

Wolfe's love-hate relationship with Jews was mixed up with his turbulent relations with Aline Bernstein. Elizabeth Nowell writes that "the influence she [Aline] had on him was incalculably great—second only to that of his parents and of his father-substitute and editor, Maxwell Perkins." Indeed, he dedicated his first novel to her ("A.B."). For her part, she later said that their relationship was "a supreme experience."[69] In some ways, however, he never overcame his ambivalence about Jews.

Firsthand experience with Nazism seems to have effected a change in him. In May, 1936, he traveled to Germany, flushed and elated with the success that translations of his novels enjoyed there. By summer, however, he came to the realization that "He had come face to face with something old and genuinely evil in the spirit of man which he had never known before, and it shook his inner world to its foundations.... Hitlerism, he saw, was a recrudescence of an old barbarism," manifested among other features, by its "racial nonsense and cruelty."[70] The disillusionment he may have suffered was climaxed on the train as he left the country, when he saw "a frightened little Jew," a fellow passenger, being held at the border because they had found money in his baggage. Wolfe wrote this incident into a short story, "I Have a Story to Tell," and incorporated it in elaborated form in *You Can't Go Home Again*. At the end of the story, Wolfe relates, "All of a sudden, I felt empty, nauseated."[71] As the train pulled out of the station, he saw the Jew look at them,

And in that glance there was all the silence of man's mental anguish. And we were all somehow naked and ashamed, and somehow guilty. We all felt somehow that we were saying farewell, not to a man but to humanity; not to some nameless little cipher out of life, but to the fading image of a brother's face... [Nazism was] a picture of the Dark Ages come again.... I recognized, at last, in all its frightful aspects, the spiritual disease which was poisoning unto death a noble and mighty people.[72]

When this story appeared in *The New Republic* in 1937, his books were promptly banned in Germany.

Another brand of anti-Semitism different from Wolfe's is "social anti-Semitism." This type is not necessarily the same as discrimination based on class distinctions, although it may be, for they are overlapping conceptions. It is more generally defined as exercised on someone outside one's peer group. For instance, when German Jews in the United States became affluent in the latter part of the nineteenth century, they at first aspired to join their peers in a pecuniary sense of the non-Jewish middle and upper middle classes. The non-Jewish groups quickly responded by enforcing the exclusion of wealthy Jews from these institutions—colleges, clubs, some occupations, vacation resorts, and the like—which would confirm their pecuniary status. The non-Jewish middle and upper middle classes were in this sense a peer group which excluded their class counterparts among Jews. Anti-Semitism was in this sense "social" rather than "class." Both Fitzgerald and Hemingway were "social anti-Semites" in this sense.

F. Scott Fitzgerald was ambivalent. His treatment ranges from realistic in *The Beautiful and the Damned* (1922), to anti-Semitic in *The Great Gatsby* (1925), to worshipful in *The Last Tycoon* (1940).

In *The Beautiful and the Damned,* a significant Jewish character in the novel is Bloeckman, a movie executive who offers marriage several times to the heroine, Gloria Gilbert. Though she consistently rejects him, he responds stoically. He is early described as a "stoutening, ruddy Jew of about thirty-five, with an expressive face under his smooth sandy hair—and, no doubt, in most human gatherings his personality would have been considered ingratiating."[73] He appears at intervals in the course of the novel, each time registering a further stage of his change into a cultivated and suave, sophisticated social type. A month after first meeting Gloria he offers marriage, "tendering her everything from a villa in Italy to a brilliant career on the screen. She had laughed in his face—and he had laughed too. But he had not given up.... She treated him rather well."[74]

He doesn't reenter the story until after Gloria's marriage. By then,

Bloeckman had grown tremendously in dignity. The boiled look was gone, he seemed "done" at last. In addition he was no longer overdressed...his right hand, which had previously displayed two heavy rings, was now innocent of ornament.... This dignity appeared also in his personality, the last aura of the successful travelling-man had faded from him.... Anthony [Gloria's husband] no longer felt a correct superiority in his presence.[75]

Several years later, after trips to Europe, "the process of general refinement was still in progress—always he dressed a little better, his intonation was mellower and in his manner there was perceptibly more assurance that the fine things of the world were his by a natural and inalienable right."[76] All this is well and perceptively observed, and signifies Fitzgerald's disinterested aim is realizing the character he was creating; it is sustained to the end. After some years, Bloeckman changes his name to Black. And when Gloria's marriage was disintegrating, her husband Anthony, obviously drunk, encounters Black in a restaurant, and charges him with trying to keep Gloria out of the movies, since he had rejected her for a part for which she was unsuited. Black with dignity tries to leave. "Not so fas', you Goddam Jew,"

Anthony says.[77] Black knocks Anthony down and has him thrown out of the restaurant. Fitzgerald's portrait of Bloeckman is untouched by bias, but would seem a faithful rendering of the intended character.

In *The Great Gatsby* three years later, from his modest beginnings Gatsby finds in the gambler Meyer Wolfsheim the channel for his aspirations to affluence. Wolfsheim is modeled on the notorious gambler Andrew Rothstein, who "fixed" the World Series in 1919 and is identified in the novel by Nick as the man who fixed the Series.[78] He is described as a "flat-nosed Jew" with "tiny eyes" and "two fine growths of hair which luxuriated in either nostril."[79] His English is accented. After Gatsby's murder, Wolfsheim is invited to the funeral, but he declines to go, even though, he said, he "raised him [Gatsby] out of nothing" and "we were like that in everything," which leads Nick to wonder if Gatsby had anything to do with the World Series fixing. Wolfsheim explains, "I can't get mixed up" in the funeral.[80] No wonder Edith Wharton wrote Fitzgerald that she was delighted with the portrait of Wolfsheim. "This reader," she wrote, is "happy to meet your *perfect* Jew." It is true, as Milton Hindus has observed, that Fitzgerald's picture of Wolfsheim is "about as realistic and objective as Marlowe's of Barabas," with no mitigation at all of his evil in personal and social relations—the "perfect" Jew.[81]

By the 1930s, circumstances combined to effect a change in Fitzgerald's ideas about Jews. On the one hand, he was repelled by Nazism. He wrote his daughter in 1938, "Please don't write mean things about Jews in open post cards! To me the Nazis are obnoxious vermin and to share any of their prejudices seems to me smallish and immature."[82] In addition, while working in Hollywood, he came to know and admire the movie producer Irving Thalberg. *The Last Tycoon* gives a favorable portrait of Thalberg in the character of Monroe Stahr. Left unfinished at Fitzgerald's death, the novel shows that the writer came to know a variety of Jews quite well while he was engaged as a writer in Hollywood.

So much did Fitzgerald admire Monroe Stahr, almost to idolatry, that his defects seem minor and like the peccadillos of a noble soul. Stahr is never named as "Jew," although his "ghetto" origin and "Jewish" elements in his background are alluded to.

His dark eyes were kind, aloof and, though they often reasoned with you gently, somewhat superior... [His] fingers... were delicate and slender like the rest of his body, and like his slender face with the arched eyebrows and the dark curly hair. He looked spiritual at times, but he was a fighter—somebody out of his past knew him when he was one of a gang of kids in the Bronx, and gave me a description of how he walked always at the head of the gang, this rather frail boy, occasionally throwing a command backward out of the corner of his mouth.[83]

Fitzgerald likened Stahr's importance in the movies to that of David Wark Griffith or Charlie Chaplin: "He led pictures up past the range and power of the theatre, reaching a sort of golden age, before the censorship."[84]

The author observes of Stahr that "he had worked with Jews too long to believe legends that they were small with money"[85] as if Stahr himself were not a Jew. He also notes that at a meeting of ten head men of the studio, eight were Jews, with Stahr the youngest, a "boy wonder at twenty-two." These Jews could not, like Stahr, do rapid cost calculations in their heads—"for they were not wizards or even experts, despite the popular conception of Jews in finances."[86] Fitzgerald's treatment is so interesting and unusual because it keeps in mind both the individual Jew, Stahr, and lore about the Jews in general. Stahr is never lost sight of as an individual. But Fitzgerald was not dazzled to blindness by Stahr, for he noted that Stahr was anti-union, and he denigrates this as "reactionary." Stahr, the author says, was a "paternalistic" employer. In his notes on the novel the author reminded himself to "Note also in the epilogue [never written] that I want to show that Stahr left certain harm behind him just as he left good behind him. That some of his reactionary creations such as The Screen Playwrights [a company union] existed long after his death just as so much of his valuable creative work survived him."[87]

Fitzgerald is another example of a sensitive writer who changed the tone of his writing about Jews once he came to know Jews personally and closely. When Fitzgerald wrote about the character of Wolfsheim, though he probably modeled him on the gangster Rothstein, he was perhaps unaware that he was uncritically falling into the stereotyped conception of the Jew of his contemporaries. For despite all Wolfsheim's evil propensities, the author did not render him as an individual. Further, the well-observed personality development of Bloeckman in Fitzgerald's first novel shows that he did not succumb to the temptations of the stereotype when he fixed his artistic attention on a character.

Perhaps the most notorious novelistic treatment of a Jewish character in the 1920s is that of Robert Cohn in Ernest Hemingway's *The Sun Also Rises* (1926). This is the writer's sole literary expedition into the Jewish character. Two aspects of the problem must be distinguished here: the quality of anti-Semitism in various characters, and the implied attitude of the author himself. The latter aspect takes on considerable significance from the fact that Cohn is by no means a stereotype, but a rounded, realized individual character.

Cohn, the author notes, came of one of the "oldest" and "richest Jewish families in New York." Before going to Princeton, "no one had ever made him feel he was a Jew, and hence different from anyone else." But he learned differently at Princeton, and it "made him bitter."[88] He became the boxing champion at Princeton in order to "counteract the feeling of inferiority and shyness he had felt at being treated as a Jew at Princeton." He derived comfort from knowing he could "knock down anybody who was snooty to him."[89] Cohn joins the expatriate community in Paris, where he becomes friends with Jake Barnes (Hemingway) and Bill Braddocks. That relationship is broken into two parts, one before and one after Cohn falls in love with the Englishwoman, Brett Ashley, whom Jake also loved frustratedly because a war wound had made him impotent. At first, thinks Jake, "I never heard him [Cohn] make one remark that would, in any way, detach him from other people. He was nice to watch on the tennis court, he had a good body, and he kept it in shape; he handled his cards well at bridge.... He loved to win at tennis.... On the other hand, he was not angry at being beaten."[90]

The relationship changes after Cohn falls in love with Brett and goes away with her for a period. After his return he joins Jake and Bill on a fishing trip to Spain and to the bullfights at Pamplona. Strains develop. "Let's not get superior and Jewish," says Bill. Jake observes to himself that Robert Cohn has the faculty of "bringing out the worst in anybody."[91] As Jake admits, he is really jealous of Cohn's temporary success with Brett, and "hated" Cohn for "barbering" to look good for her after she joins them with Mike Campbell, a British playboy.[92] Jew-baiting increases as their annoyance with Cohn grows when he moons over Brett. Bill taunts him, "Haven't you got some more Jewish friends you could bring along?"[93] After the bullfight Mike joins in the Jew-baiting with a will, since Cohn has acted like a lovesick adolescent. They are even more irritated with Cohn because he doesn't get drunk like them. Jake and Brett try without success to quiet Mike's boorish baiting. The scene grows more tense and is building to a fight, until Mike tells Cohn, "Don't you know you're not wanted? I know when I'm not wanted.... You know you didn't have a good time at San Sebastian because none of our friends would invite you on any of the parties. You can't blame them hardly, can you? I asked them to. They wouldn't do it."[94] Brett charges Mike with lack of "manners." The others—Brett, Jake, Bill—disapprove of Mike's tirade. "Nobody has any business to talk like that."[95] Mike relentlessly continues his Jew-baiting. A fight is averted. The others share Mike's feelings about Cohn's behavior. Brett tells Jake, "I hate him too, I hate his damned suffering.... What do you think it's meant to have that damned Jew about, and Mike the way he's acted?"[96]

The clash between Cohn and the others is mainly one of non-conformity with the "lost generation" life-style, which Cohn shared only incompletely and because of his personal neuroticism. The clash is accentuated by over-tones of anti-Semitism, which vary in degree in the four non-Jews. Mike and Bill manifest their anti-Semitism explicitly, Brett and Jake implicitly. Cohn is no stereotype, but an individual; his sensitivities may be related to his Jewishness, but that is far from identifying him as a stereotype.

The question remains, how is the anti-Semitism in the novel related to the author? Was Hemingway anti-Semitic? Why did he choose to include a Jewish character in this novel? The answer to the latter question is that the actual situation on which the novel is based, a period of Hemingway's life in Paris and a trip to the bullfights at Pamplona, actually included a Jew, Harold Loeb, on whom Robert Cohn is modeled. Loeb came from a wealthy, established Jewish family. He introduced Hemingway to the publisher Liveright's literary scout, Leon Fleischman, who read the group of short stories the writer wished to publish. Loeb's girlfriend was "doubtful" about the wisdom of the trip because she had "noticed Hem's anti-Semitic outbursts" observes Hemingway's biographer Carlos Baker. Hemingway did not like the tone in which the scout agreed to read the stories, and later "exploded profanely, calling Fleischman a low-down kike and a string of other epithets."[97] Fleischman persuaded Liveright to publish the stories. Later Hemingway told Loeb's girlfriend at a dinner party, "I'm writing a novel full of plot and drama. I'm putting everyone in it and that kike Loeb is the villain."[98] Baker's account makes clear that Hemingway himself was anti-Semitic. Biographical data about Hemingway and Harold Loeb tend to confirm this conclusion.

For our study cultural anti-Semitism is that species of anti-Semitism that charges the Jews with corrupting a given culture and attempting to supplant or succeeding in supplanting the preferred culture with a uniform, crude, "Jewish" culture. Considering the basic significance of such a thesis about culture, it is not surprising that a writer who introduces cultural anti-Semitism in his work assigns the Jew a critically important function in his thought and writing. "Attention to the role of anti-Semitism in a writer's work," Robert Alter has written, "may lead to a clearer apprehension of his imaginative world. If the Jews have a historical destiny, it is to be at the crossroads of trouble, and that destiny has been fulfilled time after time not only in the realm of geopolitics but also in the Christian imagination."[99] The relevant prime examples of cultural anti-Semitism in the 1920s were Willa Cather and T. S. Eliot.

Willa Cather's attitude toward the Jews was riddled with paradox. It is well known that in her fiction "she romanticized other nationalities and cultures, the Bohemians, the Swedes, the French," her biographer Phyllis C. Robinson writes, "but where the Jews were concerned she seemed to have a blind spot . . . obnoxious Jews populated her stories." But there were important exceptions like "the Biblical Hebrews [for whom] she had respect and admiration."[100] Moreover, there were a number of living Jews among whom she counted her closest and dearest friends, with most of whom she shared a profound love of music and the cultured life. Among them were the fine English pianist Myra Hess; Alfred A. Knopf, publisher of her books after 1920, and his wife Blanche; above all, the Menuhin family, parents and especially the three children, the musical prodigies Yehudi, Hepzibah, and Yalta; and the Goldsmith sisters, Pauline and Josephine, the latter the wife of Louis D. Brandeis.

Of especial importance for Cather's writing were Mrs. Charles Wiener (no first name is given Mrs. Wiener) and her husband Charles, who owned a store in Red Cloud, Nebraska, while Willa lived there from her eleventh to seventeenth year (1884 to 1890). The Wieners, neighbors of the Cathers, were cultivated French Jews, spoke French and German, and had a large library, including many books in French and German, which they made available to Willa, who spent long afternoons there. The Wieners were especially fond of Willa, and also of Willa's Grandmother Boak. The two families were warm friends, and it is obvious that the Wieners made a deep impression on Willa, which is recorded in the story, "Old Mrs. Harris" in *Obscure Destinies* (1931). It was written in nostalgic recollection in 1931, when Cather was fifty-eight and is so close an account of the life of the Cather family in Red Cloud that Robinson calls this novella "the most autobiographical story Willa ever wrote."[101] An earlier biographer, E. K. Brown, wrote that "many consider [this] Willa Cather's finest short narrative."[102] At its center is Willa's grandmother, "Mrs. Harris," but the Wieners figure in the story as Mr. and Mrs. Rosen. Mrs. Rosen is devoted to old Grandmother Harris and is also important to Vickie (Willa) in providing the means for expansion of her cultural horizons, and finally, in the story, for making possible Vickie's going to college by volunteering a loan. Brown observes that for Vickie "Mrs. Wiener's house exemplified a kind of culture she had not known, and at once recognized as akin to her spirit ... also [gave Vickie] intellectual encouragement. Mrs. Wiener was among the first to appreciate what a remarkable mind Willa Cather had and to urge her to hard work."[103]

In addition, then, to the extremely warm feeling experienced by Willa in the course of her life toward a number of living Jews, the Wieners must be counted. They had a common love of music, the cultured life, and were kindred spirits.

Why, then, the consistently anti-Semitic or hostile treatment of the Jews, except for the Wieners, in her fiction from beginning to end? We are prevented from concluding that "Old Mrs. Harris" marks a change of heart, for she returned to anti-Jewish portraiture in one of her last stories, "The Old Beauty," in 1936, published posthumously in *The Old Beauty and Others* in 1948.

Anti-Semitism appeared in her earliest writings, the vignettes she wrote in 1895 for the *Nebraska State Journal* in Lincoln when she was twenty-two. Cather "describes a baby," wrote Robinson, " 'with an unmistakable nose of an unmistakable race' grasping for a penny with which his mother tries to comfort him when he cries. 'Not an orange or a bonbon,' writes Willa, 'but a penny. He looks at it carefully on both sides as though seeing if it were genuine.' " Robinson added that "this unpleasant sketch might be overlooked except that it is the first of many stereotyped portraits of Jews in Willa's fiction."[104] This is the only image of a precocious stereotype I ever encountered.

Cather soon fitted the stereotype into the large theme of the conflict of the old and new traditions, cultures, and values and conquest by the new and materialistic. This theme of the new materialism and Philistinism lit erally buying out the old traditions is identified in part with the Jews and appears first in her first story collection, *The Troll Garden* (1905), in "The Marriage of Phaedre." A "Jewish picture dealer," Lichtenstein, born in Austria, is trying to purchase the masterpiece of an English painter despite the painter's deathbed injunction against its being sold. Lichtenstein is described as "a man of considerable discrimination" in painting, but of "repulsive personality and innate vulgarity," who spoke Jewish-accented speech conventional in writing about Jews at that time.[105]

Cather's most frequent hostile allusions to Jews in her writing occurred between 1916 and 1925, which saw publication of two short stories of this kind, "The Diamond Mine," first published in 1916, and "Scandal," first published in 1919, and later collected in *Youth and the Bright Medusa* (1925). The reason for this is speculative, since Cather destroyed or had destroyed all her letters as far as she could, and was successful with the most intimate. But in 1915 Isabelle McClung, the woman whom Willa most loved all her life, was courted by Jan Hambourg, an accomplished Jewish professional violinist, and they were married in 1915. Since Cather was a lesbian—as Robinson reveals authoritatively in her biography of the writer in 1983—the loss of Isabelle to a husband was a devastating blow. And married to a Jew! Although Hambourg, like Willa's close Jewish friends, was deeply interested in music and a great reader, apparently Willa never liked him and may even have harbored strong negative feelings. The Hambourgs welcomed Willa to their home and at times urged her to live with them. Although she declined, she did often visit and, as Robinson observes, "Willa must have seen his [Hambourg's] relationship with Isabelle as a violation."[106]

The cultural depravity of the Jew is explicitly articulated in "Scandal." In an effort to acquire social eligibility, the "department-store millionaire" Sigmund Stein tries to perpetrate a hoax on New York society. He squires a model for a time in his employ, who closely resembles an operatic diva. Stein is described as "one of the most hideous men in New York, but it's not the common sort of ugliness that comes from overeating and automobiles."[107] The story also symbolizes his effort to usurp the traditional American aristocracy in the climactic success of his efforts: he and his wife now live in "a great house on Fifth Avenue that used to belong to people of a very different sort. To Old New Yorkers, it's an historic house."[108]

Cather's personal insensitivity regarding Jews is thrown into further relief by an incident related by Robinson. In 1923 Cather was attending a performance of *Loyalties*, Galsworthy's play against anti-Semitism. "While admiring the performance," writes Robinson, Cather could "still comment to a friend about the fat Jewesses in the audience and suggest that Galsworthy might have changed the ending of the play if he had sat beside them." As for the character of Stein, Robinson asserts that he "probably owe[s his] very existence to the residue of anger Willa felt toward Jan."[109]

But Cather's resentment had more immediate expression in the comprehensive symbol of the Jew as an important influence making for replacement of the old traditions and outlook by the new, vulgar, materialistic conqueror. Not a short story but an entire novel was applied to the task, *The Professor's House* (1925), and Jan Hambourg serves as the model for the symbolic Jewish character, Louie Marsellus, in whom Cather invested her notion of the new, "vulgar," materialistic influence which was helping to force out the older, finer traditions. The idea was crystallized after the summer of 1923, which Cather had spent with the Hambourgs in their house in Ville-d'Avrey. She was careful to avoid any stereotypical traits, except for one. "There was nothing Semitic about his countenance," she wrote of Louie, "except his nose." He is not the crude Jew of the short stories but a "cosmopolitan, generous man devoted to those about him" and he has a "zest for life."[110]

The basic confrontation in the novel is exemplified in a series of symbolic opposites regarding Marsellus and Tom Outland, who had been affianced to Professor St. Peter's daughter Rosamond and had died in World War I. Outland had loved the old Western culture and older modes of American life that were giving way to industrialism and its attendant culture symbolized by the engineer Marsellus. Outland had made an invention, which he had willed to Rosamond. Marsellus, married to Rosamond, had exploited Outland's invention for an industrial use, which made him and Rosamond rich. Thus Cather brings into play the common nineteenth-century cliché that the Jew is not creative but can only exploit for money what the Christian creates. Professor St. Peter is fighting a losing battle with the materialistic new, which is pressing in upon him. Rosamond is infected by Marsellus, the Jew undermining traditional culture. "It's not just the clothes," says her sister Kathleen, " ... it's everything ... she's entirely changed. She's become Louie. He and all this money have ruined her."[111] James Schroeter pithily states the thesis of the novel: it "says pretty much the same thing about Jews as the shorter pieces—the Jew is a money maker rather than a creator, a traditionless aggressor who invades from the outside; he threatens and destroys the past; and he symbolizes what is wrong with the present ... Willa's 'message' is simply that America is falling into the hands of the Jews."[112]

The evidence indicates that Cather's ingrained anti-Jewish prejudice is joined with her resentment at Jan Hambourg's intrusion on her relationship with her beloved Isabelle McClung. In light of what we now know, I believe that, consciously or unconsciously, this influence operated in the stories of 1916 and 1919 and the novel of 1925. Cather continued to depict Jews unfavorably in her fiction until quite late in life. In 1936, when she was sixty-three, she wrote "The Old Beauty," which exhibited an unabated anti-Semitism.[113] This story deals with an event said to have occurred in 1922. At a French resort an old, beautiful, aristocratic American woman is visited by a man she knew when young. She ruminates about their last meeting two decades earlier. By a timely visit he had saved her from an attempted rape by a Jewish banker. The attempted rape of the old culture by a Jewish upstart?

How is one to reconcile these prejudiced manifestations against Jews as crude barbarians with the portrait of the kind, generous, highly cultivated Mrs. Rosen of "Old Mrs. Harris," who lived by cultural values higher than those of anyone else in the "English-speaking" town of Red Cloud? Moreover, this representation of an actual Jewish woman, Mrs. Wiener, was probably not far from the actuality, since it arose from the writer's personal experience. What is said of the Jewish Rosens, that is, of the actual Wieners, is totally at variance with Cather's characterizations of all other Jews in her fiction.

Another case of the higher scapegoating is the anti-Semitism of T. S. Eliot. Where Willa Cather blames the Jews for the decay of traditional American culture, Eliot's horizon is Western culture as a whole, and the Jews are responsible for undermining it. There is conventional anti-Semitism in his 1920 volume of poems. "Of Cooking Eggs" makes the Jewish financier, the British peer Sir Alfred Mond, the symbol of "Capital." Repulsion is expressed in "Sweeney Among the Nightingales," where Rachel's eating of grapes is described as repulsive. Similarly, in "Gerontion," sheer revulsion from the Jew as a disgusting creature is evident. The "jew" is scarcely human: he "squats"; he is not born but "spawned"; he does not grow and develop, he is "blistered," "patched," "peeled."[114] In short, the Jew is a degenerate and rootless. But he is not despicable for himself alone—he infects the inside of Western society with decay. In such attitudes toward Jews Eliot was deeply in sympathy with several anti-Semites who influenced him—Henry Adams and especially the French-Catholic pro-fascist Charles Maurras. The underlying fear of presumed Jewish disintegrating influence prompted the observation in Eliot's *After Strange Gods* (1934) that "reasons of race and religion combine to make any large number of free-thinking Jews undesirable" in the United States.[115]

Most notorious and familiar of all, and most fully articulating Eliot's notion of the disintegrating influence of the Jews on Western culture is "Burbank with a Baedeker, Bleistein with a Cigar." The poem is packed with quotations from and allusions to great literary works of Western culture, ancient and modern. The plenitude of such allusions symbolizes the great culture which is being disintegrated, as indicated by their fragmentary nature. Who is responsible? Why, "Bleistein" or the Jews, that "Chicago Semite Viennese." Not only he, but also that upstart Sir Ferdinand Klein, who robbed Britain of her past glories. Western culture is rotting—but the Jew is the one who has caused the decay.[116]

Eliot never gave public notice to the charge of anti-Semitism, but he is reported several times to have denied it in private. He once said, "I am not an anti-Semite. It is a terrible slander of a man." And Robert Giroux reports that Eliot said, "I am a Christian, and therefore I am not an anti-Semite,"[117] which some people might regard as a non-sequitur, unless the term "Christian" is strictly defined. It is quite possible that Eliot really believed he was not anti-Semitic, but merely acknowledging unpleasant facts of history, since stereotyped notions of Jews are so deepseated that one can hold them quite unaware. Whatever he may have thought, in his use of the image of Jews in his writing before the mid-1930s, he clearly regarded the Jew as the malefactor responsible for the decline of Western culture.

The array of significant—non-Jewish and Anglo-Saxon—literary figures emerging in the 1920s who, to one degree or another, manifested anti-Semitism is disturbingly inclusive. But anti-Semitism had no essential relation to modernism, as a glance at one of the seminal works of the 1920s, *Ulysses* (1922), would demonstrate. One could not ask for a more definitive literary manner of handling anti-Semitism in fiction than James Joyce's mode of deflecting anti-Jewish attitudes. In the newspaper office Mr. Deasy says to Stephen Daedalus, "England is in the hands of the jews. In all the highest places: her finance, her press. And they are the signs of a nation's decay. Wherever they gather they eat up the nation's vital strength. I have seen it coming for years. As sure as we are standing here the jew merchants are already at their work of destruction. Old England is dying." "A merchant," Stephen answers, "is one who buys cheap and sells dear, jew or gentile, is he not?" "They sinned against the light," Mr. Deasy goes on. "Who has not?" Stephen replies.[118]

In the United States, too, there were distinguished exceptions. Edmund Wilson nowhere baited the Jews. There are, for instance, a number of references to Jews in his novel *I Thought of Daisy* (1925), but nowhere does he stoop to any stereotyping or invidious overtones. There is especially a passage of several pages on "Harry Hirsch, ... a small, young Jew with very large, intense eyes, like motor headlights [Eddie Cantor?] ... doubt the son of a Rabbi or Cantor in a Synagogue." Where had he got that "new accent" that was so popular? "from the sounds of the streets? ... or simply from his own nostalgia among the dark cells and raspings of New York ... or from the cadence, half-chanted and despairing, or the tongue which the father had known, but which the child had forgotten."[119] This empathic speculation devoid of any suggestions of prejudice, was unhappily exceptional among the major writers of the 1920s.

Another exception in this regard was Sinclair Lewis. While he was at Yale, he became interested in the Jews in New Haven in connection with his job as night reporter, and wrote several articles in 1906 on the local ghetto for the *Yale Literary Magazine*. In the summer of 1906 he was a deck hand on a cattle boat to Europe, and observed Jewish crew members at their religious observances and saw how their shipmates ridiculed them. He put this experience to use in the first story for which he received pay,

"That Passage in Isaiah," in the May, 1907, issue of *The Blue Mule,* a five-cent San Francisco publication. A bearded, Orthodox Jew, Blumenbaum, is a hand on a cattle boat bound for England. He is sympathetically portrayed, as is the persecution he suffers at the hands of the crew. He is especially harassed by his crew boss Spuds. Tormented beyond endurance, Blumenbaum curses Spuds, saying God will not let such a one live. At the landing, during a fog, Spuds is terrified at the look in Blumenbaum's face in the glare of a searchlight. At the same time a loose gate swings around and sweeps Spuds off into the sea, the curse apparently fulfilled.[120]

Lewis' sensitivity on the Jewish question led him to denounce Henry Ford's anti-Jewish campaign from 1921 on. In 1922 he attacked Ford's anti-Semitism in a talk at an Evanston church, concluding that if Ford knew more of Jewish history, "he would not frighten people into believing that America was in danger of subjection by New York Jewish millionaires."[121] He once withdrew from a hotel after he learned it discriminated against Jews.

He incorporated this conviction into his literary work. His *Arrowsmith* (1925), written in close collaboration with the respected bacteriologist and science popularizer Paul de Kruif, portrays a devoted Jewish scientist, Max Gottlieb, who gained a reputation for his European work in immunology. He is driven from his native Germany because of his tactlessness, his fury at discrimination against Jews, his dissenting ideas, his eccentricity and his "religion of science," and comes to the United States. The novel's protagonist, Arrowsmith, studies with Gottlieb in Nebraska, is inspired to emulate him, and becomes his assistant. Arrowsmith "preached to himself as Max Gottlieb had once preached to him, the loyalty of dissent." After Arrowsmith does some successful research, he gives up testing his results, and feels that "in giving up his experiment... he became a traitor to Gottlieb and all that Gottlieb represented."[122] Throughout the novel Gottlieb's Jewish origin is pictured as one of the obstacles put in the way of Gottlieb's fulfilling his scientific genius.

Considering Lewis' consistent awareness of the problems faced by Jews, it is not surprising that he was prompted by Nazism to write one of the most effective, though transient, anti-fascist propaganda pieces of the 1930s, in *It Can't Happen Here* (1935). It projects to 1939 the way in which fascism might come to the United States through the experience of Doremus Jessup, editor of a Vermont newspaper. The well-intentioned Jessup is at first taken in by an American form of fascism. The fascist party sets forth a program that is anti-labor and apparently anti-wealth. All organizations are *gleichgeschaltet* and "International Jewish Finance and especially International Jewish Communism and Anarchism and Atheism" must be "barred from all activity." Further, "any Jew who shall refuse to swear allegiance to the New Testament" will be excluded from public office. There is a Jew in Jessup's town who conforms to the fascist program, and another, a "fresh kike," who resists it. "Minute Men" act against such "bellyachers as Jewish doctors, Jewish musicians, Negro journalists, college professors."[123]

Jessup's growing disillusionment is climaxed when a rabbi is murdered after the rabbi asserts that the Jews, whom the fascists would like to transfer to a "Zion" in South America, cannot see the American leader "as a rival to Jehovah." For Jessup this is "the last straw"; he refuses to knuckle under to the fascists and joins the underground resistance. However, Lewis wished to make clear that he understood that some Jews were susceptible to fascism in order to protect their wealth, as indeed Nazism in the early years showed about some German Jews. The impact of the novel was reinforced when it was quickly put into play form by Lewis and John C. Moffitt. It was produced by the Federal Theatre, and on October 17, 1936, the play opened simultaneously in seventeen cities from coast to coast. Attempts to get the story into film were frustrated because, Lewis thought, it was vetoed as "controversial" by movie "czar" Will Hays.[124]

As early as 1933 Lewis was thinking of writing a novel about the Jewish problem, but he never got around to it. Again in 1939 he wanted to do a play about anti-Semitism in the medical profession, to be titled "The Undiscovered Country," and began gathering data, but this project also was unrealized.

All these 1920s writers have this in common: they are all of North European origin, which then current racial ideas regarded as "superior." All were born between 1876 (Anderson, Cather) and 1900 (Wolfe), so that all lived through about the same phases of national development, that is, the era of mass immigration, of intense industrialization and urbanization, of jingoistic war fever and racialism. They were all subject to one of the most severe growths of anti-Semitism in the United States, climaxing in the early 1920s with the alarming spread of the Ku Klux Klan and the distribution of the infamous *Protocols of the Elders of Zion*. Under these conditions it is not surprising that major writers manifested anti-Semitism in some degree or intensity.

By the 1930s, the incalculable threat of Nazism hovered over the nation and the world. Anti-Semitism moved into its most extreme expression, the genocidal. The attitude of writers could not help but be affected one way or another. We have seen how some, like Faulkner, Fitzgerald, and Wolfe, explicitly reversed earlier tendencies to Jew-baiting in their writing. But talented writers are not necessarily humanists, and in some, like Pound, an earlier anti-Semitism was reinforced by the racism spread by Nazism, and a writer like Cummings seems hardly to understand how Nazism affected the Jews. Eliot and Hemingway never again referred to Jews in their writings after the 1920s. But writers like Edmund Wilson and Sinclair Lewis were immune to the epidemic of Jew-hatred.

3

The Depression Years: The 1930s

"PROLETARIAN" AND LABOR FICTION

Rarely did the national mood change so abruptly and radically in times of peace as after the stock market crash of October 24, 1929, which set off the Great Depression. Overnight, financial euphoria was changed to panic. In the next week alone over $15 billion were lost. As two leading historians put it,

by the end of the year the shrinkage in securities of all kinds had reached the fantastic sum of forty billion dollars. Millions of investors lost their life savings.... Business houses closed their doors, factories shut down, banks crashed, and millions of unemployed walked the streets in a vain search for work. Hundreds of thousands of families lost their homes; tax collections dropped to the point where cities and counties were unable to pay school teachers; construction work all but ceased; foreign trade, already badly hit, declined to an unprecedented low.[1]

Mortgages on thousands of farms were foreclosed as farm prices fell catastrophically. By 1932 there were 85,000 business failures and 5,000 banks suspended. Unemployment grew apace until by 1932 it reached 12 million of a population of 123 million and was still growing. By 1932 the national income had fallen about one-half from 1929 as did industrial production.

What was being done to alleviate the suffering brought on by the catastrophe? Almost nothing, and despair gripped the land. Several historians have written:

Confronted with something terribly wrong in the old systems of production and distribution, business leaders and political stalwarts saw no need for social legislation and forthright reform. Bread lines and malnutrition, the eviction of unemployed laborers, the uprooting of thousands of farm families by foreclosures on mortgages, the loss of home and job by hundreds of thousands of salaried middle-class workers imperilled capitalism and democracy, but the [Hoover] administration and its supporters were oblivious or forgetful, or bewildered. They were unwilling to sponsor reform or even federal relief that would stay starvation and check the loss of home and goods.[2]

Under these conditions, the people were not supine. After sustaining the initial shock, the electorate swept Franklin Delano Roosevelt into office in 1932, and the labor movement began a counterattack. Strikes broke out all over; John L. Lewis' militant industrial unions abandoned the passive American Federation of Labor and organized the Congress of Industrial Organizations in 1936. The sit-down auto strike against General Motors in Flint, Michigan, in 1936 set off a new wave of labor militancy all over the country. On the international scene, Hitler's assumption of power in 1933 gave rise to an anti-fascist sentiment, which was organized into a mass movement. The Nazi attempt to reduce the Jews to sub-humanity and the fascist revolt in Spain, given essential military aid by Hitler and Mussolini, spurred the movement on. But the anti-fascist movement was not strong enough to compel Roosevelt to lift the American arms embargo on Spain, and in 1938 the Spanish Republic was conquered by Generalissimo Franco with vital aid from Nazi Germany and fascist Italy. It is not easy for subsequent generations to imagine the ardor with which large sections of the American people, from liberals to Communists, embraced the Spanish-Republican cause. Matthew Josephson has written of the Spanish Republic, "I should never have believed that I would be so moved by any action taking place in a distant land, and it was surprising to see how many other Americans felt similar emotions."[3] About 3,300 American volunteers went to Spain to fight for the Loyalist cause in the Abraham Lincoln Brigade, the project largely organized by the American Communist party, but including men of varying political views from center Left to the Communist Left. Almost half lost their lives and were buried in Spanish ground.

Many writers worked in the midst of those labor and Left activities. Writers, artists, and other intellectuals were especially active in defense of the Spanish Republic. For instance, on March 1, 1937, the *New York Times* reported that ninety-eight American writers, many of them well-known figures, had signed a statement condemning the Franco rebellion. Leading writers were also active in helping the labor movement. One of the most famous of these actions was the formation of the Writers' Committee to investigate the violent anti-union actions taken against the miners of Harlan County in Kentucky in 1931. Theodore Dreiser was the active chairman of the committee, engaged in the dangerous work on the ground in Kentucky, together with other noted writers like Edmund Wilson, John Dos Passos, and Waldo Frank.

This participation by leading writers did not begin in the 1930s. Despite the fact that the radical movement was remote from general interest in the prosperous 1920s, numbers of recognized writers had become involved in labor and protest activities as the previous decade wore on. A leading Communist writer and intellectual, Joseph Freeman, wrote of *The New Masses* in its beginnings in 1926 that the group around it was small.

It was isolated from the mass organizations of the workers and from the mass of intellectuals, who, despite liberal reservations, were at this time attached to the existing system. One or two novels, occasional stories and poems, were all that American left-wing writers were able to produce in the creative field. Proletarian literature was in its propaganda stage. The handful of revolutionary writers active in the Coolidge-Hoover era devoted themselves chiefly to criticism.[4]

But perhaps more than any other single event the Sacco-Vanzetti defense campaign had aroused the writers and artists who awoke in 1927 to the threatening miscarriage of justice at the final stages of the appeal process. A number of prominent writers joined the picket line in front of the State House in Boston, and some were arrested while peacefully exercising their right of dissent. In August, 1927, ninety-three artists, writers, and intellectuals petitioned Massachusetts Governor Fuller to stop the execution, to no effect. An appeal to President Coolidge for a stay of execution also was rejected. These events made a deep impression on the writers. They composed poems, wrote novels and plays on the case, testifying to the depth of their feelings on the issue. Events like these in the 1920s were an anticipatory tremor of the literary earthquake in the 1930s.

For many writers, these experiences, post–World War I disillusionment with government and political "ideals," and repulsion from prevailing philistinism and "Normalcy" made transition to radicalism easy. In 1926 some had gone to Passaic to help striking textile workers. Several avant-garde literary journals were also radical, like *The New Masses* or the little magazines, places where anti-bourgeois and modernist writers were published alongside the politically radical. A few even joined the Communist party or were close sympathizers. Then the socioeconomic cataclysm of October, 1929, suddenly made the Left intensely relevant. Writers on the Left organized themselves into the radical writers' and artists' John Reed Clubs after the stock market crash. And as we have noted, the rape of the Spanish Republic by Franco and his fascist allies profoundly affected all sensitive people—writers and artists in particular.

By the latter 1930s perhaps a majority of American writers tended toward the Left, among them leading literary figures. As sensitive registers of their time they could not remain unaffected. They could not ignore what events at home and abroad were telling them about the structure of capitalism and the need for change. While radicalism had had a peripheral effect on them in the 1920s, it became central in the 1930s. In 1932 a statement in support of the candidacy on the Communist party ticket of William Z. Foster and John W. Ford (a Black) for president and vice-president was signed by fifty-two writers, artists, and intellectuals.

When Hitler came to power the next year and the danger to democracy became more imminent, the Communist party began a process of change. In the preceding five years the party had been hostile to ideological rivals like the Socialist party and crudely designated Socialists as "social fascists," that is, those whose policies and actions, according to the party, "objectively" aided the fascists. But it now became apparent that a broad, unified anti-fascist popular force, called the People's Front, must be established to fend off the mortal Nazi danger. To this end the party changed its program in the cultural area from a drive for "proletarian" art and literature, which demanded obligatory relation to the party and revolution, to the less stringent "progressive" literature and art of "good will" whose main thrust was militantly democratic and anti-fascist.

The John Reed Clubs, which had stressed "proletarian" literature, were quietly dissolved and replaced in 1935 with a broader, less stringent, non-dogmatic American Writers Congress. Following the public organizing conference in 1935, two more conferences were held in 1937 and 1939. The congress did indeed obtain cooperation of many leading American writers who, like most sensitive people, were seized with the need to resist fascism. But the congress proved short-lived. It was severely shaken by the Soviet-Nazi Pact in 1939, and many of its members abandoned the Left in revulsion. During the life of the congress itself there were also many defections from the ranks because of disillusionment with the Moscow purge trials and with Stalinism. Some disaffected writers remained on the Left but shifted their allegiance to the Trotskyist parties. For their part, *The New Masses,* the Communist party, and its non-party allies, the so-called fellow travelers, were unswervingly, if unconsciously, Stalinist.

One gains a fuller perspective on the leftward movements when one considers the Left tradition in this century among writers. A literary-political socialist journal, *The Comrade,* was published from 1901 to 1905. Short-lived publications followed until 1911, when the solidly based, non-sectarian *The Masses* began to appear, attracting leading writers and artists to contribute. Not strictly socialist, the journal was generally anti-Establishment in politics and art and was hospitable to rebels against the genteel tradition and its morals. The editors were socialists of one sort or another, with, however, nothing of the strict conformity of doctrine that was demanded in later years by *The New Masses.* Its pages were open to any form of rebellion, from bohemianism, Tolstoyanism, or the non-conformism of the Ash Can school of painting led by John Sloan, himself an editor of the magazine, to the open radicalism of John Reed, also on the editorial board, as well as the systematic socialism of Max Eastman, the editor. As John

Reed wrote, "Sensitive to all new winds that blow, never rigid in a single view of place in life, such is our ideal for *The Masses.*"[5] Max Eastman was the editorial mentor of the magazine from 1912 to 1917, when its anti-war stand caused it to be banned from the mails and its editors to be charged with conspiring to obstruct recruitment for the war. (Both the first and second trials ended in hung juries, and the case was finally dropped.)

No sooner had *The Masses* ceased publication in 1918 than *The Liberator* took its place with the same general outlook, except that it ostensibly dropped opposition to the war. This was again under the editorship of Eastman with Floyd Dell, who had had the same position on *The Masses,* as associate editor. *The Liberator* continued to espouse socialism with a non-sectarian outlook and its pages were open to all tendencies. But a new generation was coming up, in which Communist writers like Mike Gold and Joseph Freeman were the leaders. When Eastman and Dell gave up the editorship in 1921, Gold and Freeman became the editors. In 1923 *The Liberator* became a virtual Communist party organ, and the next year it was merged with several other Communist journals. In 1926 the radical tradition was resumed with the founding of *The New Masses.* A few Communists led it, but there were many non-Communists among its supporters. From then on *The New Masses* was to be the main vehicle of left-wing adherence to Soviet policy in connection with the Moscow purge trials, the expulsion of Trotsky from the Soviet Union, and the Soviet-Nazi Pact. While these events disaffected some important literary people, throughout the period a number of writers perceived that the Communist party was the most active and effective center in the country for fighting the Depression and for anti-fascist activity. They remained with it because they placed highest priority on the battle against these and upon defense of humanity at home and abroad.

The seeds of the literary future, however, rested rather with *Partisan Review,* which was first published as an organ of the New York John Reed Club in 1934 specifically to advance "revolutionary literature." A conflict soon developed between those who believed revolutionary literature should be an explicit tribune of political action and who rejected "bourgeois" literary influences and those who believed the artist should not be interfered with in realizing his visions. Among the latter were William Phillips and Philip Rahv, who led the attack against sectarianism and a mechanical approach to creative writing. The argument continued with increasing strain until 1935, when the John Reed Clubs were dissolved. The magazine then had no formal affiliations. It merged briefly in 1936 with *The Anvil,* journal of the Mid-west John Reed Clubs.

Phillips and Rahv finally broke with the party and in 1937 reconstituted the magazine. On the new editorial board, besides these two, were the Trotskyists Dwight Macdonald and Fred Dupee, Mary McCarthy, together with G.L.K. Morris, an abstract painter who was the magazine's financial

angel. Macdonald pushed the magazine in a Trotskyist direction, although
Phillips and Rahv never joined a Trotskyist party. *Partisan* became anti-
Stalinist, a zealous and effective promoter of modernism in literature and
art, acquired prestige, and emerged from World War II as one of the most
influential literary journals in the country. Macdonald resigned from the
board in 1943 when his anti-war views became too hard to reconcile with
the pro–World War II views of his colleagues. *Partisan* also shed its relationship to Left politics and by the 1950s was a centerpiece of the American
literary Establishment.

Throughout this period of Left literary development Jewish writers played
an increasingly important, and later a central, role. A notion of the pace
and nature of this participation can be gathered from Jewish membership
in the successive editorial boards of radical publications. In the first, *The
Comrade,* which opened the century in 1901, there were seven editors, of
whom one, Morris Winchevsky, was Jewish. Winchevsky can be called the
representative of the Yiddish-speaking sector of the radical movement—
there was as yet no English-speaking Jewish Left. Born in Lithuania in 1855,
he first immigrated to Prussia, then quickly moved to England, where he
joined the socialist movement and was the editor of the first Yiddish socialist
journal. After fifteen years in England, he came to the United States in 1894
and again took up his radical activities. He was among the founders of the
Forverts (Jewish Daily Forward) in 1897, and later of the Communist *Frei-
heit (Freedom)* in 1922. But he was also a poet, and his Yiddish poems and
songs were sung by Jewish workers all over the world. When *The Masses*
began publishing in 1911, the Yiddish-speaking socialist movement had
already struck roots in the Yiddish-speaking community and, although a
mainstay of the general socialist movement, it simultaneously had its own
separate development.

On the original editorial board of *The Masses,* only one member, Louis
Untermeyer, poet and anthologist, was Jewish. This, it will be recalled, was
still 1911. But when Eastman and Floyd Dell left its successor, *The Liberator,*
in 1921, two Jews, Mike Gold and Joseph Freeman, were the designated
editors. By the 1920s the second immigrant generation was coming to maturity and taking its place. A number of Jews had been contributors to *The
Masses* and *The Liberator.* Among one hundred contributors named in lists
in Daniel Aaron's *Writers on the Left* were about fifteen Jews—15 percent,
already a disproportionately high figure. They were among the rising leadership. When *The New Masses* took over from *The Liberator* in 1926, its
contributors spanned a wide spectrum of radical and artistic opinion; although sympathetic to the Soviet Union, few actual Communists were
among its movers. *The New Masses* began with an editorial board of six,
three of them Jewish: Mike Gold Joseph Freeman, and an artist, Hugo
Gellert. The first two, however, were the effective editors, and by 1928,
Gold became sole editor. In 1934 *Partisan Review* was established as the

publishing arm of the writers and artists organized into the John Reed Clubs, and all twelve of the original editors were Jewish, William Phillips and Philip Rahv among them.

One more set of figures will confirm the extent to which Anglo-Saxon dominance of United States literature had declined. The First American Writers Congress in 1935 included a large percentage of leading writers. When elections were held at the conclusion of the congress, Waldo Frank was elected chairman; of the Executive Committee of seventeen, eleven were Jewish, and of the National Council members, fourteen were Jews. Finally, in the summary volume of the proletarian movement, *Proletarian Literature in the United States* (1935), an anthology of work in six genres, half of the sixty-three contributors were Jewish. In the individual genres, six of sixteen in fiction were Jewish; in poetry, sixteen of twenty-nine; in reportage, three of eight; in drama, six of six; in literary criticism, five of ten. The "Critical Introduction" was written by Joseph Freeman.[6]

These figures do not by any means signify that Jewish writers dominated the front rank of American writers, although some lasting works were created by them, most particularly Henry Roth's *Call It Sleep,* which was not a proletarian novel. The proletarian movement as such was short-lived. The urgency of forming a united front against advancing fascism forced the Communist movement to modify its sectarian insistence on a narrowly conceived proletarian direction, and instead it welcomed and encouraged within its orbit a literature of wider appeal and scope. The dissolution of the John Reed Clubs and formation of the broader American Writers Congress was the organizational expression of this new approach.

On every hand the world was in crisis. The Depression resisted efforts at complete recovery. Hitlerism and fascism were an imminent international menace to the most elementary human values and culture. The sense of emergency that brought together writers and intellectuals of varying political hues (except for anti-Stalinists and Trotskyists) was conveyed by Waldo Frank in his "Forward" to the published report of the First Writers Congress.

We were drawn together [he wrote] by the threat implicit in the present social system, to our culture and to our very lives as creative men and women. We are held together by common devotion to the need of building a new world from which the evils endangering mankind will have been uprooted, and in which the foundations will live for the creation of a universal human culture. We represent many phases of thought, many varieties of temperament and of art. But these differences have served to strengthen the texture of our gathering; to enrich the fiber of our discussions.[7]

But this unity of writers was far from solid. From the mid-1930s radical writing in the United States bifurcated into the pro-Communist, Stalinist, on the one hand, and the anti-Stalinist, strictly literary, modernist wing on the other, represented in the main by *The New Masses* and *Partisan Review,* respectively. By the end of World War II and during the Cold War *Partisan* abandoned its Left character. However, general Communist influence did not cease suddenly. It continued into the 1940s, and an important novel like Richard Wright's *Native Son* (1940) was written under its auspices. It is customary to dismiss the proletarian period as a literary desert, as a hiatus in the march of American literature. There was indeed much folly and crudity in its course. But one must consider the desperate social situation and the attempt of socially responsible writers to do something about it. And there were lasting literary achievements under Left inspiration, as we shall see.

But even more was involved. In the 1930s there was increasing participation in our literature by a new, acculturated, multi-ethnic America. In that decade, as Marcus Klein has observed, there was "the democratization of the idea of authorship in America. Paradoxically but explicably, the discovery of folk mentality meant that new Americans, too, might assert cultural citizenship. In a word, this American past was just as available to the sons and daughters of the Great Migration as it was to the natives."[8] Even if the specific doctrines of the proletarian period did not survive in their original form, its function in "the democratization of authorship" was established, and American literature was never the same again. But it was the second fork of the bifurcated Left literary movement, the *Partisan Review* modernist tendencies, that governed the postwar future. In the 1940s and 1950s the literary had so far overshadowed the political in *Partisan* that the journal became an important sector of the Establishment.

But how may we account specifically for the large and disproportionate number of second-generation Jews in positions of influence on the literary scene by the 1930s? The reasons are complex. During this decade the "center of gravity" of the mass Jewish immigration was moving to the second generation, as E. Digby Baltzell observed: "As this second generation now knew the language, had been educated in the public schools, and had assimilated American values of democracy, self-respect and equal opportunity, they were ready to move with the mainstream of American life."[9] The entry of Jewish writers in such considerable numbers was a consequence of the acculturation process. But the disproportionate number still remains to be explained. It was an aspect of the remarkably rapid upward mobility of the Jews emerging from the ghetto, under conditions of the relatively open path to careers, especially in areas where discrimination and anti-Semitism were less decisively enforced. Perhaps discrimination against Jews in many areas of academic and professional life contributed to their number in self-employed intellectual vocations. In fact Jews were also disproportionately present in the fine and graphic arts and in some professions like law and medicine. The stimulus to excel seemed stronger among Jews because of their marginal position in Christian society, in which they had endured centuries of persecution and were targets of discrimination and anti-Semitism. This raised barriers to be overcome. The traditional Jewish love of and obligation toward education and learning, previously expressed in study of the Talmud and holy books, were now applied in secular channels.

In radical thought and creativity Jews were also prone to appear in great numbers because they knew poverty on the East Side in the early decades of the immigration. They were therefore immediately responsive during the 1930s to the suffering brought on by the worst depression in our history. Stemming from a working-class environment, with many even yet not extricated from the slums, they knew the suffering at first hand. They were devoid of any vested interest in the social structure that they were entering and whose performance did not recommend it. Very important, too, was the brutal fact of Hitlerism, which obviously touched Jews most immediately and often gave the initial stimulus to radicalization.

Until World War I the overwhelming mass of Jews in the United States were working-class and wage workers. Although a shift to the middle class had already begun between the wars, a majority remained working-class, proletarians. In defining this word Webster's *New International Dictionary* (second edition) cites the nineteenth-century *North American Review* to this effect: "Machinery ushered into existence the fourth estate, *proletarian* or wage earner." The definition cites other features: a proletarian is "one with no property"; he is "not possessed of capital." The idea of a literature about and for the working class was not created in the 1930s. It was already exemplified in the intensely class-conscious ballads of the "Wobblies," the radical International Workers of the World whose prime balladeer was the Swede, Joe Hill. Already in the 1920s proletarian literature was continuously discussed—under that name—by its central advocate, Mike Gold. In February, 1921, Gold had published in *The Liberator,* "Toward Proletarian Art." He looked to the proletariat to inspire "resurrection" of the arts, which he charged with exhaustion and sterility. Full of emotion and high-flown rhetoric, the article in a vague way called on the artist to identify himself with a struggling, aspiring, revolutionary people out of whom will come "huge-hewn poets, those striding outdoor philosophers and horney-handed creators" whom Walt Whitman prophesied.[10] Lacking for the most part in analytical specificity, the article was nevertheless a trumpet call to artists to join in revolutionary creativity. The article also called attention to an actual realization of proletarian art and doctrine by the Soviet *Proletkult* movement, the group of narrow, sectarian artists and cultural workers who tried, unsuccessfully, to monopolize the Soviet arts until 1932. In keeping with the general change in policy away from a sectarian to a people's front approach, the group was dissolved, to be replaced by the Union of Soviet Writers and the broader doctrine of socialist realism. In the United States this congruent change occurred a few years later with the dissolution of the John Reed Clubs and the organization of the First Writers Congress.

American proletarian literature had the following essential features. It was written from the putative workers' viewpoint, that is, it was highly class conscious. It dealt with some critical juncture in working-class life during which the workers were in struggle to gain their due vis-à-vis the employers, the capitalists, by strikes and ultimately by revolutionary action. However vague Gold may have been in his 1921 article, he was specific on this score. He pointed to the several types of action in which workers engage: "strike, boycott, mass-meeting, imprisonment, sacrifice, agitation, martyr-dom, organization."[11] Their depiction was the office of the artist. Often the proletarian novel ends with a strike during which the movement is advanced by victory and the hero is converted to revolutionary unionism or to com-munism. Sooner or later the plot is, in one way or another, involved with the Communist party. Not all proletarian writers were party members; some were sympathizers and in the later 1930s a number became estranged from the party and communism. Walter B. Rideout lists fifty proletarian writers between 1920 and 1954, of whom fourteen were Jews, that is, almost one-third. In the period between 1900 and 1920, the number of Jews had been six out of thirty-six—that is, one-sixth.

How did the Jewish proletarian novelists look on their Jewishness during the 1930s? A statement of Joseph Freeman in his autobiography states the general attitude fairly and applies to many who did not go to college as well as to those who did.

By the time we were leaving the university, [he wrote] we were no longer culturally Jews. We were Westerners initiated into and part of a culture which merged the values of Jerusalem, Egypt, Greece and ancient Rome with the Catholic culture of the Middle Ages, the humanistic culture of the Renaissance, the equalitarian ideals of the French Revolution, and the scientific concepts of the nineteenth century. To this amalgam we added socialism, which seemed to us the apex, so far, of all that was greatest in Western culture.[12]

One should probably add, more rigorously, the "progressive" aspect of this fusion of cultures. From the ethnic standpoint this was no vision of pluralism but rather of assimilation, for the socialist movement typically projected assimilation as the solution of the Jewish Question, this is, the total merging of the Jew into the major national culture. But even if the objective was assimilation, the material with which some of the artists worked was Jewish, life in the Jewish milieu, or Jews subjected to anti-Semitism. The active conjunction of anti-Semitism with reactionary viewpoints in the 1930s, especially as exhibited in Hitlerism, was so consistent that the struggle against anti-Semitism was, willy-nilly, an aspect of Left politics and agita-tion. Besides, the Yiddish-speaking labor movement was then one of the most militant. The Jew and his right to equal citizenship were thus among the concerns of the proletarian novels.

The movement can be said to have taken on a genuinely national signif-icance and have entered the mainstream of literary life with the publication, in *The New Republic,* of Mike Gold's famous review of Thornton Wilder's

The Bridge of San Luis Rey (1930). (Coincidentally, this was also the year of publication of Gold's *Jews Without Money*. Thus the Jew in the proletarian novel was present at its inception not only as author but as subject. Only after the Great Depression had rent the social fabric in 1930 could this doctrine explode into mainstream thinking.) Gold's attack showed how Wilder, in his succession of historical novels,

is the poet of the genteel bourgeoisie.... their goal is comfort and the status quo. Hence, the vapidity of these little readings in history.... Is this the language of the intoxicated Emerson? Or the clean, rugged Thoreau, or vast Whitman? Where are the modern streets of New York, Chicago, and New Orleans in these little novels? Where are the cotton mills, ... the child slaves of the beet fields? ... the stock-broker suicides, the labor racketeers, or passion or death of coal miners?[13]

Edmund Wilson, then literary editor of *The New Republic,* reported an unprecedented flood of letters to the magazine about the article. After some time he concluded that "there *was* a class issue involved in the dispute," and that "the Gold-Wilder case marks definitely the eruption of Marxist issues out of literary circles of the radicals into the field of general criticism. It has now become plain that the economic crisis is to be accompanied by a literary one."[14]

It is symbolically significant of the coming importance of the Jew in American literature in both theory and practice that this debate should have been initiated by the Jewish author of a novel about the Jewish milieu. Gold's *Jews Without Money* was reprinted eleven times in the ten months after its appearance in February, 1930, and many times since; by 1935 it had been translated into fifteen languages. This largely autobiographical-fictional account of Gold's own life on the East Side before 1916 is a searing exposure, without essential exaggeration, of American ghetto life in the first few decades of the century. The author, whose original name was Irwin Granich, had adopted the name "Michael Gold" after a Civil War veteran, a friend's uncle.

Gold was born in 1894 of extremely poor Rumanian immigrant parents. He left school when he was twelve to work at various odd jobs. His conversion to socialism came in 1914 when he heard Elizabeth Gurley Flynn, then a "Wobbly" and later a Communist party leader, talk socialism at an unemployed rally. (In *Jews Without Money* the speaker who converted him was said to be a man.) He reported on strikes and from 1917 to 1919 lived in Mexico, working and writing. Back in the United States he wrote one-act plays for the Provincetown Playhouse and then wrote for *The Liberator,* whose editor he became in 1921. In the meantime he led a bohemian life in Greenwich Village and went on to become a leader of the Communist literary movement, his leadership acknowledged by his sole editorship of *The New Masses* in 1928. But Gold never forgot his ties to the East Side and left a permanent record of this life in his only novel, *Jews Without Money.*

Despite its teetering on the edge of, and occasional lapses into, sentimentality, the book is saved by its emotional power. It would otherwise be difficult to explain its longevity. It is imbued with crude, almost unlettered class-conscious generalizations, but is also filled with deep compassion and passionate hatred for the injustice of poverty and the callousness of the ruling class and its administrators at every level. He frankly describes the negative side of East Side life, the prostitution, low-life, thieving, gang wars of Jewish and non-Jewish boys, anti-Semitism, an unlovely religious life, the *alrightniks,* a greedy Jewish landlord who perpetually postponed needed repair. But there are also moving portraits of the harassed father, finally crippled by an industrial accident, a radical neighborhood physician, other kind, humane persons, and above all, his revered mother. "I cannot forget you," he wrote. "I must remain faithful to the poor because I cannot be faithless to you! I believe in the poor because I have known you. The world must be made gracious for the poor. Momma, you taught me that!"[15]

This novel by the leading advocate of proletarian literature would seem on the surface not to conform to the criteria of the genre. But there can be no doubt of its working-class and class-conscious point of view. The key can be found in the passage just cited: his loving experience of the poor—the exploited—as exemplified in the life of his mother. Observation of the effects of poverty on the East Side led him to the conviction that the world must be changed. He gave effect to this conviction by organized activity to change the world, and this does in fact begin at the novel's conclusion. Like his protagonist, Gold had been forced by his family's poverty to end his formal education after elementary school graduation, and for several years he could only accumulate anger and frustration at the system. Then, at sixteen, he was awakened to organized effort.

A man on an East-Side soap-box, one night [he writes] proclaimed that out of the despair, melancholy and helpless rage of millions, a world movement had been born to abolish poverty.

I listened to him.

O workers' Revolution, you brought hope to me, a lonely, suicidal boy. You are the true Messiah. You will destroy the East Side when you come, and build there a garden for the human spirit.

O Revolution, that forced me to think, to struggle and to live.

O great Beginning![16]

Ironically enough Gold himself was criticized in the Communist press because the novel did not mention "labor organizations and strikes," actions like the shirtwaist makers' strike (The Uprising of the 20,000) or the Triangle Fire, both of which occurred during the period covered by the book, and because the poverty was depicted as simply accidental, not a class phenomenon. Gold replied that the critic was "too dogmatic," that proletarian literature has no "standard model," but must be imbued with "the revolutionary spirit." He answered specifically that the strikes and the Triangle Fire were simply not a part of the experience out of which he wrote. "I do not believe any good writing can come out of the mechanical application of the spirit of proletarian literature."[17] The revolutionary declaration on the last page of the novel is a logical conclusion to the events of the story in both mood and content. The book's meaning would be quite different without it. Indeed, when the book was reprinted during the Cold War, these last paragraphs were simply omitted, thereby evading the logical outcome. While the book does not mechanically conform to the usual formula for the proletarian novel, its unmistakably rebellious and class-conscious viewpoint attach it to this genre.

In contrast to the Gold novel, that of Henry Roth, *Call It Sleep*, cannot by any stretch of the imagination be regarded as proletarian, as Rideout has maintained it was, simply because Roth finally was actually a Communist. The novel is rather a penetrating revelation of a six-year-old groping toward an awareness of the meaning of sex within a cosmic context. The sole revolutionary expression in the novel is only one of the many that frame the boy's frantic quest for purifying light at the end of the novel.

"They'll betray us!" Above all these voices, the speaker's voice arose. "In 1789, in 1848, in 1871, in 1905, he who has anything to save will enslave us anew! Or if not enslave will desert us when the red cock crows! Only the laboring poor, only the masses embittered, bewildered, betrayed, in the day when the red cock crows can free us!"[18]

This expostulation is only one of a number at this point in the story and is a small part of the boy's awareness and actually peripheral to his quest. But the revolutionary invocation from Gold quoted above is the logical climax to the passion of *Jews Without Money*.

Unlike Gold's novel, which I believe to be of enduring value, another novel which cleaves more strictly and even mechanically to the proletarian model, Isidor Schneider's *From the Kingdom of Necessity* (1935), unfolds almost totally in a Jewish milieu. It now has a dated quality because of its doctrinaire approach to its characters. This cannot be said of Gold, who had a deeper, more empathic feeling for the poor and through them for Jews as such than Isidor Schneider. Gold is not bitter against Jewishness itself, as Schneider seems to be. Gold's passionate loyalty to his mother seeps into his feeling for her people. Nothing of this emerges from Schneider's novel. Schneider was one of the best-known editors and writers on the Left, but perhaps he never fully fulfilled his talent because of the rigid political guidelines within which he felt an inner obligation to work. In the novel the tension between the ethnic and class pressures upon him were so great that he tried to suppress the Jewishness in himself in order to do what he considered justice to the class aspect. A certain mechanical view of class consciousness appears, for instance, when he claims that "among Jewish workers there is an intuitive understanding that their difficult national problem will be solved finally, and only, when a proletarian revolution solves the world's economic problems." Schneider thus endows generalized "Jewish workers" with "intuitive" understanding of a tenet of classic socialist theory. He adds a wish-fulfilling, generalized assumption that they also "have a sincere admiration for radicals who strike blows, however feeble, at the system that must be overthrown."[19]

Schneider's novel, autobiographical like Gold's, opens in a Polish *shtetl* in the 1890s. At the turn of the century the five-year-old Isaac Hyman's family immigrates to the United States to escape poverty; they live in Harlem. They suffer the panic of 1907, move to a Third Avenue tenement during a strike, and take in boarders. When the strike is lost, the father, Morris, becomes a janitor in an ethnically mixed area where "the sheenies and the tar babies [Blacks] were considered fair game for the rest."[20] It should be noted that often, regardless of their attitude toward their Jewish identity, Jewish writers on the Left exposed anti-Semitism to which they were subjected. Thus a drunken Mr. Latimer begs a "loan" from Isaac's father. "If you want to prove yourselves kind Jews, you'll spare me a little of your Jewish money." To their protest that they have none, Latimer retorts, "What's fifty cents to a Jew with his mattress lining stuffed with dollars?" They persist in their refusal, and he rants, "I see you are nothing but dirty, low, goddam, moneycuddling Jews. And who do you get the money from? You get it out of us—you Christ-killing bastards! And instead of taking back our own, we come begging for it, fools and cowards that we are. We let ourselves be tied up, like drunkens, by laws the Jews pay for to save themselves, and their blood money."[21]

Issac's aspirations to be a writer are recognized early. He becomes editor of his high school paper. He joins a Zionist club as a means of meeting girls and writes for their magazine. But when World War I breaks out, he is won over to an anti-war position and to Marxism by Mendel, a fellow student. He joins a peace group and tries to register for the draft as a conscientious objector, but his draft board exempts him as an enemy alien, since he has never taken out citizenship papers. A good part of the novel is concerned with his love affair and his career as a Left writer and publisher. Along the way there are the usual unfavorable portraits of rabbis and Jewish teachers, most of whom were then indeed as reactionary as pictured, although the depiction of religious Jews is in some cases mechanically negative. The book ends with a Passover Seder at Isaac's home, and Isaac's final, convinced, wholehearted acceptance of his place in the working class. "With it, he would march, taking his place in the advancing lines, in the irresistible movement of the worker of mankind from the Kingdom of Necessity to the Kingdom of Freedom."[22]

The frequent depiction of antagonism between generations in immigration and acculturation novels mirrored its frequency in real life. The second generation, educated in the public schools, determined to avoid the factory life of the immigrant parents, entered either business or the professions. They dreaded the ridicule often accorded Yiddish-accented speech; they rejected the persistence of Old World ideas and customs and manners, which so many of their immigrant forebears never shook off because they had come as mature adults, and they resisted the rigid Orthodoxy, which many of the immigrant generation tried to impose on their children. The second generation, in short, aspired to live in the larger American milieu, to adopt American ways. All such tensions made for the clash of generations on the East Side.

In the case of young radicals, however, politics was often an added element in this conflict. Such a generational difference is depicted in Leane Zugsmith's *A Time to Remember* (1937). This novel includes exemplars, both male and female, of typical characters in labor struggle: the union stalwart and the stoolpigeon; petty bourgeois anti-union and pro-union parents, as well as conversion to radicalism. Within these models are criss-crossed special problems met within the Jewish family: consequences of a mixed marriage and conservative anti-union attitudes of the parents. Threads of the story are interwoven into the strike at Klein's (on Fourteenth Street in New York) in the mid-1930s, which was one of the landmark labor struggles of the period and one around which many writers and intellectuals rallied and were radicalized. The heroine, Aline Weissman, has become involved in this strike after she is forced to quit college because her father loses his job. But her mother is not Jewish, and problems of a mixed marriage emerge.

Aline develops class consciousness as a result of her work at the "Diamond's" department store. She become increasingly disillusioned with the triviality of the wealthy Jewish girls she has associated with from college and defends the union against them. The greatest part of the novel, however, is taken up with the union struggle at "Diamond's," and Jews are on both sides of the conflict, but the distinctive Jewish issue involved in the strike, going beyond identity, is the delusory belief of Aline's father that the Jewishness of both employer and employee somehow presupposes a common interest and understanding and that therefore labor conflict between them is not necessary. Both employer and employees at "Diamond's" were Jewish, so why the strike? Such appeals to their common Jewishness were actually often used by employers to facilitate exploitation of labor.

While class conflict was central to the proletarian novel, problems of acculturation also enter because so many of the genre dealt with an immigrant working class. And when Jews are involved, anti-Semitism often

intrudes not as artificial imposition but because it was part of the real life
behind the story. It was manifested not only by the middle-class employer
but also by the Jews' non-Jewish fellow workers. Centuries of folk anti-
Semitism were a part of the workers' heritage, as well as that of the employers. In addition, employers sometimes exploited ethnic prejudice to set
one group of workers against another. A classic example is the hostility of
the poor white in the South against the Blacks, under both slavery and Jim
Crow segregation. One small example of how such ethnic prejudice was
used to weaken the radical movement is shown in Edwin Seaver's *Between
the Hammer and the Anvil* (1939). Intra-student anti-Semitism, as well as
discrimination against Jews in the professions and the rootlessness of Jews,
have their repercussions in the student radical movement. A radical group
discusses the advisability of a student strike to protest the firing of liberal
Professor Thomson, who was faculty advisor to the Social Problems Club.
A non-Jewish member, Donithen, is reluctant to strike for fear it will hamper
his career. A Jewish student calls him a "rat." "Radicals! Faugh!" Donithen
says, and spits on the floor. " 'You goddammed little.... Kike! Why don't
you say it, Donithen? You never did want any kikes in your revolution did
you? For Gentiles only, eh?' "[23] When the student strike leader, Ezra, asks
the fired teacher to speak at a strike meeting, Professor Thomson asks Ezra
about the "bitter, self-wounding sort of sarcasm with which you just spoke.
I notice it in your writing, too. Do you think it's a peculiarly 'Jewish trait'?
I've seen too many grasping Gentiles talk about Jewish acquisitiveness as a
racial trait."[24]

Ezra then expresses a respect for traditional Jewish forms unusual in the
radical novel. He speaks of the contrast between his just deceased Orthodox
grandfather and his father.

I rather admired the old man [says Ezra]. Much more than I do his son, my father,
for instance. When I was younger, I used to hate what I thought was the hypocrisy
of his orthodoxy, synagogue after breakfast, strict observance of the Sabbath along
with top hat, Prince Albert coat and all that, when I knew him to be a very worldly
man, not at all religious as I understand the term. Not nearly so genuinely religious
as my grandmother, for instance, who would never go near a synagogue and freely
commented on her husband's ability as an actor. And yet, I don't know. I seem to
understand him better now. At least he was trying to maintain a certain form, no
matter how hollow it was becoming; tried to keep up a certain dignity and belief
in life. My father and my father's crowd gave up all that. But what have they got
in return? Nothing. Neither form nor substance. Nothing but a meaningless existence
driving ferociously toward a meaningless death.[25]

The meeting is planned, but a lawyer named Rosenfeld with inside information warns Ezra that the police mean to break up the meeting. Ezra
then tries to convert Rosenfeld to the radical cause, but the lawyer answers:

Look at me. To look at me you wouldn't think I would be first in my class, would you? After all, how can an anemic Jew with rundown shoes and patches in his pants be first in his class? What does he want to be first for? Will it do him any good? Not in the least. The Gentile firms don't want him. The big Jewish firms are closed even tighter. So what will I do when I graduate? Listen, I'll tell you what I'll do. I'll get in with a group of shysters like myself and make my living hounding people like myself for their miserable pennies in behalf of my employers. The very people who are keeping me down. That's because I'm an A—one student. If I was fifth or tenth—maybe I could get a job as a street cleaner.[26]

Another example of concern about anti-Semitism by a proletarian writer, and a hard-boiled one at that, is Edward Dahlberg's anti-Nazi novel, *Those Who Perish* (1934), last of a trilogy of which the first two were *Bottom Dogs* (1929) and *From Flushing to Calvary* (1932). The first two, which are not explicitly proletarian but are intensely class conscious, contain a few casual allusions to Jews. But after Hitler's rise to power Dahlberg's Jewish awareness seems to have awakened and issued in this excoriation of Nazism. The story, set in the United States, has many Jewish characters and subjects the wealthy Jewish bourgeoisie to devastating criticism by exposing their inglorious refusal to join, much less promote, the anti-Nazi boycott. This was indeed the case among wealthy Jews in the 1930s in this country. They agree with Hitler's fight against communism. If only he weren't also anti-Jewish, they would support him. Boaz, the main character, who himself opposes Communists and is an ardent Zionist, refuses to work with Communists against fascism; his lover, Regina, decides to cooperate with them, though she never joins the party. But the novel ends in despair, with Boaz dying after he has decided to go to Palestine and Regina has decided to stay and fight at home. She takes poison after his death, saying with her last breath, "For those who have the breath for tomorrow."[27]

Although Maxwell Bodenheim's *Run, Sheep, Run* (1932) has a number of Jewish characters, some of them Communist party members, nothing of Jewishness enters the story. The first third is concerned with what might be called "Love in the Party." Except for identification by their Jewish names and occasional Yiddish-inflected English, the book exemplified the widespread indifference to their Jewish identity of many in the party. Waldo Frank's *The Death and Birth of Daniel Markand* (1934), a story of the struggle of a middle-class person from an affluent background and a place in the establishment to ally himself with the proletariat, is written with the indifference to Jewish identity one might expect from a non-Jewish author. There is occasional mention of Jews in this manner. A conventional Jewish traveling salesman in the South engages in a lunchroom discussion and defends striking miners in a company town, but finally agrees, "I guess they're a rum bunch all right, ... violent, eh?" Another discussant thinks the miners would be all right if it weren't for incitement by "Godless foreign agitators," and the waitress adds, "A lot of Jews from Europe or New

York." The Jew "winced and smiled sweetly up into her face, 'May I have another slice of that delicious pie, dearie?' "[28] A number of other Jewish characters appear later, but Jewishness is apparent only in their names and description as such. The author's attitude toward Jews is not altogether clear. At the least, one may observe little self-identification as a Jew.

Albert Halper, who came from immigrant parents in Chicago, was in his early novels no less indifferent to his Jewishness than Waldo Frank of wealthy German Jewish New York parents. *Union Square* (1933) has both Jewish and non-Jewish characters, but Jewishness does not figure at all. *The Chute* (1937) is the story of the radicalization of a young Jew in a highly mechanized mail order house in Chicago where the author himself had worked as a young man. It contains naturalistic description of Jewish characters and customs in their less lovable aspects deriving from ghetto conditions. However the toughness evident in Halper's proletarian novels did not dominate the collection of his earliest short stories, *On the Shore* (1934), which were sympathetic and nostalgic pictures based on his Chicago boyhood. He had been writing for the *Menorah Journal* during this early period and had then accepted his Jewish material as valid for literature. Like other Jewish writers, Left and non-Left, Hitlerism reawakened his sense of Jewishness. He had been disaffected from the Left by the late 1930s, and in *Sons of the Fathers* (1940) he returns to a friendly and warm attitude toward the early Chicago milieu in which he grew up. The life of an immigrant family from 1892 is sketched, their move from one place to another to escape anti-Semitic harassment of the children, and the story follows the familiar acculturation pattern of the second generation. Though the personal relations within the family are idyllic, their lot in the world is harsh and the attitude toward Jewishness positive.

The frequency of the Jewish character in the proletarian novel stems in part from the fact that so many of the proletarian novelists were Jewish and consequently called upon their personal experience for their material. Furthermore, much of this writing is set in large cities like New York or Chicago where Jews formed a fairly great percentage of the population and were especially active in union struggles. Many Jews were leading figures in the general radical movement, as well as in labor unions. The problem of Jewish survival almost never entered the content of this fiction because almost all these authors acquiesced to the prevailing socialist view that the future of the Jews lay in assimilation, and that this was both a desirable and necessary ultimate resolution of the Jewish Question, soluble only under Socialism.

Of all the non-Jewish proletarian writers perhaps John Dos Passos was almost entirely immune from stereotyping: he treated the Jew as an individual, fallible like anyone. He never joined the Communist party and was indeed estranged from it after 1934, but his *USA*, his masterpiece, is one of the most enduring proletarian works. Earlier, in *Manhattan Transfer*

(1929), which foreshadows some of the innovative techniques in *USA*, several Jews are peripheral characters, accurately observed. The career of Harry Goldweiser, a successful theatrical producer, is recapitulated as an example of one type of upward mobility. "I thought," Dos Passos has him say, "I was going to be a lawyer. All us East Side fellers thought we were going to be lawyers. Then I worked as an usher one summer at the Irving Place [Theater] and got the theater bug.... Ten years ago I was a ... clerk in ... Erlanger's office, and now there's lots of 'em whose shoes I used to shine in the old days they'd be glad to sweep my floors on West Forty-Eighth."[29] He would like to do great things for the theater but "the people of this country won't let you do anything for 'em. All they want's a detective melodrama or a rotten French farce.... Well a showman's business is to give the public what it wants."[30] Another Jewish character, Jake Silverman, is arrested for "using the mails to defraud."[31]

Dos Passos shows an unusual knowledge of the generational conflict in the Jewish immigrant community. A girl tells her mother that she refuses to return to her husband, "the dirty brute." Her mother tells her to return to him. "But I aint a Jew any more," she replies. "... This aint Russia; it's little old New York. A girl's got some rights here"[32] Another Jewish mother has trouble with her children. Her daughter Anna Cohen ("A homely lookin kike, she says to herself"[33]) is on strike. Mrs. Cohen laments for her children:

Oy, what for have I raised four children that they should all of them be no good agitators and street walkers and bums...? Benny in jail twice, and Sol God knows where making trouble, and Sarah accursed given up to sin kicking up her legs at Minsky's, and now you, may you wither in your chair, picketing for the garment workers, walking along the street with a sign on your back.... Why don't you go to your work and keep your mouth shut, and draw your pay quietly?[34]

Finally, a common anti-Semitic complaint of the time is introduced in the after-dinner conversation in a WASP household. "I tell you, Wilkinson, New York is no longer what it used to be when Emily and I first moved up here about the time the Ark landed.... City's overrun with kikes and low bred Irish, ... In ten years a Christian won't be able to make a living. ... I tell you the Catholics and Jews are going to run us out of our own country."[35] The books ends with a great labor march, with "hoarse voices singing *Die Rote Fahne* in Yiddish" and talk of the Revolution as the "only hope for the worker."[36]

There is no taint of anti-Semitism in the work of Dos Passos. On the contrary, his trilogy, *USA* (*42nd Parallel* [1930], *Nineteen Nineteen* [1932], *The Big Money* [1936]) strongly fortifies the impression of his earlier work of a total absence of ethnic prejudice. There are only a few casual allusions to Jews in the first novel, *42nd Parallel*. But in the next two the Jewish radical, Ben Compton, is a central character who early repudiates his Jew-

ishness but does not lose his Jewish identity in the eyes of the world. "The
old people were Jews but at school Benny always said he wasn't a Jew, he
was an American because he'd been born in Brooklyn ... and they owned
their house." His father was observant and "kept the Sabbath like their
fathers,"[37] but he felt contempt for the rabbi and the synagogue.[38] When
Ben's brother Izzy becomes a boxer, their father disowns him. After grad-
uating from high school, Ben leaves home and works on a construction
gang in Pennsylvania. When the crew strikes and Ben joins, his anarchist
friend Nick Gigli bursts out laughing and tells Ben "to quit his kidding,
funniest thing he ever heard of, a kike walking out with a lot of wops. Ben
felt himself go cold and stiff all over. 'I'm not a kike any more'n you are.
... I'm an American born ... and I'm goin' to stick to my class, you dirty
crook.'" Later Ben goes back home and joins the Socialist party. His father
is disgusted: " 'Phooy ... radical jews,' and made a spitting sound with his
lips. ... The old man cursed Ben and Ben left home."[39]

It is apparent from Ben's thoughts and early career that Dos Passos knew
the Jews of his time in their variety. In particular, he shows the generational
antagonism caused by radicalism in the second generation, as well as the
ubiquity of anti-Semitism. Ben works with the International Workers of the
World in the West, joins the free-speech movement, and is brutally beaten
by police with the incremental, "He's a kike, beat him again for me."[40]
After being released from the hospital, he returns east to raise money for
the Defense Committee and decides to study law in the office of a radical
lawyer, Morris Stein. His father is delighted, for, says he, "A clever lawyer
can protect the workers and the poor Jews and make money too."[41] When
the Russian Revolution breaks out, "There was a feeling of carnival all
down the East Side and in the Jewish Sections of Brooklyn."[42] While Ben's
mentor in law, Stein, approves of United States entry into World War I,
Ben is a conscientious objector and is arrested for speaking at an anti-war
meeting; at twenty-three he is sentenced to a ten-year jail term. He does
not return to the story until late in the final volume, *The Big Money,* when
he falls in love with the central figure in that volume, the Communist Mary
French. When they visit Ben's family in Coney Island, Mary can see that
"they all admired Ben ... ; he was the bright boy, the scholar, but they felt
sorry about his radicalism as if it was an unfortunate sickness." After the
visit Ben tells Mary, "Well, that's the Jewish family ... some straitjacket."
She replies, "But, Ben, it's got its good side. ... They'd do anything in the
world for you ... my mother and me we really hate each other."[43]

Still other phases of Jewish life are explored in the relations of Mary
French with her "best friend" in high school, Ada Cohn, whose father was
a prominent Chicago lawyer. Mary's mother was displeased with the association and argued with her father, a doctor, about it. It was only because
he was "so shiftless that her only daughter was reduced to going around
with Jews and every Tom, Dick and Harry." Her husband replies that "it's
only on account of Mary's being a friend of the Cohns' that they've given

me their practice.... They are nice kindly people." When Ada comes to Vassar, Mary is in her second year and "horrified to catch herself wishing Ada hadn't come. Ada had gotten so lush and Jewish and noisy, and her clothes too expensive and never just right. They roomed together and Ada bought most of Mary's clothes and books for her because her allowance was so tiny. After Ada came, Mary wasn't popular the way she'd been, and the most successful girls shied off from her."[44] The friendship endures through the parted ways of life of both women, and toward the end of the story, the improvement in status of Jews in a big city is signaled by the small alteration in Mary's mother's attitude toward association with Ada. She tells Mary, "you know, I've never approved of your friendship with Ada Cohn. Out home we are probably a little old-fashioned about these things. Here she seems to be accepted everywhere. In fact, she seems to know all the prominent musical people." Her second husband, a judge, adds, "Ada Cohn has a heart of gold. I find her a sweet little girl. Her father was a very distinguished lawyer. You know, we decided we'd lay aside our prejudices a little."[45]

Other Jewish characters flit in and out of the novel. Dos Passos further demonstrates the clarity of his attitude toward Jews by his encounter with the anti-Semitic Henry Ford, the subject of one of his "profiles."

The decade also saw a continuation of what we have called the socialist or labor novel, which differed from the proletarian in that it bore no relation to the Communist party nor did it require a climactic "conversion" or strike. Unlike the proletarian novels, whose focus was rather sociopolitical, these novels were usually centered on various aspects of acculturation, but exhibited deep involvement in the (non-Communist) socialist movement. Hyman Cohen and his son Lester together authored *Aaron Traum* (1930), one of the last of this earlier tradition, although Lester Cohen in the 1930s was numbered among the pro-Communist writers. *Aaron Traum* is, however, primarily Bundist in inclination, a view that is especially close to the older generation to which the father belonged, and the book itself belongs in spirit to the pre-1930s period. The titular hero immigrates at eleven in 1886, works exhaustingly in sweatshops, and lives in a vividly described dire poverty. He falls in with a group of the Russian intelligentsia working in the shop and is initiated into anarchism. The political and intellectual ferment of the time on the East Side is described: "knotty groups stood in the mean streets, arguing about capitalism, socialism, Henry George, Single Tax, Herbert Spencer's *First Principles,* and nearly everything else under the sun."[46] Aaron reads widely. The variety of careers of Aaron's generation is exemplified in one brother who marries the boss's daughter and gets partnership in a factory; another becomes a violinist; another a boxer. Aaron participates in strikes, but the Panic of 1893 breaks the union and

The East Side streets ... were swollen with people. The women slunk about with shawls, stopping to exchange dolorous nods and make inquiry. The children grew faint at games. The men straggled about, formed groups, argued, ranted, harangued, (and in Rutgers Square) Don Quixotes tilted at established windmills of the world. There were Knights of Labor, Commonwealers, Grangers, Populists, Free Soilers, Single Taxers, Socialists, Unionists, Anarchists, Atheists—the medicine men of a world-wide malady, each with a different pill you had to swallow before all would be well.[47]

The documentation of East Side life is especially dense in this story. Several significant aspects of second-generation life are exemplified in Aaron. One is the passion for education that permeated the East Side. Deprived of schooling by the poverty of his parents, Aaron educates himself with broad reading, especially during the predictable "slack" periods in the garment industry. Aaron was "one of hundreds and thousands of the East Side young men thus occupied. In tenement kitchens, in basements, at newspaper stalls, in little stores—everywhere were young men studying, trying to escape the captivity of the sweatshop. Here an old tailor was stitching late into the night to help a son through City College, sisters were sewing brothers through law school, many a poor finisher blinded her eyes in the hope of becoming a doctor's wife."[48] Another characteristic feature was Aaron's embrace of socialism as "the only means of removing the rust of care from the human soul."[49] It was said that "a young man had socialism knocked into his head by policemen's clubs or by the constant street corner speeches of the East Side."[50] The Cohens describe the troop of young men picking up newspapers for distribution to work their way through college. The trip downtown to pick up the papers is "the travelling university."[51] Still another aspect of East Side life in the story is the division of class loyalties within a single family. Aaron has become a union activist and in time finds himself pitted against his employer-brother in union negotiations. This naturalistic novel fully exploits this technique to convey a rich picture of East Side life.

Decline of socialist militancy and cooling of socialist convictions among some Jews as the new century wore on is illustrated in Konrad Bercovici's *Main Entrance* (1932). Hirsh Aaron has become prosperous since his immigration in the 1890s, and his three sons and one daughter become professionals. The daughter, a worker in the theater, goes to the Soviet Union and returns because she is unable to endure the rigors of revolution. Her brother is a left-wing Socialist during World War I, is imprisoned as a conscientious objector, but finally moves toward the right-wing socialists because "there were more Gentiles...on that side." He calculates that "Gentile friends were a better social asset than the young men of his own people would be. The Jews were all extremely radical-extremists."[52] "From a well-behaved, quiet, middle class Jewish matron, their mother had changed herself into a blatant, loud, over-dressed and over rouged, vulgar, middle-aged, gigolo-questing woman."[53] The portrait of acculturated Jewish life in this novel is not attractive.

Denser in its documentation of radicalism is Joseph Gollomb's *Unquiet* (1935). It records the rejection of Jewish ethnicity by radicals of both generations, Russian revolutionaries and American socialists. While still in Tsarist Russia, the underground revolutionary, Grisha, discards his Jewish identity so far as possible. When anti-Semitic Russians beat his father and little nephew David, Grisha is too busy writing an article to come to their aid. His brother-in-law tells Grisha, "Go look at the old man who gave you house and schooling! You can finish your article later." Grisha replies, "Old men should stay at home." But "Home is no protection for a Jew in Russia." Grisha's article is too important—"there is no foolishness in it about 'Jews' and 'Gentiles.' And when the working class learns its lesson, perhaps they will find something better than to fight each other. There will be no need for you to punch peasants on the nose, my hero!"[54] In fear of the Tsarist police, the family flees to America and lives in a Suffolk Street tenement on the East Side. The second-generation son of the family, David, resists Grisha's rejection of Jewish identity and, indeed, his placing of religious Jews among the class enemy. The author brings out the deliberate, provocative affront which adherents of this view visited upon their religious Jewish neighbors. Still, David is attracted to socialism, whose activities on the East Side are sympathetic with the group of East Siders at City College who organize a "Breadwinner's College," but not like the "Educational Institute" (Educational Alliance) under the dominance of benevolent people from "uptown." The socialist objective was "emancipating the working class of the whole world, not directly through revolution, but by the route of education."[55]

So pervasive was the currency of the labor theme in the novel during the 1930s that even the staid Jewish Publication Society brought out a novel with a labor theme in Beatrice Bisno's *Tomorrow's Bread* (1938). However, this novel did not in the end look to the labor movement for a solution to social problems. The story follows an immigrant in the 1880s through a fluctuating career as labor leader and businessman; he ends his life in frustration, despite his early achievements as a labor leader and his later monetary success. The impression left by the book is the ultimate futility of the labor movement as an answer to the human predicament.

IN THE JEWISH MILIEU

Pervasive as was the interest in the proletarian and labor novel in the 1930s, acculturation and immigration novels seemed to be an inexhaustible genre in that and succeeding decades. And just as the proletarian novel left a permanent legacy to American literature in works like Mike Gold's *Jews Without Money,* James Farrell's *Studs Lonigan* trilogy, John Dos Passos' *USA* trilogy, Richard Wright's *Native Son,* and John Steinbeck's *Grapes of Wrath,* so also did the Jewish acculturation novel of the 1930s in Daniel

Fuchs' Williamsburg Trilogy, Henry Roth's *Call It Sleep,* and Meyer Levin's *The Old Bunch*. One needs to observe that except for Steinbeck's, all the novels in the first group are also in some way concerned with Jews.

The diminishing sensitivity to ethnic identity in many of the generation growing up in the 1910s to the 1930s was aroused to a sense of ethnic self-respect and self-defense as the murderous anti-Semitism of Nazism became ever more vicious and echoes of Nazism began to be heard in the United States. Numbers of refugees from Hitlerite Europe found refuge in this country, including some of the most talented creative minds in Germany; leaders in science, scholarship, and the arts were among the refugees, and most were Jewish. They fructified their areas of activity in this country. Several factors therefore contributed to the heightening self-identification of American Jews: the persistence of traditional barriers to complete acculturation, which saw the Jew as somehow alien in a Christian society; increasing defensiveness in the face of Hitlerism; and the influx of refugees from Nazified countries. So pervasive a part of the American experience had the Jew become that his experience could not help finding expression in literature, whether in general labor struggles or in the variety of special situations facing the Jews, which ranged from anti-Semitism to their rising achievement in many areas of American life. Most Jewish writers, at some time in the course of their writing careers, turned to their Jewish origins for fictional material.

So frequent and acceptable had such material become that in the 1950s Leslie Fiedler could write, "The patterns of Jewish speech, the experience of Jewish childhood and adolescence, the smells and tastes of the Jewish kitchen, the sounds of the Jewish synagogue have become, since 1930, staples of the American novel." Fiedler goes on to report that "by the end of the thirties . . . there were some sixty American Jewish writers who could be called without shameless exaggeration 'prominent.' " In addition to Abraham Cahan, Ludwig Lewisohn, and Ben Hecht, who belong to earlier periods, Fiedler adds, were 1930s writers like Edward Dahlberg, Leonard Ehrlich, Daniel Fuchs, Meyer Levin, Henry Roth, Waldo Frank, Maurice Samuel, Isidor Schneider, and Michael Gold; these, in his opinion, are "worth remembering." The last two, he added, are "at least symptomatically important."[56] The further winnowing of time and possibly also changes in taste over the past few decades would perhaps alter this list. I may add as outstanding in the 1930s novels of the Jewish milieu by Jewish writers those of Gold, Fuchs, Henry Roth, and Levin, as well as the earlier, and to my mind, undervalued, *Haunch, Paunch and Jowl* by Samuel Ornitz. The quality of the novels of Daniel Fuchs, Henry Roth, and Meyer Levin, each so altogether different from the other in tone and outlook, requires that we scrutinize their novels more closely than others in this section whose long-run interest is mainly documentary.

Daniel Fuchs

One of the most talented of the Jewish writers to emerge in the 1930s was Daniel Fuchs. Born and bred in the Jewish slums of Williamsburg, Fuchs earned his living as a substitute school teacher and wrote during summer vacations. From 1934 to 1937 he published three novels, the so-called Williamsburg Trilogy, *Summer in Williamsburg* (1934), *Homage to Blenholt* (1936), and *Low Company* (1937). He recalls that they sold 400, 400, and 1,200 copies, respectively. Desperate to escape from his wretched environment, weary of his teaching, discouraged at the commercial failure of his novels, he left for Hollywood where he has been a successful movie script writer ever since. Recognition of the quality of the novels came gradually, and in 1961 all three were republished in a single volume.[57] They are now considered among the lasting works of the 1930s. Although set in a working-class neighborhood, the novels are clearly not of labor or proletarian interest. The only view of the Communist party is through the distorted spectacles of the first novel's most pathetic character, Cohen, who joins the party for reasons of personal therapy and leaves when it fails him. Fuchs is quite explicit about his overall aim, to discover the cause of the misery of life in Williamsburg: "You must pick Williamsburg to pieces until you have spread them out on your table.... Take ... the different aspects that are pertinent. Collect them and analyze."[58] The result is a naturalistic novel in which the depressing, frustrating, deprived lives of the characters are unsparingly set forth. The milieu of all three novels is almost totally Jewish, and no anti-Semitism appears. Harsh though the approach is, there is an underlying tone of compassion for the victims of a generally inhuman material environment. No hope for escape is held out by the author, although in actuality he himself did escape to Hollywood.

The central character of the first novel, *Summer in Williamsburg*, is Philip Hayman, a twenty-year-old college student in the summer before his senior year, who is patently the spokesman for the author. Others are Philip's Uncle Papravel, a petty gangster with aspirations toward the big time, who affects suavity and consideration but is actually ruthless in ruining a bus competitor so as to gain a monopoly for his employer. Harry, Philip's older brother, works with his gangster uncle to escape poverty but finally he can't take the murder and illegality entailed in his uncle's operation. Also interesting are Tessie, with whom Philip has an affair, rejecting her offer to continue it after she marries a traveling salesman; and Davey, the teen-age leader of a Jewish gang who tries to emulate the gang leaders of the movies, leading his companions in their fights against Irish and Italian gangs. There is, too, Philip's father, a principled man, honest to a quixotic degree. His creed is that "a man must be honest, must do no harm to any one, but work at his trade justly and honorably. A man must be upright."[59] He wants "his sons . . . always to follow a straight path or they might just as well not have been born."[60]

Philip's mother is kind, maternal, the peacemaker of the family. As in so many novels of Jewish life of the first few generations, Fuchs gives such an affecting, exact description of the Friday twilight candle-lighting ceremony by the mother as to arouse nostalgic memories in those who witnessed the rite. Philip

watched without seeming to watch, his mother light one candle with a match, and use this as a taper for the other two. This was, perhaps, a simple thing, but he always observed the ritual, and it affected him. . . . Then she covered her head with a napkin, placed her fingertips to her eyelids, and moving her lips in a murmur, withdrawn for the moment and apart from the world, she recited the ancient prayer. There was always something strange, a little awesome, in the spectacle.[61]

Fuchs' unfavorable attitude toward the Communist party, which was a significant presence in the life of 1930s writers, is conveyed through the experience of the futile, inadequate, frustrated, pseudo-intellectual Cohen. His humiliating experience at a party drives Cohen to an unsuccessful attempt at suicide. Philip's musing over Cohen's predicament leads him to think: "Yes, Cohen was a shlemiel, but wasn't Philip's father also a shlemiel, wasn't poor Meyer Sussman who killed himself weeks back a shlemiel? Wasn't Philip himself? And wasn't it supremely true that the only wise ones were people like his Uncle Papravel, . . . people who accepted conditions as they were and made the most of them in their own way?" Fuchs ends as he began, without added wisdom, even if the intervening picture is vivid and moving. "People in tenements," Fuchs concludes, "lived in a circle without significance, one day a duplicate of the next until the end, which occurred without meaning but accidentally, cutting the procession short as pointlessly as Cohen's life had been cut. People were born, grew tired and calloused, struggled and died. That was all, and no book was large enough to include the entire picture, to give the completely truthful impression, the exact feeling."[62] The writer could only, Fuchs had said at the opening, "Collect and analyze."

The Fuchs surrogate in the next novel, *Homage to Blenholt,* Max Balkan, is still futilely seeking a way to escape from Williamsburg. Max attends the funeral of Blenholt, the commissioner of sewers in Brooklyn, who stands to the provincial Max for one avenue of power and arouses fantasies of Tamberlaine in the young man. Max's father pathetically recalls his claim to glory in his earlier role of King Lear in the Yiddish theater. Max indulges in a fantasy of gaining wealth from selling bottled onion juice and is deflated by the rejection of his fatuous scheme. Fuchs' womenfolk are down-to-earth and do not share the fantasies of the men, but rather deflate those dreams, as when Max's mother brings her husband down to earth by calling him

"Mr. Fumfotch." Max finally reconciles himself to imprisonment in Williamsburg as a shipping clerk. The conclusions of the first novel are only confirmed in the second.

The third novel of the trilogy, *Low Company*, succumbs to hopelessness and the inhumanity of man to man. The characters "knew well [that] the world...was bitter and low, humans were always miserable in their relations with one another, but it was an old tale."[63] The organizing frame of the novel is a candy store–lunch room in Neptune Beach (that is, Brighton Beach) and its habitués. It is full of remarkably detailed local color and naturalistic description, and all its characters come to a bad or frustrated end. All its human relations are centrifugal: each person flying away from the other, with hardly any satisfactory human relations anywhere. One of the main threads of the story is the fate of Shubunka, a curiously sensitive man who is the master of a chain of whorehouses. Big city gangsters try to take over the prostitution "industry" by forcing the small entrepreneurs like Shubunka to give up their houses to the monopolists. Shubunka is loath to give up what he has worked hard to achieve for eight years, and is threatened with death.

One of the few touches of human kindness in the novel, even though momentary, emerges from Shubunka's predicament. He appeals to Lurie, proprietor of a woman's clothing store, for shelter from the gangsters in his apartment away from Neptune Beach. Realizing the danger to Shubunka, Lurie persuades him to leave the city, and as he observes the brothel keeper walk to the subway, he realizes that Shubunka, too, "had a conscience and recognized in his own peculiar way the justice of his fate, above all, feeling with pity his [Shubunka's] complete wretchedness, Lurie knew how it had been insensible and inhuman for him, too, to simply, to hate Neptune and to escape from it." He realizes that he knew people there "in their lowness and had been repelled by them, but now it seemed to him that he understood how their evil appeared in their impoverished, dingy lives and, further, how miserable their own evil rendered them. It was not enough to call them low and pass on."[64] But this note of compassion is submerged in the prevailing frustration and hopelessness, isolation, ugliness, and sordidness of most of the lives of the characters.

The novel is extremely competent and tightly structured in the meshing of the characters and events leading to their several catastrophes. The milieu is a self-enclosed Jewish world and a totally secular one. Although not explicitly so, it is unmistakably Jewish in lives and speech of the characters. The essence of its meaning is given in the epigraph of the book, a passage "From the prayer said on the eve of the Day of Atonement,"[65] the plea for forgiveness for an exhaustive catalogue of sins committed in the year past. Fuchs' outlook was locked into negativity, but did not recognize the possibility of a fresh start with more positive prospects after the blowing of the *shofar*.

Fuchs stopped writing novels and instead wrote short stories which were published in well-paying magazines; then he achieved a prosperous life in Hollywood as a movie writer. From 1936 to 1975 he occasionally published other stories, gathered with some unpublished material in 1979 in his collection, *The Apathetic Movie Scribe*.

Henry Roth

Like Fuchs, Henry Roth had to wait for several decades before receiving general recognition. His *Call It Sleep* was first published in 1934, the same year as Fuchs' *Summer in Williamsburg*, but unlike the Fuchs book, it sold out its first printing of 1,500 and went into a second printing. Yet that was all until it was finally reprinted in hard cover in 1960 and in a widely sold paperback edition in 1964. To some extent the perspective of several decades was thus winnowing out the best work of the 1930s. When it first appeared, *Call It Sleep* received very favorable reviews, except for the Communist press, which criticized the novel in a single paragraph review in *The New Masses*. (Roth himself was a Communist party member.) "It is a pity," concluded this notice, "that so many young writers drawn from the proletariat can make no better use of their working class experience than as material for introspective and febrile novels."[66] However, letters of protest at this dismissal of a fine novel appeared, and a month later a second review in *The New Masses* by Edwin Seaver gave the book an intelligent appraisal: "If there is a better, a more purposeful rendering of an East Side proletarian childhood than that contained in *Call It Sleep*, I have yet to see it."[67] Yet despite a favorable reaction in the general press, the book was allowed to pass out of print and generally out of mind.

But not altogether, for it had an underground reputation that occasionally surfaced. In 1942, for example, we find Marie Syrkin, then an associate editor of *Jewish Frontier*, writing of *Call It Sleep* that it "has been hailed as the most talented novel written by an American Jew. It is an extraordinarily brilliant portrayal of life on the East Side.... Henry Roth has the equipment of a major novelist, which can be said of no other American Jewish writer."[68] Alfred Kazin and Leslie Fiedler, in their contributions to the *American Scholar*'s symposium in August, 1956, on the one most neglected book of the last quarter-century both named *Call It Sleep*. (Despite Kazin's high opinion of the novel, he did not include consideration of it in his *On Native Grounds*. Nor did he even notice Cahan's *The Rise of David Levinsky*. At that time American-Jewish literature was generally assigned a peripheral place in American literature.) Walter B. Rideout, in his study of the proletarian novel in 1956 characterized the book as "the most distinguished single proletarian novel."[69] While I do not hold the novel to be proletarian in the strict 1930s sense, for it is not political at its center, a case could be made for its leading place among that decade's fiction set in a working-class milieu. The late Harold A. Ribalow, who anthologized and wrote for many years on American Jewish writers, was instrumental in getting the book reprinted. An extensive scholarly bibliography has gathered about the book since.

Roth himself was brought to this country at about age two by his mother to rejoin his father. The family lived on the East Side until the boy was about eight, and then moved to East Harlem. Henry was a moody child and read fairy tales obsessively. In City College he first majored in science, but his interest gradually shifted to literature. He graduated in 1928, and was then living with the noted Professor Eda Lou Walton of New York University, to whom the novel is dedicated. She early perceived his talent. By 1930, with the encouragement of Walton, he began to write *Call It Sleep,* which was finished by 1933. In that year he joined the Communist party, "a time when," as Roth later said "intellectuals were beginning to gravitate toward the left almost without exception, and I along with the rest."[70] Through the influence of a friend of Walton's the novel was published in 1934.

The novel is set on the East Side from 1911 to 1913. It concerns two years in the life of a six-year-old immigrant boy, David Schearl, who obsessively loves his gentle, sensitive mother, Genya, and hates and fears his dour, unhappy, sadistic father, Albert—a typically Oedipal situation. Living with the family is Genya's sister Bertha, an overwrought, sloppy, uncouth, foul-mouthed, earthy, frustrated young woman who loves David and whose hatred of Albert is returned in good measure. The novel is beautifully structured about symbols of David's Oedipal situation, which he associates with fear of sexuality. In the first section, "The Cellar," David's family lives in Brownsville. The dark cellar of his tenement, with his fantasy of rats and the unknown symbolizes his terror. It is associated with the dark of a closet where the ten-year-old neighbor Annie initiates the terrified boy into sex. This terror is reawakened by the unsuccessful sexual advances of Luter, his father's friend and foreman, toward David's mother, overheard by the boy. The second prime symbol is "The Picture," a cheap print which Genya buys because it stands for her life in the old country home. There she had a frustrated love affair with a Christian church organist before marriage to Albert. The family has now moved to the East Side, at Ninth Street and Avenue D, where the remainder of the novel takes place. Their house has no cellar, and the key symbol has become the picture because David's terrors are now created by the revelation of the secret relation of Genya and the organist. Genya's sister has just emigrated from Europe and lives with the Schearls, so that the mutual hatred of Albert and the ill-favored Bertha is a constant source of tension. There is nothing nostalgic in the view of life in the *shtetl* as recalled by Genya and Bertha, or, for that matter, of East Side life as relentlessly depicted in the novel. Bertha's expulsion from the house by Albert is prevented only by her prospective marriage of convenience to a widower with five children, Nathan Sternowitz, who promises to buy a candy store for Bertha to manage while he continues his work as a leggings cutter. David overhears the prying Bertha extract from Genya the secret of her relationship with the organist. This knowledge—or rather, half-knowledge—on David's part triggers renewed tension and terror, which David associates with the picture, whose significance for his mother he guesses.

The third prime symbol is "The Coal." David is now going to a *heder* (described with extraordinary fidelity), where he overhears the rabbi expound Isaiah's encounter with God. "But when Isaiah saw the Almighty and His terrible light—Woe is me! he cried. What shall I do?...I, a common man, have seen the Almighty. I, unclean one, have seen him! Behold my lips are unclean.... But just when Isaiah let out this cry—I am unclean—one of the angels flew to the altar and with tongs drew out a fiery coal.... And with that coal, down he flew to Isaiah.... And the instant that coal touched Isaiah's lips...you are clean!"[71] This mode of purification and release takes hold of David's mind, and he passionately wishes to study the passage. When some Irish boys initiate David into the magic that would ensue from inserting a zinc sword between the trolley tracks to connect with the electric current (an event I sometimes witnessed during my East Side boyhood), David inserts the sword. "Like a paw ripping through all the stable fibres of earth, power, gigantic, fetterless, thudded into day! And light, unleashed, terrific light bellowed out of iron lips. The street quaked and roared, and...the short zinc sword...fell back, consumed with radiance."[72] When David tries to explain to the rabbi the connection between the event and the passage from Isaiah, the rabbi exclaims, "Fool!...God's light is not between car tracks!"[73]

But the event is repeated in the final, climatic symbol of the book in "The Rail." David's fear of Albert intensifies after Albert has ordered him to accompany him on his milk route and watch the wagon while Albert is delivering milk. Two men steal several bottles of milk. On his return, Albert, insane with anger, pursues the men and beats one into insensibility. He terrifies David into promising not to reveal the incident to Genya. Seeking release from fear on the roof (the symbol of light as opposed to the dark of the cellar), David meets a Catholic boy, Leo, who persuades David to arrange an assignation with the older of Bertha's step-daughters, Esther, in her cellar. As an inducement he offers to give David a crucifix and praying beads. " 'The beads make you lucky,' he [Leo] said. 'Don't have to be scared of anything.' "[74] The deal is consummated and Esther's sister, Polly, informs on them to her father. David is unnerved during his *heder* lesson and blurts out to the *melamed* that he is adopted, the child of a church organist. The *melamed* hastens to inform the boy's parents of his "impure" origin as does their brother-in-law Sternowitz who rushes to reveal David's iniquity concerning his daughter. David fears to go home and wanders through the streets. In a Joycean passage, David links the purification of the glowing coal of Isaiah with the brilliant light of the sword in the rail: "Yes, wasn't scared ... When? Sword in the fire."[75] He finds a milk ladle, and plunges it between the tracks, and then,

Power! Power like a paw, titanic power, ripped through the earth and slammed against his body and shackled him where he stood.[76]

Described in a poetic passage of great intensity, the short circuit knocks him unconscious. He is taken home, and by that time the confusions introduced by the reports of the rabbi and by Sternowitz have been dissipated. When Genya asks him why he had gone to the car tracks, he says he doesn't know. "He couldn't tell now why he had gone, except that something had forced him."[77] But he is tranquil. He has undergone a profound purgation. "He might as well call it sleep ... and feel, not pain, not terror, but the strangest triumph, strangest acquiescence."[78] "The Rail" was finally the symbol of release from the fears and pain that had wracked the boy in his Oedipal predicament.

Besides the fine structure, both narrative and symbolic, the novel has several other striking features. Although the influence of James Joyce's *Ulysses* is evident in a number of passages of stream-of-consciousness, they are not imitative but a valid, effective use of this new technique. The internal viewpoint of the novel is that of the boy David, but at the same time the characters and events retain their objectivity. Indeed, the characterizations are definite and individual. Genya, Albert, Bertha—all are sharply defined. Bertha especially is drawn with richness and subtlety. (For instance: the earthy Bertha is having her teeth extracted. The dentist removes one. "Doctor Goldberg had told her to spit, she had spat—not at the cuspidor beside the chair but at Doctor Goldberg."[79]) David's association with his peers, Jewish and non-Jewish, rings with authenticity. If there is any such thing as the American-Jewish novel, this is it, for it is pervaded by reality as the Jew of the time lived it, as immigrant Jews immersed in the folk mores and their ever-present sense of difference from non-Jews.

The language has unusual poetic power. Roth's feeling for language appears in one of the unusual features of the novel, its realistic rendering of immigrant and slum dialects and its contrasting translation of Yiddish into beautiful English prose. English as spoken by working-class Irishmen and Italians and others is set forth phonetically with considerable accuracy, but these are familiar enough. What is unusual, is the immigrant English of the Yiddish-speaking boys, which reflects Yiddish word order as well as the shape of words modified by the more familiar Yiddish. For example: "See, I tol' yuh I had sumtin tuh show yuh. See, like dot it closes ... he didn't hea' it, cause ev'ybody wuz sleepin'. Rats on'y come out innuh da'k, w'en yuh can't see 'em, and yuh know ... dey comin' f'om de cellah. Dots we'n dey live innuh cellah—all rats."[80] Or: "So w'y wuz yuh lookin in de Chinkee-

Chinaman's windeh."[81] Most interesting of all, however, is the manner in which Yiddish, which is the predominant language in the story, is rendered in a beautiful, poetic English, respectful of the dignity and literacy of the original spoken language. The English has one trait which marks it as a translation of Yiddish, frequent direct translations into English of Yiddish idioms, and sometimes suggestions of Yiddish word order.

The issue here is delicate because of the widespread use in entertainment and humor of Yiddish phrases as occasions for humor. Instead, Roth gives conversational Yiddish speech a seriousness which does not permit of risibility. Some examples: "No, they'll know the black hour [*shvartz yur*] hasn't seized me."[82] "Woe me" [*veh's mir*].[83] "Your man [or husband] [*dein mann*] is asleep."[84] "The light before my eyes grew black" [*shvartz vor die eugen*][85] "A black year befall you!" [*A shvartz yur off dir*].[86] "Shah! Be butchered" [*Sei geharget*].[87] "Where was learning, veneration of parents... deep in the earth" [*teef in drerd*].[88] "Do as I tell hammering the samovar" [*khoken mir a cheinek*].[89]

It must by now be apparent why the novel is not proletarian in the sense of the 1930s, for although an authentic picture of Jewish working-class life, it concentrates on penetrating deeply into the psychology of the child and is saturated with the peculiarly Jewish mental attitudes of the immigrant Jew. Yet it would be a great error to judge the novel as therefore parochial or particularistic, for it has a universality derived from deep exploration of the particular in which general human problems are illuminated. In this case the particular is the mind of a young boy in an acute Oedipal situation, or, less technically in a distorted relationship with each parent—excessive dependence on the mother, total rejection of the father—with the overtones of child sexuality which constitute the Oedipal character of the situation.

The author himself said in 1979 that it "was a very Jewish book; all the elements in it are very Jewish, and yet, it was written by somebody who no longer felt Jewish."[90] This is a striking, if unconscious, tribute to the artist in himself. For it means that Roth was able to distance and successfully convey his material for artistic purposes without at the same time losing its passionate content. The creative power of the story is seen in the author's statement in another interview in 1977 that "none of it is autobiographical, or all of it is autobiographical, in the sense that no incident in it does not have some real base somewhere, either in my own life or often in what I heard or saw....However, the total structure is not autobiographical. Everything is arranged in order to obtain a novelistic structure."[91] Since Roth by his middle twenties had not written very much before, though he had devoured whole libraries, one can only conclude that a great intuitive artist was at work here.

Why, then, did he not go on to further creation? His high reputation as a novelist rests on this single novel, just as Ralph Ellison's rests on *The Invisible Man*. The answer is elusive. Roth has told interviewers that he began another novel in which he tried to depict the development, as a socialist, of a man who was an illiterate and devoted Communist party member. He wrote about one hundred pages and was given an advance by Max Perkins at Scribner's, but then ran up against what seemed an insuperable writer's block. In later years during the McCarthy period, while he was still a party member, he burned this manuscript together with "a couple of very, very valuable journals."[92] Further efforts at writing were unrewarding, and he gave up. He married, during World War II worked as a precision grinder, and afterwards moved to Maine. Why had he given up writing? "You could name a whole slew," he said in 1977, "who one after another stopped being creative writers. I thought at first each one was blocked for some unique personal reason or other, but apparently it was ... social.... The 30's, ... disabled an entire generation of writers." More or less responsibility for this is often assigned to the Communist party's rigid restrictions on content and manner, which hobbled the creative imagination. When asked if party demands and conditions in the United States and Europe had contributed, Roth generally agreed: "Trying to write ... with an eye on the revolution, or on the Party, trying to write with a maximum of social consciousness was not the kind of thing that I was cut out for. Nevertheless I felt compulsion to do so, and since I couldn't do it," Roth asserts that *Call It Sleep* was "not a proletarian novel."[93] It has been suggested that the short circuit of the third rail in the novel was an unconscious prophesy of Roth's own literary sterility after 1934, and he seems to agree. "Look at the symbolism of *Call It Sleep* at the end. A shunt is thrown across the third rail.... Communism intervened as a way of solving the problems of humanity, as a way of absolving me from being a Jew. But it didn't work. It didn't work for anybody. That was the shunt."[94] Yet, Roth remained in the party until the 1960s.

Renewal came with the Six-Day War in 1967, when he was sixty-one. A remarkable thing happened—with his return to Jewish consciousness prompted by the war came a rejuvenation of his literary activity. "When Israel defeated the Arabs in a matter of a few days," he said, "my exaltation knew no bounds.... I experienced a resurgence of my long dormant literary vocation." He has become a Zionist and active worker for Israel. He has visited Israel twice, in 1972 and 1977, and together with his wife led the activities of the work for Israel in the Jewish community of Albuquerque, New Mexico, where they lived. At the same time he continued to write, but "Israel is my main concern now," he says, "and any work of literary merit that I can achieve must be in her behalf, to muster sympathy and support for her struggle for survival and security."[95] The latest word in a 1979 interview seems to be that he is writing a work on his own maturing process—"the diaspora youth leaving his Judaism, or attempting to ... get as far away from it as possible. And then, against that, the old man, in a counter statement, in a counter movement, ... because returning is impossible, reuniting with Judaism in the form it has taken now in the State of Israel."[96]

Meyer Levin

This writer's *The Old Bunch* (1937), like the books of Mike Gold, Daniel Fuchs, and Henry Roth, is invaluable for documentation of the first few immigrant Jewish generations in the first three decades of the twentieth century. As a work of art, *Call It Sleep* can hardly be challenged as the finest of the four. As for *The Old Bunch*, Meyer Levin has himself designated his novel as "sociological," an example of "studies of Jews in American society, trying to produce positive values."[97] It makes no pretense to high art and is a straightforward account of a group, or "bunch," of friends, Levin's contemporaries, who were growing up in the 1920s and early 1930s in the Jewish section of Chicago. Levin's novel is the Jewish counterpart of James T. Farrell's concurrent account of the corresponding Irish side of Chicago in his trilogy, *Studs Lonigan* (1932, 1934, 1935). Levin adopted his concept of the novel from his conviction that the "family unit" was not "the determining human relationship" of his peers, but rather "the surrounding group, the bunch, as perhaps even more important than the family in the formative years." This was especially the case, he held, with "the children of immigrants" whose "life-values were determined largely through their group relationship."[98] Levin did not always have a positive Jewish awareness. While still in high school, his first published story was one about "ghetto shame," repudiation of his origins.[99] In 1925 he went as a journalist to cover the opening of the Hebrew University in Jerusalem, stayed on a kibbutz for a half-year, and in 1930 published the first novel in English about a kibbutz, *Yehuda*. He also translated and rewrote a collection of Hasidic tales.

Levin was attracted to the Left in the early 1930s but was always a critical adherent and never joined the Communist party. However, he published a proletarian novel, *The New Bridge*, in 1933. *The Old Bunch* is not itself a proletarian novel, since it gives a naturalistic portrait of a group of young, growing Jews without an explicit ideological framework. His book is rather in the tradition of the American-Jewish novels of Abraham Cahan, Ludwig Lewisohn, and Mike Gold, all of whom he acknowledges as influences. Like Farrell's trilogy and John Dos Passos' trilogy *USA* (1930, 1932, 1936), Levin's is a "collective" novel, that is, it does not center on one or two characters, but rather follows the life of each of about a dozen members of "the bunch" from adolescence to their thirties. Some half-dozen girls are also depicted, but the boys dominate the action. Their fathers' occupations range from that of ordinary shop worker to small shopkeeper to small factory owner, but some do not undergo the struggle for sheer survival as do Mike Gold's East Side characters. The later experience of the various members of the bunch is wide-ranging—artist, scientist, small businessman, big manufacturer, unscrupulous politician—and their political directions vary from Left to Right. These political divisions do not appear until two-thirds through the book, when there are strikes during which police brutality radicalizes one, while another becomes a grasping, vulgar anti-union man-ufacturer. The Zionism in the novel is critical, reflecting the author's own preference at the time for a cultural rather than a political Zionism.

The attitude of Joe Freedman, a sculptor who goes through some of the experiences of Levin himself in Paris and Palestine, and was probably the author's spokesman, exemplifies problems of acculturation. In his college drafting class he sits next to the non-Jew "Blondy," who is "one of those clean-cut, typically American-looking boys, with a right-angled jaw and cool blue eyes. . . . A kind of taken-for-granted fellowship existed between Joe and Blondy. What Blondy had, what Joe knew he could never have, was this complete acceptance of, and by, his environment. With him, Dan-ville (Illinois) seemed exactly the right place to have come from, his house probably the rightest place in Danville."[100] The University of Chicago was something new, thought Joe, was something "he hadn't met before in his life" growing up in a Jewish environment. "It was as though this were inner America, but America was made up of dagoes, Irish, Poles, Jews, the bloody nineteenth ward, and back o' the yards, and Maxwell Street [the Jewish area] and Little Italy. . . . This was like a homely dining room assembled of odd pieces, but by people who couldn't be wrong. Here were these houses with their white-pillared porches, and they were right, and he was wrong."[101]

On the distaff side the seven girls attached to the bunch assemble when one of them marries one of the boys. Their parochial stereotyped view of non-Jewish boys emerges from their conversation. "Listen, those *shkotzim* [non-Jews] are after only one thing. . . . You can trust a Jewish fellow but you can never trust a *sheigitz* [non-Jew]—But suppose it was a fellow you really liked. Suppose you were really in love with him.—You wouldn't marry a Gentile, would you?—I certainly would if I wanted to.—Aline, your mother would die.—She'd get over it.—Well, it never works out.—I'd go out with a *goy* but I wouldn't marry one."[102] Another experience, only too typical for the period, is that of Mitch Wilner, the medical scientist who has already done valuable work and is encouraged to apply for a research post at the Mayo Clinic. He is rejected with no reason stated. "Fellows had warned him, hinted, but he laughed it off saying that a man's Jewishness might be the deciding factor against him when all else was even. But they never refused a man who was really tops! . . . There could be no other reason, and still he couldn't believe it."[103] Another manifestation of anti-Semitism under less dignified circumstances was the case of another of the boys, Dave (Runt) Plotkin, a shyster lawyer with underworld connections. He is living with a gold-digging non-Jewish woman whom he forced to his bed by giving her money for an abortion. After cohabiting for three years, he suggests marriage. "She stared at him. 'What the hell would I want to marry you for? What a laugh!' " She is overcome with laughter. "Well, what's so funny?" "Why you—. . . you little Jew runt.' "[104]

If there is any unity in this one-thousand-page novel, it is simply the fact that all its characters are in their several ways struggling with the problem of acculturation, finding a place in the non-Jewish world. The radical viewpoint with which Joe Freedman ends the book is simply one among others, and not an organic part of some design of the book as a whole. Indeed, one ends the novel with the feeling that it could go on almost indefinitely through the rest of the lives of its characters. This is another way of saying that it has no strict artistic form—it simply is not that kind of novel. It is what one might call a pluralistic, rather than unitary, story in which the characters are not connected by esthetic necessity.

Nevertheless, *The Old Bunch* is one of the memorable novels of the decade, and perhaps the most fully documented of any novel of acculturation. Since acculturation is a process, any one segment of it is different from others, so that the documentation is for the most part valid for the dozen or so years it encompasses, from 1921 to 1933. And because it was a candid portrait, some Jews and Jewish organizations were disturbed, a not uncommon response to fiction depicting Jews as less than perfect. There were sermons preached against it in temples and, Levin reports, it was "described in some of the Jewish press as a degradation of our people." The author was invited to lunch by a representative of the Anti-Defamation League to discuss criticism of the book. This disapproval largely receded, and Levin wrote in 1950 that "this was the outstanding American Jewish novel of its generation."[105] At least, it can be agreed that this was *one* of the "outstanding American Jewish novels of its generation."

Levin's next novel, *Citizens* (1940), is centered on the involvement of one of the "old bunch," Mitch Wilner, now a doctor, with the Memorial Day Massacre of strikers in Chicago in 1937. This book is clearly a proletarian novel (though not listed as such by Rideout) in that it gives a highly sympathetic treatment to the labor movement and even shows favorable attitudes of workers toward Communist party members. Unlike *The Old Bunch*, the milieu is the labor movement rather than the Jewish community, and most of the characters are non-Jewish. Levin refused to comply with the publisher's suggestion that "the story would be much more American if this doctor [Wilner] were not a Jew,"[106] which is sufficiently revealing of the commercial view of popular sentiment toward the Jew. Since the 1940s nearly all Levin's work has been devoted to Jewish fiction and lately, predominantly to Israel. In the post–World War II period Levin spent part of each year in Israel, where he died in 1981.

Others

Our picture of the 1930s should be completed with a brief look at some novels that offer documentation of the several other aspects of Jewish life in America at the time. Some explore family origins in the old country before emigration and trace the Americanization process in the new world, especially in the second generation, and others are set entirely in this country.

Although Charles Reznikoff was essentially untouched by the proletarian movement, he was an active adherent of labor Zionism and was editor of its organ, *Jewish Frontier,* from 1955 onward. He attained distinction primarily as a poet, and we shall return to him in our discussion of Jews in poetry. But he also wrote an acculturation novel that so impressed the young Lionel Trilling that he called it "the first story of the Jewish immigrant that is not false" and said it was "not merely a fine but a truer story than previous attempts in the field of American immigrant Jewish fiction." It was, he said, superior to "Mr Michael Gold's admirable and moving *Jews Without Money.*"[107] It is more "realistic" and less "romantic" than the Gold novel. Reznikoff's *By the Waters of Manhattan* (1930) was, like so many of its kind, autobiographical. The first half is devoted to the hard life of his mother in the *shtetl* and, later, in the United States after she came here alone. The able, bright Sarah Yetta Volsky aspires to education but is frustrated and has to work in the sweatshop. She marries and lives in poverty. Her son Ezekiel is at the center of the second half. He goes through high school, reads copiously, and after high school opens a bookshop in Greenwich Village. His liaison with a customer does not leave him any less frustrated than his mother had been.

It is apparent that this is a somber, not to say depressing, novel with little lightness. It is indeed, as Trilling noted, a "realistic" picture of immigrant life: there is no nostalgia here. The first half is written in an extraordinarily direct and simple, unembellished prose which was not, however, banal. But the second part, in which the travail of Ezekiel is concentrated, takes on a lyric quality which bespeaks the poet. Such a sentence as this suggests the quality: the design of his friend "Jane's kimono had probably been modelled on a leaf or a flower, but the copyist had obscured its meaning so that Ezekiel saw only patches of colored felt stretched with tinsel."[108]

Trilling's high praise has not thus far been vindicated by posterity. The novel seems dull and has made little impress on subsequent writing. If it has survived at all, it is because of Reznikoff's distinction as a poet, which was considerable. It is curious that in 1930, when Reznikoff had been identified with the Objectivist school of poetry for at least a decade, Trilling took no notice of his poetry in the review. Further, Trilling's judgment of the immigrant—or, we might say, acculturation—novel as so generally a failure and "false," a charge he associated in his review with the failure of "Theodore Dreiser and Upton Sinclair,"[109] points to Trilling's literary prejudice, later reiterated with respect to Dreiser in an essay in *The Liberal Imagination*. It is here laid bare by his coupling of Dreiser and Sinclair as novelists.

The persistence of the second-generation Jews' awareness of their roots in East Europe was still strong in the 1930s, even though immigration had been practically cut off in 1924. Irving Fineman deliberately set out to promote knowledge of the immigrant background of Jewish forbears in *Hear, Ye Sons* (1933). The protagonist, Joseph, born and married in Poland, conscripted into the Tsar's army from which he escaped to the United States, is a successful lawyer and sees to it that his children are aware of the life he led in the *shtetl*. He casts a nostalgic glow over that life, even on his *heder* experience as a boy. In answer to questions asked of the *melamed*, he says, he "got a stinging blow and the reproof, 'Little heathen! Ask no questions! How often must I tell you?' " In retrospect the author gives this dogmatic tyranny an apologetic and obscurantist interpretation. As we saw also in Anzia Yezierska's later years, he says,

Only now in the days of my old age do I see how just was his maxim. For many's the question I have asked in my time to which the only answer is painful or silence: why with the good must there be evil in this world, why with happiness must men endure all manner of suffering; why must life end in death? . . . "Ask no questions!" answered my teacher unmindful of my tears, his lank curls winging to and fro as he resumed Israel's deathless story, halting only to reach with his ferrule for the knuckles of some drowsy little scholar whose head had sunk down upon an outs-tretched arm.[110]

As with Yezierska, Fineman's nostalgia overcomes his critical sense, and he ends by being an apologist for obscurantist aspects of Orthodox life.

For the rest, like so many acculturation novels—and here they were only mirroring reality—his children attain positions of note in American society: a famous construction engineer, a well-known social worker, another killed in World War I, a concert pianist, and finally the self-hating one. This last is an English professor at Princeton who "is not, I understand, taken for a Jew. He is accepted, nay welcomed, in the best, most exclusive academic circles. He will marry, I have heard, a gentile."[111]

But there are distinctions within assimilationist tendencies. Fineman's English professor is at one self-hating extreme, but by no means all assimilationists are self-hating. They may simply prefer a minimum Jewish identification without animus toward Jews or Jewishness, and there are gradations between. However, novels like Nat J. Ferber's *One Happy Jew* (1934) seem to overlook such distinctions. The prosperous Marmelstein family, fugitives from Hungarian anti-Semitism, flee to America, where, Marmelstein "told himself a thousand times, the Jew is spared suffering and humiliation merely because of his miserable heritage."[112] All his sons change their names and marry gentiles. Only the "one happy Jew" among them remains Jewish, lives on the East Side, and does educational work among his people. But the effort of his family to renounce their Jewishness is frustrated by the coming of Hitlerism. However, this fast-paced novel in the end reduces to a cartoon of the problem.

Just as there is no suggestion of the current radicalism in Ferber's novel, so also Louis Zara's *Blessed Is the Man* (1935) tends toward a conservative outlook. The novel traces the rise of Jake Krakauer in the usual manner from peddler to store owner to affluent chain store owner to bank director to financier. There is perhaps a too detailed family chronicle of a happy marriage with its five sons taking their place in American life: one loses his life in World War I, one becomes a doctor, one a radical, one marries a non-Jew. Jake is a good family man, decent in his personal relations, and also a political conservative and an anti-union businessman. Zara made his contribution to the celebration of the tercentenary of Jewish settlement in the United States in 1654 with his *Blessed Is the Land* (1954), a historical novel of this first Jewish settlement centered about its best known member, Asher Levy. The book ends: "Blessed are those that created for us a new land of milk and honey."[113]

No portrait of Jews in the 1930s would be complete without some attention to the socially important presence of Jews in the film industry in Hollywood. A broadly satirical picture of the crude, undignified effort to ape the philistine, prosperous Christian middle class—or to outdo it—is Aben Kandel's *Rabbi Burns* (1931). The nouveau riche temple Judaism of Hollywood's Jewish community is ruthlessly satirized, as well as its attempt to assimilate to conventional superficial, materialistic Christian life. This is developed through the study of a young, "modern" Hollywood rabbi and his wealthy, upwardly mobile congregation. For them Judaism is a veneer of pseudo-religious feeling over an affluent middle-class life. Spokesman for the author is Adam Krasoff, a journalist who edits the local Jewish weekly in an effort to build it into a national journal. He is contemptuous of the Reform Rabbi Marvin Burns (né Moishe Bernstein), born on the East Side and Anglo-Saxonized. The rabbi is a despicable, slick hypocrite and a pompous orator whose religion is empty. He is also "spiritual advisor" to a large movie company. The rich, old established German Jews of the town had not admitted the Eastern European Jews to their synagogue. The latter therefore proceed, with Rabbi Burns, to build a temple modeled on a movie palace combined with a recreation center. The several types of "new rich" Jews are depicted, together with their love affairs.

The assimilationist concept of these Jews is epitomized in the author's characterization of one of them:

It was one of his business and religious doctrines that Jews should always be stylishly dressed in a Gentile community.... By dressing well, they helped to efface themselves as Jews, except, of course, for those unfortunate characteristics which were ineradicable. [He] practiced many other externals in behavior, speech, and appearance, all of them calculated to make the Jews more palatable to the Gentile. And it was his proud boast that some of his best friends were Gentiles.[114]

The novel has narrative pace and is engaging, but the characters and situations are too pat and almost a "set-up" for the author's criticism. The novel now has interest only as a document of the period.

ATTITUDES OF THE 1930s

Anti-Semitism in the United States is not independent of Europe. On the contrary, it is closely related. Thus, in both places three peaks of anti-Semitism in the past century occurred at about the same time, as John Higham has shown. In Europe, the first period of especially intense anti-Semitism came in the late 1880s and 1890s with the emergence of Adolf Stoeckel in Germany and Edouard Drument in France; the second with the currency given to the *Protocols of the Elders of Zion* in the post–World War I period, 1919 to 1923; and the third with the coming to power of Hitler in the 1930s. In the United States there were parallel developments: the first saw the emergence of populist anti-Semitism, the intensification of anti-foreign agitation following mass immigration, and the qualitative change in anti-Jewish discrimination, social and economic; the second period witnessed the unprecedented campaign of Henry Ford's *Dearborn Independent* and its serialization of the *Protocols* and the rapid rise of the Ku Klux Klan.[115]

This mutuality is most vividly exhibited in the third period in the 1930s with echoes in the United States of the dominance of Nazism in Germany. Between 1933 and 1939, Oscar Handlin has noted, there were about one hundred anti-Semitic and, we should add, pro-fascist organizations in this country. Demagogues like William Dudley Pelley, Gerald L. K. Smith, Gerald Winrod, and many others flourished. The arch-demagogue Father Charles E. Coughlin drew millions to his weekly radio talks fulminating against the Jews, and his journal *Social Justice* further disseminated his pro-fascist and anti-Semitic views. Anti-Semitism was even expressed on the floor of Congress by such men as John Rankin. In the 1930s, also, as E. Digby Baltzell has observed, "Discriminatory practice against Jews—in education, in employment, in white-collar jobs, and in the professions—continued, and in many areas became more intensified."[116]

If anti-Semitism was becoming more intense during the Depression and Nazi influence was increasing, contrary tendencies were also operating. While desperate economic circumstances were providing fertile soil for the demagogue, they were also radicalizing others who were too deeply rooted in humanistic values and the democratic tradition to be misled by prevalent attempts at scapegoating the Jews. These saw anti-Semitism for what it was, a means of distracting people from the actualities from which they were suffering. Among these were most writers, Jewish and non-Jewish, and both groups exposed anti-Semitism in their fiction. There were other writers—and some leading ones like Ezra Pound—who were persistently anti-Semitic, but they were few. Some of those who had indulged in anti-Semitism in the 1920s revised their opinions under the impact of Nazism. And we have seen how the Jewish proletarian writers exposed anti-Semitism in their fiction.

However, it appears that Jews were virtually taboo in the popular fiction of the 1930s and early 1940s, or, if they were mentioned, it was in some invidious or inferior connection. Popular magazine stories were targeted to interest a mass readership, and therefore the publishers and authors took the greatest care to avoid doing battle with any presumed prejudice of that audience. Evidence of the ethnic character of the fiction supplied to the mass audience became available in 1945. The Bureau of Applied Research published its survey of the treatment of minorities in popular fiction of "the most widely read magazines" during the two years of 1937 and 1943. Scrutiny of 198 short stories in those two years showed that "Prejudice against minority peoples in this country is widespread."[117] In these stories, Blacks and Jews were "disapproved"; Mexicans, Italian Americans, and Japanese Americans were regarded as "out groups"; even Irish Americans were "sometimes not accepted as 'good Americans.' "[118] Among the 900 characters identified in these stories, "minority and foreign groups were seldom represented," and only ten of the characters were Jews. Heroes, heroines, or major characters were seldom drawn from minority or foreign groups. Each minority had its stereotype, including that of the "sly and shrewd Jews."[119] The researchers concluded that not only did "Americans" receive "better treatment, both qualitatively and quantitatively, than the minority groups," but that even among the foreigners treated, the Anglo-Saxons and Nordics, who were still "foreigners," were best treated, European and Oriental groups next best, and the worst was reserved for Blacks and Jews. "The Negroes and Jews *never* appeared as heroes or heroines. No Negroes or Jews were depicted as members of the armed forces. They had the lowest occupational rating. They constituted the only group with more disapproved than approved traits. In short, of all the distinguishable groups of characters in mass magazine fiction, the *Negroes and the Jews are depicted least favorably*" (emphasis added). The researchers hold that these stories were written without conscious malice, but responded to what were considered the needs of easy commercial appeal. This does not mean that such stories are harmless. As the researchers believed, over a period this "serves to activate the predispositions of a hostile or even an indifferent audience."[120]

While this fiction makes no pretense at sophisticated art, it is obvious that an immense change has taken place since the 1940s and 1950s on what are permissible attitudes toward Blacks, Jews, and all minorities. What is striking about the non-Jewish proletarian writers of the 1930s is not only that they ignored this taboo, but that they clearly condemned anti-Semitism in their fiction as it emerges from its context. They were aware of the usual concomitance of anti-Semitism with reaction, and its usefulness in furthering reactionary causes. The question arises from the above survey and the contrary practice of most serious writers: were they ahead of their times in treating Jews as they did in their fiction, or were the popular fiction writers and the editors and publishers who dictated the treatment of minorities in

magazine stories behind the times? Was the popular audience ready for fully
human treatment of Jews and minorities in the 1930s?

Serious novelists paid little attention to this commercial notion of re-
maining silent on the "controversial" subject of the Jews in the country.
On the contrary, the general tendency among non-Jewish writers was to
include Jews in their fiction and especially to condemn anti-Semitism explicitly or implicitly. One outstanding example is the unequivocal condemnation of anti-Semitism apparent in one of the enduring novels of the decade,
James T. Farrell's trilogy, *Studs Lonigan* (1932, 1934, 1935). In the lower
middle-class Irish milieu of Farrell's Chicago, ethnic prejudice was rife. Studs
Lonigan's father Patrick tells the family they must move. "When we bought
this building," he muses, "Wabash Avenue had been a nice, decent, respectable street for a self-respecting man to live with his family. But, now,
well, the niggers and kikes were getting in, and they were dirty, and you
didn't know but what, even in broad daylight, some nigger moron might
be attacking his girls. He'd have to get away from the eight balls and the
tinhorn kikes. And when they got into a neighborhood, property values go
blooey."[121] Studs as a boy belongs to a gang whose only non-Irish, Jewish
member is Davey Cohen, who even joined the gang on their Jew-baiting
expeditions, though he was not happy about it. They would rove "in little
Jerusalem" looking for "hooknoses" and "Christ-killers." They beat up
Jewish boys—"Take that for killin' Christ."[122] Davey goes along for a "gang
shag," but when his turn comes, the promiscuous Iris "wouldn't let a kike
touch her" and she calls him "a dirty Jew." The humiliated Davey wanders
about the city, full of hostile thoughts against the Irish. They were "dumb,
...always had to fight with their fists... couldn't use their noodles." He
thought himself "so much cleverer than the Irish,... a race of beer guzzlers,
flatfeet and boneheads. Why, they even had to take a Jew Christ,...and
make an Irishman of him.... The dumbest Jew was smarter than the smar-
test Irishman."[123] Davey can no longer endure the life and runs away from
Chicago.

In the second volume, *The Young Manhood of Studs Lonigan,* the young
Irishmen continue to harass Blacks and Jews. On one street they go "searching for niggers," create a disturbance, and throw "bricks into the windows
of houses where they thought niggers lived." They find a ten-year-old Black
boy, take off his clothes and burn them, "made him step on light matches,
urinated on him, and sent him running off naked with a couple of slaps in
the face."[124] Their treatment of Jews is no less gallant. At a football game,
they plan to disable the star of the opposing team, "Jewboy Schwartz."
After several attempts to knock him out, "Weary" jams his knee deliberately
into Schwartz's groin, but still Schwartz plays on. They finally disable
Schwartz, and fear they have killed him. He survives, but can play no more
football. When one of Schwartz's teammates tells Weary, "Play football
and quit squabbling. You half killed my buddy," Weary replies, "And I'll

kill you, too, kike!"[125] The teams fight, and the game is called off. Another instance of mindless anti-Semitism involves another of the gang, Tommy, who holds up a Jewish man. When this man wants his money returned, Tommy complains that "the Jew is sore, and threatens to press charges if he don't get his money back. You know, these Jews, always wanting their pound of flesh."[126] When one of the neighborhood Jewish boys Philip Rolfe plans to marry Studs' sister and converts to Catholicism, Studs remarks, "You know, he's Jewish, and I always make it a point never to trust a Jew, but I finally am convinced that he's one white Jew, if there ever was one. And accepting the faith, well, I suppose we oughtn't to call him a Jew any more. He's on our side of the fence."[127]

The influence of the current neo-fascist movement is manifest in the final volume (1935). The "radio priest Father Moylan," obviously patterned on the pro-fascist Father Coughlin who broadcast from Detroit and was especially influential in the Middle West, is invoked to flay the "Jew international bankers." Studs' father tells Studs, "The stock markets are manipulated by the Jew international bankers."[128] On another occasion, he says "the Jew international bankers...are squeezing every penny out of America and Americans."[129] When Studs' father loses all his money and business in the Great Depression, "he heaped a curse on the Jew international bankers. They didn't want America to collect its just debt from Europe. If America did, they wouldn't make enough greedy profit. That was why there was a depression."[130] With a naturalistic technique Farrell is ruthless in exposing the severe limitations of his fellow Irish neighbors at the time, and their mindless prejudice against the Jews and Blacks is shown as an element of that narrow, anti-social viewpoint. That this attitude was not universal among the Irish is demonstrated by Farrell himself, who was one of them but their compassionate and sensitive critic.

Far less socially responsible was the attitude of the bohemian expatriate, Henry Miller, at the time in Paris. Henry Miller's attitude to the Jews is ambiguous, if not ambivalent. His equivocal manner of alluding to them is indicative of an emotional confusion toward them brought on by unextirpated traditional prejudice. In the bohemian Paris of his *Tropic of Cancer* (1934), his friend Borenstein "puts on that he is a Pole, but he is not, of course. He is a Jew.... In fact, all Montparnasse is Jewish, or half-Jewish, which is worse," and he details their names. "The Jews are snowing me under.... Of them all the loveliest is Tania, and for her sake I too would become a Jew. And I am ugly as a Jew. Besides, who hates the Jews more than a Jew?"[131] On the other hand, he presents a striking, if melodramatic, metaphor of the Jewish predicament.

For the Jews [he wrote], the world is a cage filled with wild beasts. The door is locked and he is there without whip or revolver. His courage is so great that he does not even smell the dung in the corner. The spectators applaud but he does not hear. The drama, he thinks, is going on inside the cage. The cage, he thinks, is the world. Standing there alone and helpless, the door locked, he finds that the lions do not understand his language. No lion has ever heard of Spinoza. Spinoza? Why they can't even get their teeth into him. "Give us meat!" they roar, while he stands petrified, his ideas frozen, his *Weltanschauung* a trapeze out of reach. A single blow of the lion's paw and his cosmogony is smashed.[132]

This half-romantic, half-real, half-comprehending statement of the Jewish situation is typical enough of ambivalence. Ambiguity and ambivalence also appear in Miller's statement that "the first people to turn to when you're down and out are the Jews. I had three of them on my hands almost at once. Sympathetic souls. One of them was a retired merchant who had an itch to see his name in the papers; he proposed that I write a series of articles under his name for a Jewish daily in New York."[133]

Theodore Dreiser

A notorious case of anti-Semitism in a major American writer is that of Theodore Dreiser. He was born in Indiana and lived in the Middle West until he moved to New York in 1894. As a journalist and writer there he inevitably associated with Jewish colleagues. Jewish characters hardly figure in his fiction, but in his only play, *The Hand of the Potter* (1919). There is no evidence of animus against the Jews in the play. Mike Gold later explained how Dreiser came to write the play. Dreiser told Mike Gold that "he had himself long wanted to write an East Side play, but felt unsure of the milieu." Gold readily then guided Dreiser through the East Side and to his tenement home for a Friday Sabbath evening ritual and meal. The occasion, wrote Gold, "was all simple and friendly and you could tell that Dreiser was a good human being." Gold was impressed by the play, and "how well he'd grasped the character of the Jewish immigrant life . . . [and] created a group of real tenement people such as I lived among."[134]

But there is clear evidence a few years later that Dreiser was anti-Semitic. In a letter to H. L. Mencken—a kindred spirit in this respect—dated November 5, 1922, he wrote that "New York is to me a scream—a kyke's dream of a Ghetto. The lost tribe has taken over the island." This sentiment was reiterated in the same year to others in letters—he didn't care for New York—"Too many Jews."[135] To another: "To [sic] many unidealistic Jews. Hence the old, vivid, searching idealism is gone."[136] Like so many anti-Semites, his attitude toward Jews was dual—admiration and contempt. He admired their talent but deplored their presumed invidious traits. "Just think what they have achieved," he explained to a friend, but, adds his biographer W. H. Swanberg, "In private he swore maledictions on them, swore they could never be trusted!" His quarrels with his Jewish publisher Horace Liveright "often set him off on violent diatribes against Jews in general."

In 1930, he told the *Jewish Journal* of San Francisco, "the Jews are one of the greatest races which ever stood on earth." But on the other hand, he complained, "You Jews want to be a race which envelops the earth. You'd like to have your fingers in every pie."[137]

In 1933 Dreiser went public with his anti-Semitic sentiments. He was then on the editorial board of the monthly *American Spectator* together with George Jean Nathan, Ernest Boyd, James Branch Cabell, and Eugene O'Neill. Jews were very much in the mind of the world that year, for Hitler had gained power in January. Beginning in the January issue, the magazine ran frequent articles on the Jews. The confused and inadequate current grasp of the basic issues among literary people emerges from most of these articles. The editors themselves contributed to this year-long discussion in the September issue with a transcript of an "Editorial Conference (with wine)." The tone of the discussion is generally light though the subject is deadly serious. Dreiser sets the problem: "The world's problem with the Jew is not that he is inferior, but that he is superior. He is altogether too successful in the professions and in all other branches of the arts and sciences."

My real quarrel with the Jew [he says] is not that he is inefficient or ignorant or even unaesthetic. It is really that he is too clever and too dynamic in his personal and racial attack on all other types of persons and races.... the Jew, to me, particularly in the realm of commerce and some practical professions, wherein shrewdness rather than creative labor is the chief issue, might well be compelled to accept a handicap-limitation as to numbers in given lines. Thus 100,000 Jewish lawyers might be reduced to ten and the remainder made to do farming.[138]

In this ingenious way, Dreiser weaves elements of the stereotype into his argument. Then follows more discussion of Dreiser's central thesis about the Jews—the solution to the Jewish "problem." Their aggressive, overweening situation in the world could be overcome by their foregathering in a state of their own.

The entire discussion reveals that all these writers shared in one degree or another what would be unthinkable in a publication today. It did not arouse any immediate public response. Meanwhile, in private, Dreiser continued to fulminate against the Jews. A friend noted in his diary that, after a dinner, Dreiser

started knocking the Jews, out of a clear blue sky. Hitler was right, he said. Something had to be done about this question. The Jews were all right but shouldn't live with others. Let them have their own country, but Palestine, he admitted—that was a difficult place, not the right place for a highly civilized race like the Jews. But England would be glad to create a larger Jewish country in South Africa. Let the Jews all go there and be happy.[139]

By early 1935 Dreiser's books had been banned in Germany. In a letter dated January 14 (1935), Dreiser notes the ban and wonders if it is because the Nazis think him a Jew, as many people seemed to believe. Perhaps they think so, he writes, because of his "Jewish tragedy—*The Hand of the Potter*—which had quite a run in Germany." The same day he also wrote of this to Mencken, asking if there was "any procedure" he could apply "to disabuse the [German] authorities" of this false notion.[140]

The issue finally burst upon the public in *The Nation* of April 17, 1935, with Hutchins Hapgood's article, "Is Dreiser Anti-Semitic?" Hapgood, author of *The Spirit of the Ghetto* (1902), there revealed that *The American Spectator* had refused to publish his letters complaining of the "anti-Semitic slant of the general argument." Instead, Dreiser wrote Hapgood a letter which "horrified and astonished me." The rest of the article is the text of the letters exchanged between them. Dreiser reiterates the views expressed in the symposium, and adds, "If you listen to Jews discuss Jews, you will find that they are money-minded, very pagan, very sharp in practice, and . . . have the single objective of plenty of money." Jewish lawyers lack integrity. Jews refuse to "fade into" the country they inhabit. The Jew should seek a land of his own. Hapgood replied that Dreiser's letter might have been "written by a member of the Ku Klux Klan or a representative of Hitler," and he challenged Dreiser's assertions about the Jews. "For you," wrote Hapgood, "who ought to be a leader in our civilization, to take this barbarous attitude is to me inexplicable on any decent ground." Once again Dreiser returns to justify his view. He thinks the Germans should have "negotiated" with the Jews and "the powers of the world for land and social opportunities of an equal character elsewhere." Indeed, an international conference should be convened, added Dreiser, to discuss a solution to the Jewish problem. Once again Dreiser calls for the Jews to be furnished with "an entirely adequate country" and "loans and equipment necessary to start them upon an independent and, as I see it, certain to be successful and even glorious career as a nation." Either that, or total assimilation, he adds. In his final reply, Hapgood calls the first scheme "obviously impossible of realization" and the second, assimilation, "actually going on but impeded by anti-Semitism."[141]

This relentless exposure of Dreiser's anti-Semitism could not be ignored by *The New Masses,* for Dreiser was then sympathetic to communism. In an article, "Dreiser Denies He Is Anti-Semitic" two weeks later, the paper reported several discussions of Dreiser with *New Masses* representatives and writers. At the first meeting, Dreiser "withdrew nothing" and even "added further to the confusion." A second meeting was no more fruitful. The article noted that Dreiser ignored the fact of the existence of classes among the Jews, of poor and rich, and they charged that his views were "almost identical with the propaganda used by Hitler and his followers to promote Nazism." They finally succeeded in getting him to admit a few "contradictions in his stand." They regarded as "inadequate" a statement which accompanied the article, but did not give up hope that he would "regain his traditional place as a fighter for human liberty." Dreiser's accompanying statement asserts his belief in the class distinctions among Jews and the identity of the interests of Jewish workers with all workers. He also repudiates any use of his words by Nazis and dissociates himself from Hitler and fascism.[142] An editorial on May 8 in *The Nation* agreed that Dreiser had "retracted almost nothing" and agreed with *The New Masses* statement that "anti-Semitism is not something that can be temporized with or toned down."[143] Two pages of letters on the matter also appeared in the May 15 issue of *The Nation*.[144]

Mike Gold did not let the issue rest. Gold's identification with the Jewish poor was intense, and he was outraged at Dreiser's obstinate and irresponsible confusions. His article in *The New Masses,* "The Gun Is Loaded, Dreiser," warned the eminent writer that "the times are dangerous . . . for childishness," and asserted that Dreiser "can now undo this damage only by years of devoted battle against anti-Semitism and fascism." He called Dreiser's Nazi-like "slogans . . . an American tragedy, infinitely worse that that which befell Clyde Griffiths." He scolded Dreiser for failing to distinguish poor exploited Jews from rich Jewish exploiters, and reminded Dreiser of their tour of the East Side years before. He chides Dreiser for calling on Jews to be "pure Americans" by reminding Dreiser that he is the son of immigrant German parents. While Gold believes Dreiser's repudiation of Nazism, he emphasizes that "any theory of nationalism which forces cultural assimilation of its citizens is a big step toward fascism." Although Gold himself "sees only good in assimilation," he disagrees with Dreiser's pointing "his chauvinist gun . . . at the Jews, and saying, 'Either assimilate or get the hell out.' "[145]

All this discussion seems to have made no impression on Dreiser. On June 27, 1935, he wrote to Sergei Dynamov, editor of the Soviet *International Literature,* and reiterated his approach to the question. Alluding to the discussions that had occurred, Dreiser wrote, "I have not changed my viewpoint in regard to the Jewish programme in America." There are those concerned with the Jewish problem, he writes, "who have no programme to offer"—as if combatting anti-Semitism and supporting full equality were not a "programme." Complaining that Jewish "peculiar race drift in their management of the movies in this country" has also managed to introduce Catholic censorship of the medium and thus strengthened the Catholic church in the United States, Dreiser ends by enjoining the recipient that the letter is "confidential and private."[146] The confusion is deep as ever half a year later in his letter of January 7, 1936, to Heywood Broun. The Nazi "need for social separation" from the Jews is not criticized, but rather their method of dealing with it. The Nazis "should have offered them territory, payment for their property, and transportation, under such terms as the world would consider economically fair!"[147] In 1939 he was in debt to his publisher Simon and Schuster for almost $10,000 and several years behind in delivering a novel contracted for, and he suspected that they—Jewish publishers—were part of a plot to remove his books from the market because of his "anti-Judaism," as he said. In a letter to a non-Jewish friend enjoined as "strictly private," he asked for a list of "fairly recently organized non-Jewish publishers."[148]

Did Dreiser ever arrive at a clear view of the problem of anti-Semitism? The critic F. O. Matthiessen, in his biography of Dreiser, wrote that he "grew into a humane philosophy largely through fighting within himself the most destructive prejudice of our time, anti-Semitism. . . . Not until 1939 had he purified his thought to the point of speaking out forthrightly against social torture of any group, or race, or sect for reasons of difference in appearance or creed or custom."[149] One only wishes this had been true. But Matthiessen was too charitable. After Hitler's invasion of Poland in 1939, Dreiser wrote to Mencken, "I begin to suspect that Hitler is correct. The president [Roosevelt] may be partly Jewish. His present animosity toward Hitler has already resulted in placing America in the Allied camp—strengthening Britain's attitude and injuring Germany in the eyes of the world. The brass!"[150]

Thus Dreiser must be included in the overlong roster of great writers who were inveterate anti-Semites.

4

The Jew at War: The 1940s

Anti-Semitism over the centuries has proven to be a most flexible instrument. It has been remarkably adaptable to the diversionary needs of rulers or aspirants for power in a variety of periods with their special circumstances and potentiality for anti-Jewish charges. In the Middle Ages, for instance, the Jew became closely associated with the Devil and supernatural forces of evil and with necromancy as well as with the profane usurer practicing the forbidden traffic in money. The economic stereotype of the passion for money has straddled many periods. In the post-Enlightenment period, while Jews were granted civic and legal equality, the charge of dual loyalty could not be suppressed. Under these circumstances they were regarded as aliens in the country of their settlement, and they were suspected of being more loyal to the Jewish people than to the state in which they lived. With the rise of the labor and revolutionary movements under capitalism Jews were simultaneously accused of being revolutionaries and bankers bent on controlling and gaining the world's wealth.

Since warfare has been a constant of social experience, appropriate anti-Semitic accusations were introduced to help divert the populace from the rigors of war. Jewish loyalty in wartime was suspect. Jews were often denied even the right to serve in the military. Where they were allowed to serve, it was widely believed that they managed to evade fulfillment of dangerous duty, of service altogether, or were cowardly. The issue arose in the United States when the first Jewish settlement was established in New Amsterdam in 1654. Peter Stuyvesant and the city council refused to grant the Jews citizenship and excluded them from the city guard. The reasons: "the disinclination of and unwillingness" of the local guard "to be fellow soldiers with the aforesaid nation [the Jews]," and because of their lack of citizenship.[1] But those who charged that the Jews typically evaded their obligation to serve in their country's wars were, like all anti-Semites, not bothered by the facts. The Jews, they said, connived either to stay out of front-line duty or to keep out of the forces altogether.

This stereotype was so widespread that even the otherwise tolerant Mark Twain was temporarily victimized by it. In his article "Concerning the Jews" (1899) he charged that the Jew has "an unpatriotic disinclination to stand by the flag as a soldier—like the Christian Quaker." When a documented, official set of figures showing Jewish participation in all United States wars was made available to him, he retracted the libel in an article, "The American Jew as Soldier" in 1904, in which he called a "slur" the view that "the Jew is willing to feed on a country but not to fight for it." This was false and "ought to be pensioned off now, and retired from active service."[2]

Jews did in fact serve honorably in all the wars of the United States. They fought with distinction in the Revolutionary War, and such figures as David Salisbury Franks and Solomon Bush attained the rank of lieutenant-colonel, while Benjamin Nones, an ardent patriot and deeply conscious Jew, renewed his short-term enlistment a half-dozen times. But the falsity about Jewish evasion of war duty dies hard. Thus, in an 1891 article in the *North American Review* a Civil War veteran wrote that in his eighteen months of combat duty he could "not remember meeting one Jew in uniform." He had heard of no Jewish soldiers at the many recruiting stations he visited after recovery from a war wound, nor did he ever encounter anyone who had met a Jewish soldier.[3] On reading this the Jewish scholar Simon Wolf undertook to set this slander to rest forever. In 1895 he published his closely documented and researched *The American Jew as Patriot, Soldier, and Citizen*, in which he gave names and figures for participation of Jews in the country's wars up to that time. (It was this book which induced Mark Twain's correction cited above.) During the Revolutionary War Wolf found forty-six Jewish soldiers in a Jewish population of about 3,000. During the Civil War he concluded that Jewish soldiers fought on both sides, with 7,038 on the Union side and 834 on the Confederate side. Thereafter Jewish organizations and scholars reported the figures of Jewish participation. About 4,000 Jews volunteered for service in the Spanish-American War or in the state militias. In World War I more that 200,000 served in the armed forces, of whom over 9,000 were officers; 1,132 received citations and decorations; three were awarded Congressional Medals of Honor, and 147 won Distinguished Service Medals or Crosses. And, contrary to anti-Semitic rumor that Jews were safely tucked away in the Quartermaster Corps, they were present in higher proportion in the infantry and had actually a proportionately lower representation in the Quartermaster.[4]

Allusions to Jews were less frequent in the fiction of World War I and less important to the plot than in the avalanche of war books following the Second World War. Where the Jews in the First World War were mentioned, they were not only treated by their fellow soldiers with the usual slanders, but some slanders were added appropriate to the special circumstances of that war. Peculiar to that war was the charge that Jews were "pro-German." Before the United States was drawn into the war in 1917 on the Allied side, East Side immigrants who hated Tsarism did tend to sympathize with the German antagonist of the Tsar, and the Jews of German origin were also inclined toward the German side, but once the United States entered the war, the Jews gave it their full loyalty.

In his early novel, *Three Soldiers* (1921), John Dos Passos speaks through the anti-war, radical Jewish soldier, Eisenstadt, who is baited as a Jew by his fellow soldiers and who agitates for an end to the war to be followed by revolution. Later Eisenstadt is court-martialed for some unexplained reason—probably his outspoken political talk—and one of his fellow soldiers conjectures, "I bet that kike Eisenstadt turned out to be a spy."[5] How customary this association of Jews with spies was in World War I was also illustrated in a passage from James T. Farrell's *The Young Manhood of Studs Lonigan* (1934). One character says, "Hey, there's that Jew punk, Stein. His old man speaks German; I'll bet he's a German spy."[6] In neither case does the author share these ignorant sentiments.

One constant anti-Semitic stereotype in all wars is the accusation of evasion of service. In connection with World War I we have seen how a character in Sherwood Anderson's *Dark Laughter* indulges in this stereotyping, as did Faulkner's character in *Soldier's Pay* (1926). Again in "Death Drag," Faulkner depicts a reckless Jewish stunt flyer who answers someone's question as to whether he flew in World War I, "Why should I be a flyer in a war?"[7] On the other hand, Faulkner, decades later in *The Mansion* (1959) has a Mississippi bigot surprised to learn that a New York Jewish Communist, Barton Kohl, was actually killed flying an old crate for the Spanish Loyalists in the Spanish Civil War. The author's own deep respect for Kohl is evident in the context.

For a number of reasons the Jew received more extensive and complex treatment in the novels of World War II. The sheer quantity of fiction published about this war was imposing: one researcher writes that "almost three hundred war novels were published" between 1941 and 1949 alone,[8] and many included Jewish soldiers. And no wonder, for almost 600,000 Jews served in the armed forces. They were in all branches of the service, and it was a rare unit which did not have at least a few Jews. Of 35,157 Jewish casualties, over 8,000 were killed. Jews were awarded 2 Congressional Medals of Honor, 74 Distinguished Crosses, 37 Navy Crosses, and 2,391 Distinguished Flying Crosses.[9] The Jewish soldiers were mainly second-generation Jews who had grown up during the Depression and were rapidly becoming acculturated. In the 1930s Jews were already, of course, becoming writers in ever-increasing numbers, and many young Jewish writers emerged after the war. A number of the established Jewish writers of the 1930s were too old to serve, and many young writers began their careers by drawing on their war experience, as was also largely true of the young non-Jewish writers.

One could not read far into the war novels of World War II without being struck by the ubiquity of Jewish characters in them regardless of the ethnic origin of the author. And whenever Jewish characters appear, almost always at one time or another they meet with anti-Semitism in some form. There were several reasons for this. Considering the stubborn persistence of stereotypical conceptions of the Jews over the centuries, even during prosperous times, as demonstrated by many post–World War II studies, stressful war conditions might be expected to bring out prejudices. This was especially true of a civilian drafted army, wrenched from their private lives, in which soldiers from every walk of life and every class and stratum of the nation were thrown together at random in all the services in forced close association. Many met Jews for the first time in the army and had always imagined that Jews conformed to the unpleasant stereotypes. For their part, Jewish soldiers were confronted with the bitter irony of being subjected to anti-Semitism while fighting a war where the enemy was using anti-Semitism as a prime tactic.

Involuntary proximity with Jews was exacerbated by the upsurge of anti-Semitism at home in the 1930s and its extension into the war years.

Between 1933 and 1939, [writes Morris U. Schappes] there were 114 anti-Semitic organizations formed, and 77 of them were still active in 1940. Towards the end of the [1930s] decade the radio-priest, Charles E. Coughlin, was reaching an audience of ten million with his anti-Semitic propaganda from Detroit, and . . . his magazine *Social Justice* . . . used the forged Protocols of the Elders of Zion as a guide. . . . In addition the German-American Bund, the Silver Shirts and the Black Legion were among the organizations that added the storm-troop flavor to their anti-Semitism. . . . Hoodlum violence was added to demagogy. . . . The propaganda was vicious and reflected all the social tensions caused by the economic crisis.[10]

Under the strains of the Great Depression, from which the nation recovered only through war production, and the sinister influence of Nazi anti-Semitism and anti-Jewish agitation at home during the 1930s, millions of soldiers entered the armed forces primed to vent their frustrations on the Jews. It quickly became apparent that anti-Semitic demagogy had not been without effect. It was also evident that masses of United States soldiers were confused about the reasons for the war, as the official concern of the army demonstrated after some months of war. The fact that anti-Semitism was an earmark of the Nazi enemy did not seem to make much difference to large numbers of soldiers. Hence the strange paradox: while condemnation of Nazi treatment of the Jews was official policy, there was an upswing of anti-Semitism in the United States armed forces. Although the proto-fascist movements within the country were stopped after entry into the war, the prejudices they had fostered lingered on.

This condition was not, of course, limited to the armed forces. Evidence of Jew-baiting on the home front appeared in several short stories. In Irwin Shaw's "Act of Faith," a father writes to his soldier son in France:

Wherever you go these days—restaurants, hotels, clubs, trains—you hear talk about the Jews—mean, hateful, murderous talk. Whatever page you turn to in the newspapers, you seem to find an article about Jews being killed somewhere on the face of the globe. And there are large, influential newspapers and well-known columnists who each day are growing more and more outspoken and more popular. The day that Roosevelt died I heard a drunken man yelling outside a bar, "Finally, they got the Jew out of the White House." Some of the people who heard him laughed, and nobody tried to stop him. . . . I know the poison was spreading from Germany before the war and during it, but I had not realized it had come so close.[11]

Delmore Schwartz wrote a short story on this theme, "A Bitter Farce," which has the ring of personal experience. While teaching English composition to navy personnel at Harvard during the war, his first-person narrator experienced "innumerable anxiety feelings which had their source in events which had occurred for the past five thousand years." In this obvious reportage Schwartz's students exhibit an almost reflexive racism and anti-Semitism. A Miss Eberhart writes, "there is something about Jews that other races can't stand. It always comes out sooner or later. Some Jews are charming people, but even the best are not liked, because, well, they are demanding, grasping, almost unscrupulous about the way they get what they want." In conversation with the teacher about the composition, the girl senses his disapproval of her racism and affirms, "No crack was intended." The disquieted teacher assigns an essay on tolerance by Louis Adamic. A student named Murphy joins the discussion and tries to attribute stereotyped traits to the Jews, for "there is something wrong with a lot of Jews." In the ensuing discussion, Murphy blurts out that the Jews are "traitors by inheritance." So little did Murphy comprehend of the ensuing discussion that he finally complained to the teacher that "they shouldn't have put such essays [as Adamic's] in the textbooks. They're troublemakers."[12]

Ignorance of the aims of the war, among them the turning back of the global threat of fascism and exposure of exploitation of anti-Semitism to further fascism, among other things, led to misunderstanding. Louis Falstein, in his *The Face of a Hero* (1950), wrote out of his experience as a tail gunner that while the Jewish narrator knew he was fighting fascism because he "hated Hitler, hated fascism, and feared they would come to America," his crewmates "fought on nothing. They fought without anger." They had no notion of what the war was about "for the army had kept our cause a deep, dark secret."[13] The soldiers were aware that the Jews were especially a target of the Nazis; yet, this did not seem in many cases to affect their own negative attitude toward Jews as Jews. The evidence for such awareness was only too apparent in the common charge that this was a "Jewish war," that the war was being fought for the sake of the Jews. How widespread this notion was is evidenced by its frequent appearance in the war novels. The war writers were not copying from one another: they were writing out of personal experience.

Anti-Semitism provided ignorant, disgruntled, and reactionary soldiers, who resented having to serve in a war they didn't understand, with a ready-made scapegoat. (This is a classical example of scapegoating.) In Norman Mailer's *The Naked and the Dead,* Sergeant Gallagher, who had before the war joined "Christians United" (the Christian Front) and sold "Father Killian's [Father Coughlin's] magazine" is angry at leaving his family and career for the army. He resents "getting your head blown off . . . for what, for what? Goddam Yids, fight a war for them."[14] And in Stefan Heym's *The Crusaders,* Jew-baiter Dondolo tries to taunt the half-Jew Bing into a fight, but Bing refuses to be provoked because "it was more important to fight the Germans than Dondolo." "It's because of people like you," replies Dondolo, that he had to leave his family. "Bunch of Jews get themselves into trouble and the whole American army swims across the ocean. This fellow, Hitler, and Mussolini, too, . . . we should be fighting with them, against the Communists."[15] In a barracks conversation in Irwin Shaw's *The Young Lions* the Jew-baited Ackerman is told that "You people got us into this war."[16] And in an air force novel, Saul Levitt's *The Sun Is Silent* (1951), casual conversation among the flight crew, one of whom is Jewish, asks, "Why are the Jews fighting this war? . . . I want the truth. . . . It's because of what Hitler did to the Jews. . . . It's revenge, that's what it is."[17]

The charge of "Jew war" was only an adaptation of the scapegoat technique to the specific features of World War II. In addition soldiers in these novels run through the gamut of clichés about Jews and war. But an exceptional feature of some of these novels was their representation of the modes of response of several Jewish soldiers toward the fact of their Jewishness in a hostile atmosphere, from the self-hating to the self-accepting. The fact that this was done by non-Jewish, as well as Jewish, authors indicates how far we had come from the incidental treatment of Jewishness encountered in the World War I novels. It was Hitler, of course, who made much of the difference. Jews were forced into the center of public awareness by the variety of anti-social crimes and the Nazi threat to civilization.

Among the numerous war novels were a number written by Jewish writers who had been soldiers in the various armed services. Some of these writers had already begun writing in the late 1930s and early 1940s while others opened their writing careers with their books about the war. They wrote notable fiction based on their experience in the war. It is not surprising that they were preoccupied, among other aspects of their war experience, with the anti-Semitism they encountered among their fellow soldiers.

Many World War II novels contain consciously anti-fascist characters and are centered about anti-fascist sentiment. This is especially true of Mailer's

The Naked and the Dead (1948) and Stefan Heym's *The Crusaders* (1948).
Both also make clear the association of anti-Semitism with pro-fascism. In
the Mailer novel, several different attitudes of Jewish characters toward
their Jewishness are vividly presented.

Mailer's best-selling novel catapulted him into general public notice and
immediately marked him as a coming American writer. More than three
decades later this novel still stands up as one of the best about World War
II. It concentrates on the action of an infantry platoon in the Pacific war.
The novel is an intense and informed work of anti-fascism, but its sociopolitical significance is not artificially imposed on the characters. They remain fallible human beings, profoundly human. Depiction of their relation
to fascism is therefore human rather than predominantly ideological, while
the author's hatred of fascism is intense. For him the literary problem lies
in depicting a complexity of motivation, especially in his pro-fascist characters. The fascist General Cummings is closest to the pure ideologist, but
the soldiers Craft and Gallagher, anti-Semites and actual pro-fascists, are
shown as frustrated personalities who strike out at the easiest available
targets—Jews in this case—to sustain the superiority of their self-image.

The central theme of the novel could be interpreted as the fumbling
resistance of what is decent and democratic in men to the social and individual aggressions of the fascist mentality. A subordinate but important sub-
theme is the characters' relation to anti-Semitism as an index of their fascist
or anti-fascist viewpoint. The problem of anti-Semitism is focused in two
characters, Roth and Goldstein. Roth is a "droopy" person ridden with
inferiority feeling because of his Jewishness, and is deeply desirous of approval by his Christian fellow soldiers. He is glad he never learned Yiddish.
At the same time he has a false sense of superiority because he acquired a
college education, but he is not respected by his fellow soldiers. Goldstein
is altogether different. He is genuine, decent, sensitive, and a competent
soldier, perhaps the most admirable figure in the entire novel. He is much
offended by the anti-Semitism he meets, but unlike Roth, he turns "his face
to the wind."[18]

The anti-fascist conviction of the author is the clear and unequivocal
premise of the story but the pro-fascist and anti-Semitic figures dominate
the novel. The anti-fascist protagonist is the vaguely left-wing, worldly wise,
disillusioned Lieutenant Hearn who, for the first half of the book, serves as
an aide to the division commander, General Cummings. Cummings is a
fascist with explicit, elaborated ideology and fascistic postwar plans. Hearn
despises the field officers in his mess, with their hatred of "kikes, niggers,
Russians, limeys, micks."[19] After he finds association with his general and
with them no longer tolerable, Hearn becomes a platoon commander in a
combat unit; he is killed on a patrol by a sadistic non-commissioned officer
who resents Hearn's effort to spare the men a useless ordeal.

Anti-Semitism is directed at the two Jews by their fellow combat soldiers, who differ only in the degree of their hatred. Most important is the Boston Sergeant Gallagher, whose pro-fascist mentality is most extensively analyzed and who is in some ways the novel's most significant character. He is perpetually angry; before the war he was politically active but frustrated in his job aspirations. He is influenced by current Catholic pro-fascists and is psychologically the most penetrating achievement of the story in its portrait of his petty bourgeois fascist mentality. He blames the Jews for all his failures and is quick to bait them. When his wife dies in childbirth, he quickly concludes, " 'I bet a fuggin Yid was the doctor. . . . The Yid killed her.' It relieved the tension he was feeling." During the excruciatingly hard and dangerous mountain patrol—an account of which is one of the finest bits of World War II writing—the exhausted men must leap across a four-foot gap. Soon after he had called a resting Roth a "Jew bastard," Gallagher extends his hand to catch Roth as he leaps across. In mid-flight Roth sees "Gallagher's face staring in surprise at him, and then he slipped past Gallagher's hand"[20] into the yawning gap below. The remorseful Gallagher later accuses himself of killing Roth and feels he had sinned and would be punished for it.

The climax for Goldstein comes differently. When he is assigned with others to the laborious task of carrying a wounded soldier out of the jungle on a stretcher, his fellow bearers are angry at their job. The wounded man has a stomach wound and cries out for water but Goldstein refuses it, knowing that it would kill him. Goldstein is cursed as a Jew for his apparent heartlessness by the others, who are ignorant of the water's effect. When Goldstein is asleep one of them succumbs to the wounded man's entreaties and gives him water, and the man dies soon thereafter. Their exhausting labors have been vain. Goldstein had sustained himself by recalling his grandfather's saying, "Israel is the heart of all nations," but when the suffering man dies, Goldstein thinks, "the heart of all nations has died." While bearing the excruciating burden of the dying man, Goldstein believes that the heart suffered with the body, and that futile suffering kills the heart. He thinks,

the heart could be killed and the body still live. All the suffering of the Jews came to nothing. No sacrifices paid, no lessons were learned. It was all thrown away, all statistics in the cruel wastes of history. All the ghettoes, all the soul cripplings, all the massacres and pogroms, the gas chambers, lime kilns—all of it touched no one, all of it was lost. It was carried and carried and carried, and when it finally grew too heavy, it was dropped.[21]

Despair over the futility of the past sacrifices of the Jewish people under the blinding glare of the Holocaust seems to be Goldstein's revelation at the moment of the death of the "heart" that he has just undergone.

While Mailer's novel is pervaded by ambivalence and psychological complexity, Stefan Heym's *The Crusaders* (1948) is less "modern," but more politically sophisticated and focused with respect to the issues of World War II. The aim of the novel is embodied in the central character, Bing, a half-Jewish refugee from Nazism who was serving in the psychological warfare corps of the American army and was determined to get at "the truth of the war."[22] The novel follows the operations of Bing's unit through the French and German campaigns. Through the lives of its many characters the novel centers about the forces working against realization of the anti-fascist aims of the war. A main thread of the story is the exposure of the links between international cartels, fascism, and American big capital. Post-war investigation had indeed confirmed the existence of such a linkage, which is personalized and perhaps somewhat schematized in the novel. Heym had experienced fascism at first hand before emigrating from Germany to the United States; he shows the fumbling anti-fascism of some Americans and the fascist sympathies of others. (Heym returned to East Germany in the 1950s.)

As the story develops, some Americans are shown to be working against democratic war aims. The connection between anti-Semitism and fascism is exposed through the character of the vicious anti-Semite, Sergeant Dondolo. He is a fascist sympathizer and black marketeer who sells his army wares through a Frenchman, Sourire, who is in turn an agent for the expatriated Russian cartellist, Prince Yasha Bersekin, who is being wooed in a business way for postwar business connections by an agent of American finance capital, Major Willoughby. Their anti-Semitism is not treated as an isolated phenomenon directed solely against the Jews, but as part of the pattern of the fascism of the period.

There is nothing of specific Jewishness in Bing, except his half-Jewish identity. But after he is killed, one of the moving moments of the book occurs when another Jewish soldier, Abramovici, says Kaddish over him, "bending, straightening himself, and bending again. From his lips came words that rose and fell with his swaying, '*Yiskadal veyiskadash shemah rahboh . . .*' " prayer for the dead. Like Bing, he is a refugee, and is sympathetically treated. He tried "to look like a soldier ever since he got into the army," but his physique, the bulge in the middle that prevented his pants from staying up, made this difficult.[23] He demonstrates, however, that he can act like a good soldier under fire. Then there was Traub from Rivington Street in New York, whose knowledge of Yiddish made him useful in talking to a Russian escapee from a concentration camp, who had learned Yiddish from old Jews who had died there, and whose Yiddish was used in communicating with captured German soldiers. As with nearly all Jewish characters in many books of World War II, their Jewish identity is related primarily to anti-Semitism. Almost all are acculturated with varying degrees of intensity of identification as Jewish, but few, if any, embrace Jewishness as a full, rich ethnic culture. For most of them, an absence of anti-Semitism, or a total removal of anti-Semitism, would reduce their sense of Jewish identity to the vanishing point.

This is certainly true of the several Jewish characters in Irwin Shaw's *The Young Lions* (1948). Like *The Naked and the Dead,* this novel was a best seller; unlike Heym's or Mailer's novel, Shaw's can be called commercial, that is, it is written with an experienced eye for mass readership. One is not inspired with a sense of the integrity of its characterizations nor does it convey fascism in anything like the articulated form offered by both the Mailer and Heym novels. Shaw seems to have become a commercial writer by 1948. His story revolves around Noah Ackerman, but a second Jewish soldier of a different kind, named Fein, appears briefly as a pendant to Ackerman, the "heroic" Jew. Fein was so big as to be physically intimidating. Even though he was not popular, he seemed indifferent to everything and everyone, and was left alone. He advises passivity in the face of anti-Semitic offense. Ackerman's macho answer: "I want every Jew to be treated as though he weighed two hundred pounds."[24] Fein is an easily expendable character and indeed passes out of the story early.

The center of the story is neither the war itself nor anti-fascism, as in the Mailer and Heym stories, but rather Ackerman's personal encounter with anti-Semitism. The infantry company to which he is assigned was thoroughly anti-Semitic, presenting every type, from the know-nothing on, all except Fein and a leftist theater director, Whitacre. The men echo the usual clichés about Jews making money at home out of the war and even about Jewish domination of the world by a cabal of rabbis. The Jew-baiting of Ackerman escalates until ten dollars are stolen from his barracks bag. He posts a notice saying he doesn't want the money, but only "to take my satisfaction, in person, with my own hands." The reply comes quickly, signed by the ten largest men in the company. "We took it, Jew-boy. We're waiting for you." Noah enlists a reluctant Whitacre as his second, and stipulates he will fight each in turn until one of them is knocked out of the fight by him. Since this is unlikely, Ackerman takes on one after another; he is fearfully mauled; he lands in the hospital several times. Not until his combat with Number Ten does he succeed in knocking out his antagonist. He expects that his moral victory will inspire respect from his fellow soldiers, but they turn away and ignore him. He deserts, and a month later gives himself up, with the explanation that he felt "it impossible for me to live among them" after his futile effort to prove himself worthy of their respect. But calmer thought prevailed, and he concluded that "I must fight for my country."[25] When the full story is told to the authorities, it is decided to drop charges if he agrees to return to his company, which he does. Three of the most intense anti-Semites signal a continuance of their baiting, and he threatens them with a recently purchased spring knife, saying he will use it against anyone who tries to lay a hand on him. From then on his life in the company is tolerable, and he develops a deep friendship with one of the non-Jewish soldiers.

If this scenario sounds like melodrama, it is. After five fights, "his face was crooked and lumpy, and one ear was permanently disfigured in a flat, creased cauliflower. His right eyebrow was split, and a white scar ran diagonally across it, giving the broken eyebrow a wild, interrogating twist."[26] In the reading it strikes one as Hollywood bravado and gratuitous violence. The quixotic Noah is not highly credible. Without underestimating the extent of anti-Semitism in the army during World War II—and nearly every Jewish soldier must have experienced it, as the present writer did—it seems an incredible stretch of probability that the punishing string of fights would have been allowed to go on within the realities of an army company. The macho sequence of events around the fistfights is a commercial rather than an artistic approach to the novel's problem.

The novels examined thus far record anti-Semitism in the ground forces of the army in Europe and the Pacific, but it was no different in the air force. Three air force stories, all by Jewish writers who were themselves members of the air force writing out of personal experience, ring changes on the theme of anti-Semitism. The central characters of all three are airplane personnel, two are gunners, one a navigator, and all experience anti-Semitism with varying degrees of severity.

The Jewish air gunner, Ben Isaacs, appears in Louis Falstein's *Face of a Hero* (1950), a deeply conscious anti-fascist story that relates his trial of courage in acting on his convictions in the war against fascism. His army experience becomes a test of convictions, self-respect, and selfhood in the struggle to overcome the fear and horror of participation in aerial warfare. How dangerous it was is attested by the fact that only Ben and one of his original ten crew members survived. He had emigrated at fifteen from Russia to the United States and knew anti-Semitism and even pogroms as a child. While in this country he had "almost forgotten that being Jewish carried any stigma." Ben admired the courage of his crewmates, who "fought on sheer guts, with hardly any knowledge of the causes of the war." Falstein makes that terror of death from the air real in his gripping descriptions of combat, one of the most striking features of the novel. By the time of his last mission, Ben is at last free of the paralyzing fear of death, and was "intoxicated by the thought of self-conquest."[27]

Ben's crewmates resent their participation in what they regard as a "Jew war." They occasionally slip into this locution in his presence and then try to apologize. They express surprise that he does not have "a desk job like most Jews?" Ben bids them look around and see other Jewish gunners. The charge, he says, "is a lie." Although Ben found, he says, "no Jew-baiting among flyers," there was "some among orderly room commandos." But even among flyers it "slipped out." When his crewmate Dooley makes an

Italian laundress pregnant, Ben asks him if he knows she is sick. Ben is told to "mind your own business, you Jew bastard! Don't go taking the wops' side against your buddies. . . . We don't want no wop lovers in this barracks." On another occasion Ben's crewmates abort their visit to Italian laundresses when they come upon them entertaining a Black corporal. Ben stays to apologize to the laundresses and the corporal. On another occasion the crew is waiting for services at the graveside of a crewmate, and Italians are digging the grave. They hurry the diggers on. "I never seen a lazier bunch of people than the Eyties," says one. "Niggers is lazier," says another. Dooley then races to the defense of the Blacks because of their superior performance as the 99th Fighter Squadron. This was, says Dooley, "an all-nigger outfit. And if it wasn't for them chasing off the ME's that day we got hit over Graz, maybe you wouldn't be here." Ben "felt keenly" the prejudices of his crewmates against the Italians. He looked for "some way we could atone for the indignities we heaped upon them and the humiliation we caused them. We fouled their beds and bought their sisters. They had greeted us with kisses and roses when we first came. . . . We became the loathsome *Americani*. They had hoped we would clear out the *fascisti*."[28]

Like Falstein, Saul Levitt was an aerial gunner and a conscious anti-fascist. His *The Sun Is Silent* (1951) registers similar encounters, though his gunner-hero Harry Miller experiences more intense anti-Semitism than Ben Isaacs. After all his bitter experience in combat and on the ground with his fellow soldiers, Harry concludes: "A war against fascism. If only you could feel a wall behind you. But nothing is guaranteed. Let me in, it's the brotherhood of man, isn't it? It's a war against fascism, isn't it? It's the best war against fascism available, isn't it?" Harry had been brought up in the family of a radical, Socialist father, and had had his early experience with anti-Semitism when, at sixteen, he was rejected for a job because he was Jewish. "Harry," his mother asks him, "why they hate the Jews so much? They take it in with their mother's milk, this feeling?" Much of this unthinking, widespread anti-Semitism was latent, with some half aware of it. Once, when Harry's crewmate Gluck went out with Harry, he said, "I'm gonna tell you something, Harry. You know something. . . . I don't like Jews, but you're O.K." He couldn't understand why Harry replied, "Go f—— yourself, Gluck." But Harry did go to town with him because, "This anti-Semitism of Gluck, he felt, was something Gluck had acquired somewhere, . . . but did not quite believe. Miller wasn't quite sure."[29]

Another variety of uncertain anti-Semitism emerged when a pilot, Masters, told Harry about a Jewish pilot who had passed flight training before the war. To achieve this, the Jew "had to be twice as good . . . *and this guy was twice as good.*" Harry believes the story was told to him "with neither sympathy nor compassion, merely a curiosity." Harry believed he "was saying a number of things at once: *Why was the man there in the first place? Wasn't it unusual for him to be that good? Why didn't he stay home and try to make money?* Masters hadn't cared about the Jewish pilot one way or another. But Masters had admired him for sticking to it." But there is no question about the explosive anti-Semitic intention of a crewmate, Krolik, from a mining town. The men of the crew discuss an impending strike of miners at home, and all express ignorant anti-union views, while Harry defends the strikers. Krolik resents Harry's views, and resorts to scape-goating: *"What the hell are you doing here, Miller?* Listen, Miller, do you think it'll make people feel different about Jews—*whether they got killed in action or not*—.... They'll keep on saying in a coal camp and everywhere else, *all Jews are alike in or out of uniform."* When a crewmate blunderingly tells an anti-Semitic joke, Miller feels "as if he were being told a funny story by an executioner."[30] Like Falstein's Ben, Miller does not allow the ignorant prejudices of his crewmates to blunt his own conviction that he can take his place in fighting fascism.

There's a narrower focus on the Jew as air officer in Joseph Landon's *Angle of Attack* (1952). The story of navigator Irwin "Win" Hellman is, according to the author, based on an actual incident in the air war. Win comes from Brooklyn and is the only Jew among the airmen of the story. Anti-Semitism enters the story about halfway through and is at the center for the remainder. On a bombing mission near Vienna several crewmen are killed and the plane is chased by three Nazi fighters. The pilot signals surrender. Win takes command, believing the plane can escape. He gets unanimous agreement from the crew and they succeed in fleeing after shoot-ing down one of the Nazi fighters. The all-Black 99th Group fighters at last escort the plane home safely. (Although the fighters didn't receive the initial call for escort, the pilot calls them " ... sonsabitches ... stupid goddam nig-gers.") In evading capture after the pilot had signaled surrender, and in downing a Nazi fighter afterward, the crew had transgressed the sacred rules of air combat, and this is revealed at the debriefing after the plane's return. The enemy radio tells the story over the air and lets Win's group know that they will now be a special target in combat. Win is Jew-baited, and expresses his surprise to his close friend, Navigator Macy—"I didn't expect to catch it here."[31] He tells Macy that he was afraid to be captured even though he had been wearing dog tags with a non-Jewish name. What did not come out at the debriefing was that he was saddled with the entire responsibility for the affair, since his crewmates simply did not volunteer the information that they had all been consulted and had agreed to the escape plan. It never does become publicly known that the crew had approved Win's proposal to evade, and in an imperfect way Win's story is a parable of the Jew as scapegoat. On a later mission, Win's plane is shot down and he is killed.

Markedly different from nearly all other war novels, Herman Wouk's *The Caine Mutiny* (1951) is a defender of the armed forces establishment and in reality a critic of other war novelists' critical view of conventional values. Although Wouk deals with a naval episode, his book is in effect a paean of gratitude to the regular armed forces for withstanding the initial thrust of the war before the nation could fully mobilize. There is nothing wrong in recognizing this service of the defense establishment, but this hardly exempts it from criticism, which is in effect what Wouk attempts in this book. He misleads the reader so that the climactic reversal at the end comes as a shocking surprise. The novel won the Pulitzer Prize in 1952 and dominated the best-seller lists for two years. It was also made into a successful movie and play.

The crucial situation, it will be recalled, was Lieutenant Maryk's seizure of command of the *Caine* from Captain Queeg at the dangerous moment of a typhoon when Queeg seemed to be paralyzed and irrational with fear, and Lieutenant Keith then acquiesced to Maryk's takeover. From Queeg's point of view this was mutiny; from Maryk's viewpoint this drastic action was necessary to save the ship and its men from disaster. The event is described in some detail, but the layman is hardly in a position to judge the truth.

The real villain of the story is Lieutenant Keefer, an intellectual and novelist who is engaged in writing a war novel. Wouk's spokesman is Barney Greenwald, a lawyer in civilian life, who is dragooned into defending the mutineers against their deposed Captain Queeg. Greenwald makes it clear that Keefer had planted the seed of mutiny by exploiting the suggestibility of the other officers. Wouk's anti-intellectual bias is unconcealed, and the plot takes advantage of the layman's innocence of technical aspects of seamanship. If the narrative hero of the novel is the young Lieutenant Keith, Wouk's own hero is Captain Queeg. At the denouement, Greenwald says, " 'The wrong guy was on trial.... I'm ... ashamed of what I did.... Queeg deserved better at my hands. I owed him a favor, don't you see? He stopped Herman Goering from washing his fat behind with my mother.... Here's to you, the *Caine*'s favorite author, and here's to your book.' He threw the yellow wine in Keefer's face."[32]

What was behind Barney's real feelings? He comes to the dinner celebrating the acquittal of his antagonist quite drunk, has no intention of staying, but has come to lecture the celebrants on the truth. "The reason I'd make Old Yellowstain [Queeg] a hero is on account of my mother, little grey-headed Jewish lady."[33] He was thinking what the Nazis would do to her if they were not stopped.

Life, it seems, was very simple, to Barney and, by valid extension to his creator, Herman Wouk. The case he set up in his anti–anti-war novel is too pat, and is an attempt to manipulate a credulous reader.

Non-Jewish writers also included the Jew in their novels relating to the war, as well as exposing anti-Semitism during the war and immediately before and after it. We add here several examples.

Anti-Semitism in the regular army just before World War II is one important theme of James Jones' *From Here to Eternity* (1953), set in Pearl

Harbor before the Japanese assault and culminating in the attack itself. The problem is treated with insight, and Jones' own condemnation of anti-Semitism is conveyed through his protagonist, Prewitt. Two types of Jewish self-hatred are exemplified in the characters of Sussman and Bloom. The first wishes to obliterate his Jewishness and fuse with the others, while Bloom is defensive about his Jewishness to the point of paranoia, desperate to be accepted as a man without the Jewish label. Jones develops Bloom's train of thought to explain why he will soon take his own life, frustrated as a man and as a Jew: "He had wanted to prove to them a Jew was no different than anyone else. He had meant to *make* them admit it, for once, but he had failed."[34] So in the end, Bloom was really like Sussman; both obsessively wished to be accepted. Bloom differed only in that he would not ignore slurs to his Jewishness as Sussman did but was hypersensitive to the point of paranoia. Yet both alike desperately craved acceptance.

Bloom hopes to gain acceptance by his fellow Christian soldiers through winning the heavyweight boxing championship for his regiment. He is continually roused to violent rage by anti-Semitic slurs. But before he can prove himself, he paranoically misinterprets Prewitt's kindness toward his dog and Prewitt's irritated reply to his thanks. For his own part Prewitt too is dangerously frustrated, and the lack of understanding on both sides leads to a fight. Prewitt wins, and Bloom is humiliated by the defeat: he never will gain acceptance now, and he commits suicide. Prewitt had wished to reassure Bloom that he had not fought him as a Jew, but he is confined to the stockade for some infraction before he can get to Bloom. Both men, thought Prewitt, had taken on the wrong target. In a bar he is complimented for taking down the "Jewboy." He turns away "feeling a little sick in the hollowness of his stomach. He didn't hit Bloom because Bloom was a Jew. Why did they always have to make a racial issue of it all the time?"[35]

What is notable about the World War II novel by non-Jewish writers was the author's freedom from ambivalence or ambiguity in condemnation of anti-Semitism, either explicitly or in context. This is in contrast to the attitude of authors in some of the World War I novels. In this respect the world had moved forward in the intervening years.

Divergent from the usual pattern of treatment of Jews in the post–World War II novel by non-Jews are James Gould Cozzens' *Guard of Honor* (1948) and John Horne Burns' *The Gallery* (1947). The first includes several Jewish characters but at no point alludes to their Jewishness nor is there any suggestion of anti-Semitism. The second introduced a Jewish character as a saintly person.

Cozzen's story is set in an air force base in Florida while the war is going on. Three of the characters are Jewish, so identifiable only by their names. A Women's Army Corps Sergeant Levy is depicted as a tough and efficient soldier blindly loyal to her lieutenant. A Captain Solomon, who has his pilot's wings, is a professional promoter and public relations type who does

not figure importantly, but one of the central characters of the novel is Chief
Warrant Officer Botwinnick, called "Botty," who is an honorable, efficient
administrative officer, really an office boy for the other officers. Seven men
are killed because of a mistake Botty made, and he offers himself for punishment but his fate is left in the air at the novel's end, and there is no
suggested connection with his Jewishness. One implicit sub-theme in the
story is criticism of some officers' treatment of Blacks. The Cozzens novel
would lead us to conclude that there were some military environments in
which Jewish soldiers were in no way differently regarded from any others.
On the other hand, possibly Cozzens preferred not to get entangled in anti-
Semitic plot elements.

John Horne Burns' novel, surely one of the finest about World War II,
is set mostly in Naples in August, 1944, much of it in the Galleria Umberto,
an arcade in the city. Burns intends this as a microcosm of the world, and
he offers a group of "portraits" in the "Gallery," "who became," wrote
Burns, "... synechdoches for most of the people anywhere in the world."[36]
The final, and in a way climactic, "portrait" is called "Moe"—a Jewish
Second Lieutenant Moses Shulman, an ex-taxi driver from Brooklyn, who
is convalescing from a wound received in combat and is about to return to
the line. On this last night before his return to combat he is convinced he
will be killed when he returns to the fighting. He goes through a series of
encounters that reveal a sweet, generous, saint-like character, seemingly
guided by Martin Buber's ideal of human relations and sometimes raised
to such transcendence as to lose touch with human reality.

On his last day before returning to the front Moe wanders about Naples.
He disarms several mildly anti-Semitic encounters with kindness and sweet-
ness and tries to divert a refugee Jewish officer from his vengeful feeling for
what he has suffered. In the PX he is moved by the obvious fatigue of an
Italian sales girl to bring her unbidden a cup of coffee. "You're the first
man today who treated me like a human being," she tells him,[37] and agrees
to meet him after work. Moe wanders about Naples before meeting her.
He is certain he will be killed when he returns to the front tomorrow, but
he is strangely composed at the prospect, which evokes tears in an Italian
airman he meets. "Are you such a strange man because you're a Jew or in
spite of it?" the Italian asks. "You are a just man ... You are a good man
in 1944," he adds.[38] Also in his wanderings he chats with an Italian child
and is deeply moved at her "helplessness and desperation ... My God, how
cruel ... If I live, I'll do something about all this ... something."[39]

At their meeting Moe and the Italian girl Maria find in each other respect
and love and human dignity. Both are moved by the deep tragedy in which
the world is engulfed. "There is a shadow over all the earth," she says,
"with no promise that it will ever lift by the cloud's passing away from the
sun ... Only from you have I sensed what hope could mean."[40] She offers
to hide him so he won't have to go to the front, but he refuses. When they

part, he knows he will never return, and he is indeed killed by a German in the fighting. Moe, then, is Burns' symbol of a desperate effort to hold on to one's humanity, to kindness, to human decency in the midst of a cynical abandonment of all humane values, with each person ruthlessly abandoned to his own gratifications. Although the violation of precious values is rampant in war, it is not total, and Burns means Moe's relations with other human beings to stand for the hope for human dignity that Maria sees in him. Actually, it is not too much to say that, to Burns, Moe is a primitive Jesus figure.

If one had hoped and expected that victory over fascism, in which anti-Semitism was a cardinal tenet of the fascist enemy, would witness an immediate diminution of anti-Semitism at home, one was doomed to disappointment. This recession of anti-Semitism did indeed take place some years later, but for different reasons. But in the few years following the war's end, the prejudice so rife during the war itself was to continue. Prompted to action by this ugly residue of the war, a few Jewish authors rose to do battle. Their effort did indeed create a sensation. Two of them made their point by the device of subjecting a non-Jew to anti-Semitic harassment. Several demonstrated that self-hating Jews cannot evade anti-Semitism by renouncing their Jewishness.

5
Jewish Anti-Semitism: The Problem of Self-Hate

For over two thousand years the Jews have been afflicted with numbers among them who wish to transfer their identity to that of their host people. Their lack of a national state before 1948 and the worldwide persistence of anti-Semitism in all its varieties, economic, political, and social, have caused them to be regarded as an alien people nearly everywhere they settled. Many have succumbed to the all-too-human tendency to avoid the ineligibilities attaching to their alien status and, as they thought, to head off anti-Semitism by religious conversion to a socially approved faith or by renouncing or concealing their Jewish origin. This tendency has become stronger since Emancipation opened these escape routes wide and equality before the law protected such changes. The problem often became acute when a Jew wished to intermarry. Before Emancipation, when ghettoization prevailed, such changes were undertaken only by the adventurous, but were beyond even the range of thought for most Jews.

The term "self-hate" has been applied to those who are born Jews but feel negatively or antagonistically toward their fellow Jews and Jewishness in general. Such a person may not be in a position to deny his Jewish origin or to separate himself from other Jews. Thus it can coexist with acceptance of one's status as a Jew as a fact of life while one entertains the notion that the world would be better off if there were no Jews. This species of Jew is the Jewish version of the anti-Semite.

The term "self-hate" is of recent coinage. There is not even a listing of the term in the Second Edition of *Webster's Dictionary* (1913), even as late as its 1945 printing. The term is probably a translation of the German *Selbsthass*, first used in Theodor Lessing's *Der Judische Selbsthass* (1930). As Clement Greenberg has pointed out, the phenomenon is "strictly speaking, more self-doubt and self-contempt than actual self-hatred" and "is better defined as 'the Jewish inferiority complex.' "[1] But the term self-hatred has gained a certain currency with its specific meaning of Jews rejecting other Jews and oneself as a Jew as analyzed by the German émigré social psychologist Kurt Lewin in his essay, "Self-Hatred Among Jews" (1941). Lewin used the term broadly to apply to both groups and individuals. Group manifestations are the hostile feeling in Europe of German Jews for the East European; and in the United States, of the established Spanish Jews for the German immigrants of the mid-nineteenth century, and of German Jews toward the Eastern European Jews of the mass immigration. We have encountered many instances of these prejudices in the fiction we have examined.

However, Lewin has overlooked the distinction between rejection, on the one hand, by an individual Jew of *all* Jews and Jewishness, and on the other hand, of one group of Jews by another group of Jews. The first is individual renunciation of Jewish identity and ethnicity, the other social dissociation of, usually, one class of Jews by another class. In the latter case, for instance, middle-class German Jews used to look down upon immigrant East European Jews of the working class, or even Jews of this group who had only recently risen from the working class and had not yet acquired middle-class manners. But in the case of the "self-hating" Jew it is Jewishness as such which is rejected. The difference becomes clear when one recalls that middle-class German Jews usually retain close association with their fellow German Jews as fellow Jews, which is far from the self-hating rejection of Jewishness. It is well-known that German Jews in Germany wished to reduce the visibility of the *Ostjuden* just as the German Jews in the United States, during the mass immigration and later, resented being identified with the uncouth ghetto Jews. They tried to reduce the visibility of the immigrants by settling them, if possible, in small cities or rural areas, without much success.

Middle-class, established, acculturated Jews were fearful that anti-Semitism might be generated by the presence of numerous newer Jews with their residue of ghetto mentality and language singularity. This drew them closer to one another as Jews, since they did not hate Jews as such but only disapproved and were contemptuous of the strange lower-class Jews from Eastern Europe, whom they called "kikes," an appellation they introduced. But among these middle-class Jews were also some who wished to dissociate themselves from Jews altogether. Confusion on this point is possible if Lewin's concept of "self-hatred," which includes both types of attitude, is adopted uncritically. In our discussion, therefore, *we shall use the term exclusively to refer to those who reject any identification with the ethnic group of their origin.* Especially despised by the established German Jews, and even by many assimilated Jews generally, was the audible stigma of Yiddish, the language usually used by the new immigrants, which was often regarded as an ill-sounding, vulgar "jargon." Such middle-class Jews were perhaps unaware of, or ignored, the existence of a large and growing significant literature in this "jargon," which is today indisputably recognized as a language in which a universal literature was created. The real reason for the rejection of the language was its association with the segregated life of the *shtetl* and the ghettos of American cities, which stamped Yiddish speakers as unacculturated Americans.

In terms of understanding the Jewish community, therefore, and the behavior of American Jews, the distinctions I have tried to draw here take on considerable significance. To illustrate the distinction as it is exemplified in literature, we shall first examine a novel exemplifying each type. The first is Vera Caspary's *Thicker than Water* (1935), and the second is Ben Hecht's *A Jew in Love* (1928), to be followed by a number of examples of the latter type.

The Caspary novel epitomizes the relations among the three major Jewish immigrations, the earliest Sephardic of the seventeenth century, the German of the mid-nineteenth, and the Eastern European mass immigration of the late nineteenth and early twentieth.

The Caspary novel vividly illustrates the haughty attitude of the proud Piera family toward both German and Eastern European Jewish newcomers and the "decline" of the family through its "dilution" by intermarriage with both "inferior" groups. As the pecuniary fortunes of the family go down, they are rescued and enhanced by Ashkenazi spouses. The Pieras could trace their ancestors back many centuries to rich and powerful patrons of art in Spain and Portugal, and the first Piera had come to the United States in 1660. In the 1880s the family is settled in Chicago. Rosalie Piera is about to marry one of those "newcomers to America, the aliens, and barbarian Germans, half of whom never knew their great-grandparents' given names." Never had Rosalie's mother "thought her beloved daughter could consider a suitor of German descent." Even worse, another daughter marries Julius Smith (né Sliwoski) who conceals his Polish origin until his mother appears; she wears a *sheitel* and speaks Yiddish! The haughty Pieras regularly refer to their German and East European fellow Jews as "kikes." The author records that,

with the exodus of Jews from Russia and Polish Russia in the two decades since a bomb had been hurled at Alexander II [1881], bitter prejudice had arisen among American Jews against their Russian co-religionists. This bitterness did not ferment so rapidly in the Middle West as in Eastern cities where the greatest number of immigrants settled. But gradually as they came to Chicago, as the section around Maxwell Street grew crowded with uncouth, unclean strangers sputtering a gutteral jargon, the solid citizens felt their security threatened, their place in the community, the respect of their Gentile neighbors, their social position and their prosperity.[2]

Just as the Sephardi condescended to the Germans, the Germans in turn looked down upon the East Europeans. In the 1920s, one of the family married the "kike" Sam Chodorov, and the younger generation realize that at least the aristocratic Sephardi are scarcely known as such any more. In this competent and rather slickly written story the moving force of the narrative is intra-Jewish class prejudice.

There is no subtlety in the Jewish self-hatred depicted in Ben Hecht's *A Jew in Love* (1928). A clearer case could hardly be found. It is doubtful if Ben Hecht was aware of this or would grant it. He seemed unconsciously anti-Semitic. He may rather have viewed his characterizations as cleverly cynical, but this was a rationalization: in reality it was self-deceptive and shallow. The description of his central character, Jo Boshere (born Abe Nussbaum), is given in terms that would be appropriate for *Der Stuermer*, and Boshere's revulsion from his Jewish appearance gives the book its central theme—"this biologic handicap he sought to overcome"[3] by exploiting women sexually, especially non-Jewish women. He is a monster of corruption, not only with his wife and Jewish mistress, but especially with his blonde, non-Jewish lover Tillie, from whom he plots to extort obsessive love to compensate for his appearance. He heartlessly, cruelly, cynically manipulates his women to feed his egomaniacal erotic plots. The story is profoundly self-hating and anti-Semitic.

Boshere, at thirty, is a dark-skinned little Jew with vulturous and moody face.... The Jews now and then hatch a face which for Jewishness surpasses the caricatures of the entire anti-Semitic press. The Jew faces in which race leers and burns like some biologic disease are rather shocking to a mongrelized world. People dislike being reminded of their origins. They shudder a bit mystically at the sight of anyone who looks too much like a fish, a lizard, a chimpanzee or a Jew... [Boshere had] an uncomfortably Semitic face, a face stamped with the hieroglyphic curl of the Hebrew alphabet.... [He had]...the look of a Prince Charming in the midst of a pogrom.[4]

How confused Hecht is appears from his observation, in the midst of this anti-Semitic, self-hating description, that "The Jew face is an enemy totem, an ancient target for spittle and, like a thing long hated, a sort of magic propagandist of hate." If there is any doubt of this confusion, Boshere took in Tillie "the niggerish delight of the Jew in the blonde."[5] The mood of the radical brother of his Jewish mistress Alice Stein "struck Boshere as that of a rascally Oriental during a horse trade."[6] Boshere's sister Esther, an ardent Zionist, had a "cowl nose, nigger eyes, red rubber lips and Spanish jaws ... and beside her, Boshere's ugliness appeared as a species of perfection."[7]

That a Jew should be "charming looking" in such a context is anomalous to the author. Of Dr. Julie Goldstein, writes Hecht, "[That] this charming looking man about whom hovered so engaging and brittle an air of ancient princeliness should be named Goldstein was one of those farcical accidents with which Jewish nomenclature abounds—a product of racial caste degeneration which injects its ghetto history into the names of its poets, artists, elegantes and philosophers."[8] The precise meaning of this "racial caste degeneration" is unclear. It can only mean that the "charming" feature cannot be derived from his Jewish forebears, but only from a non-Jewish admixture, a "degeneration" because mixed with the Jewish. And Goldstein's wife Sara receives from Hecht the dubious compliment of possessing "that calm, undemeaning servility which lights the love of the true Jewess."[9]

We have no reason to suppose that Hecht's own view of the Jew when he wrote the novel was different from that expressed by Boshere in his discussion with his sister Esther. Its tone and import are the same as the author's own description of Boshere. She has been collecting money for the Jews of Palestine, and Boshere berates her for "running around like a half-witted *yenta* raising nickels for a lot of God damn stinking Jews in Palestine." She answers, "You're ashamed to have me associated with the Jewish cause because it reflects on you. It reminds people that you're a Jew." His reply is that "I'm no more Jew than kangaroo. I'm Boshere. I have no connection with Jews . . . this Jew consciousness is because I once had it. It's the consciousness of not being a normal social human being. . . . Once in a while a Jew comes to light whose ego is stronger than his label, who has enough brains, character, genius to lift his soul out of the God damn slimy stranglehold of Jew consciousness."[10] One has a deep suspicion that Hecht believes he is describing himself here. Sixteen years later Hecht was himself to become an extreme Zionist, awakened to his Jewishness at last by Hitlerism. He became a leading propagandist for the right-wing terrorist Irgun Zvai Leumi and was instrumental in raising large sums for their activities. In 1944 he published *A Guide for the Bedevilled* in which he confesses to the astonishing fact—if it is a fact, which seems incredible—that "I lived forty years in my country without encountering anti-Semitism or concerning myself even remotely with its existence."[11] This included the 1920s, it may be recalled, when anti-Semitism was overt and widespread. Although a journalist in Chicago, he was apparently unaware of Henry Ford's anti-Semitic campaign in the *Dearborn Independent* and the period of Ku Klux Klan strength, especially in the Middle West.

But in his autobiography, *A Child of the Century* (1954), there is still no evidence that he was really aware of the anti-Semitic character of *A Jew in Love*. He calls Boshere "this worthless fellow, who cost me so much trouble with Jews who do not like the word 'Jew' used in a title,"[12] thus ignoring the point of the criticism, namely, the Jew-baiting aura of the book and the character of the Jew he depicts. Yet he named this novel as one of the five books he had written for which he still cared. He had, he writes, "always considered myself un-Jewish. My un-Hebrewizing had been achieved without effort or self-consciousness. I would have said in the days before I came to New York that I was a Jew by accident, and that I had shed this accidental heritage as easily as ridding myself of some childhood nickname. . . . I met anti-Semitism only through Jews who were more open to its distress." But in New York he came "to look with pride on what was obviously a Jewish-dominated culture."[13] But one looks in vain for any recognition or acknowledgment of the self-hating nature of his favored novel.

Like Hecht's Boshere, the self-hating Jew aspires to identification with the dominant ethnic majority group, and professedly adopts and projects upon the Jew the stereotypical view. This phenomenon of minimizing or trying to eradicate one's original ethnicity is not unique to the Jews. It may be found in any minority group subjected to a threat of discrimination on grounds of origin, evidence the not uncommon name changes in many groups to approximate the Anglo-Saxon. Except perhaps for short periods, the entire phenomenon was far less severe among these non-Jewish ethnic groups. No other group has had as long or drastic a history of persecution that additionally had a strong religious component (Jews as "Christ-Killers"). Other immigrant groups were mostly Christians. True, during some periods of American history various Christian denominations, such as the Quakers in the seventeenth century or the Catholics in the nineteenth, were victimized and became targets of discrimination for their fellow Christians. But these prejudices were temporary while anti-Semitism has endured for several thousand years.

Another source of confusion is the charge of self-hate against a Jewish author who deals with "negative" features of Jewish life, as if Jews were immune from such features or could be harmed by the exposure of such features. Excessive caution may be involved in condemning such writing as inciting or abetting anti-Semitism by providing fuel for the case made against the Jews. Often a realistic portrait of Jewish life is taken as a self-hating expression. Hypersensitive, overprotective Jewish critics have in fact greeted almost every attempt to face the realities of Jewish life squarely in literature as self-hatred even before the term was invented. Indeed, many significant novels of Jewish life, beginning with Cahan's *The Rise of David Levinsky,* have been so treated. Ornitz's *Haunch, Paunch and Jowl,* Gold's *Jews Without Money,* Levin's *The Old Bunch*—all were criticized by some Jews as representing Jews in an unflattering manner and indicating self-hatred on the part of their authors or as being injurious to Jewish welfare. These critics feared that exposure of unfavorable aspects of Jewish life would lend credence to charges by anti-Semites and hence reinforce anti-Semitism. A longer perspective has shown that such criticism is mistaken, for we now look back on such fiction as providing some of the most revealing pictures of how Jews lived in their time. Their durability as social documents is symptomatic of their superiority to the common run of fiction. Our discussion of these novels earlier by no means found rejection of Jewish identity by their authors but a determination to face the negative as well as the positive realities of the life they had experienced.

The concept of self-hate can be further clarified by examining other examples perhaps less clear-cut and unambiguous than that of Ben Hecht's Boshere, a self-hate clearly shared by both character and author. There are, however, problematic and ambiguous cases like those of Jewish writers such as Nathanael West, Norman Katkov, and Jerome Weidman. There are also authors whose self-hate was usually *not* shared by their authors, authors whose purpose was explicitly to expose self-hatred, writers like Ludwig Lewisohn, Budd Schulberg, Jo Sinclair, and Myron S. Kaufmann.

Like several other notable writers of the 1930s, such as Henry Roth and Daniel Fuchs, Nathanael West had to wait several decades after his early death in an auto accident in 1940 for general recognition. His four novels sold poorly and were reissued only in the 1950s. If rejection of anti-Semitism is not as categorical as we should like from a Jewish writer such as Nathanael West, it is in part because he was an artist who identified the Jews with the commercial spirit of his father, a successful real estate agent. In part, too, it was a consequence of West's aspirations toward an aristocratic status in general American society, which is hard to reconcile with his radicalism. In fact, his attitude toward the Jew was confused and complex. When he took out a passport in 1926 on the eve of a Paris trip, he legally changed his name from his original Nathan Wallenstein Weinstein to Nathanael West in order to present a more aristocratic front there. He tended to identify Jewishness with Orthodox Jewish religion, in which he did not believe; and he also tended to hold that commercialism was specifically associated with Jewish life.

In his eagerness to minimize his Jewishness, he even denied that there was any such group as the Jews. A friend reported, "He held and underwrote his opinion with facts and figures, that the original Jewish people had wandered so far and blended so deeply into the blood of the countries they found that it was senseless to identify them as a blood strain." In other words, he had no conception of the Jews, or any other socially coherent group as having an ethnic character, even if composed of many "blood strains," as most peoples are.

Yet, to complicate matters further, West never did or would deny that he was Jewish. When he attended Brown University in the 1920s, he longed to join a fraternity, but Jews and Catholics (I assume that Black membership was "no problem" because no Blacks, or at least very few, attended college) were excluded from membership. He had good reason to resent anti-Semitism. Quoting the same friend: "He knew more about it [anti-Semitism] than any man I have ever met." At Brown he regarded himself as a "Jewish outsider" but also as "a Jew and a non-Jew at the same time." His creed was that of the literary intellectual adherent of French and English modernism. "His feeling about his minority status," concludes his biographer Jay Martin, "had long since been translated into a sense of superior status as part of the elite minority of well-dressed men, of the gentleman and the author. He had become Nathanael West."[14]

There were some resemblances between his attitude toward Jewishness and toward radicalism. Most of his friends were Communists or left-wingers. He was himself drawn to radicalism but never became a member of the Communist party. He tended to distance himself from the ideological doctrines and, of course, the dogmatism of the Communists and was sardonically amused at the concern for the poor evinced by the Hollywood Communists in contrast to their lavish mode of life. But he was immersed in radical activities, from his participation in the Writers and Artists Congresses to fund raising for the Spanish Loyalists. His attitude toward radicals, therefore, was ambivalent, accepting their practice but not necessarily their theory. So, also, he denied his Jewishness in theory but accepted his Jewish identity in practice. In both cases he operated on the basis of his basic conception of himself as a person detached from what he considered the follies and foibles of those with whom he shared some kind of identity.

The several aspects of West's ambivalence about the Jews are exemplified in his novels. His writings are not free from occasional stereotypical allusions to Jews. In *A Cool Million* (1934), a searing satire of American life, especially in its susceptibility to the pro-fascist demagogues of the 1930s, a fascist organization called the "National Revolutionary Party," wearing "leather shirts," advertises "Ezra Silverblatt" as "Official Tailor" to the party selling "everything for the American fascist at rock bottom prices." The novel is couched in a style parodic of the dime novel or Horatio Alger story, when the young hero is jailed for trying to rescue an innocent girl from a bawdy house. The next day, "a small man of the Jewish persuasion entered his cell. 'Have you any money?' said this member of the chosen people."[15] He is Sam Abramovitz, obviously a predatory shyster lawyer, and when Lem rejects his service, the lawyer threatens him if he doesn't pay for this unsolicited conference. Another Jewish character is the bizarre interior decorator, Asa Goldstein, who has no personal traits except for an extraordinary power to imitate any historical style of decoration, from American colonial to any regional American style. His main assignment is to furnish the rooms of a bawdy house, each in a different American regional style, a mode of satire, one would suppose, of varieties of American nostalgia callously exploited for commercial purposes by a Jew in accordance with West's invidious conception of the Jew.

On the other hand, West also amply satirizes anti-Semitism, among other ethnic prejudices. In *Miss Lonelyhearts* (1933), the titular hero stops for gas at the "Aw-Kum-On Garage" in Connecticut telling the attendant about deer he had seen at a pond the day before. "The man said that there were still plenty of deer at the pond because no yids ever went there. He said it wasn't the hunters who drove out the deer, but the yids."[16] In *A Cool Million,* the young hero Lem becomes associated with the ex-President "Shagpoke Whipple," who has been jailed for bank malfeasance. Shagpoke doesn't blame "the mob" for thus repaying him for his services to the nation, but rather "do I blame Wall Street and the Jewish international bankers. ...It was Wall Street working hand in hand with the Communists that caused my downfall." Shagpoke addresses a crowd. Why are there unemployed? "Because of the Jewish international bankers and the Bolshevistic labor unions, that's why." Shagpoke informs another audience that "here in Detroit there are too many Jews, Catholics, and members of unions." In the Mississippi River town of Beulah, "all the inhabitants of Beulah who were not coloured, Jewish, or Catholic assembled under a famous tree from whose every branch a Negro had dangled at one time or another." Shagpoke is introduced to "Southerners, Protestants, Americans." They are assured he "ain't no nigger lover, he don't give a damn for Jewish culture, and he knows the fine Italian hand of the Pope when he sees it." In the riot which followed "the heads of Negroes were paraded on poles. A Jewish drummer was nailed to the door of his hotel room. The housekeeper of the local Catholic priest was raped."[17]

West felt no personal attachments to his Jewish identity or Jewishness, and occasionally falls into conventional stereotyping, but his *A Cool Million* is a devastating satire on American gullibility to demagogic reactionism, in which anti-Semitism is a useful element.

While self-hatred is present in some degree in West, that of Norman Katkov in *Eagle at My Eyes* (1947) is patently self-torturing and guilt-ridden. The author is as much confused as his central character, Joe Goodman, who has no greater comprehension of his situation as a Jew at the end than at the beginning of the story. The writing is journalistic, more like a newspaper report of the suffering of Joe as a Jew in the toils of love for the non-Jewish Mary Simpson whom he cannot leave despite his conviction that intermarriage is not viable. Katkov was a Midwestern journalist, and the locus of his story is St. Paul. Like his creator, Joe Goodman is a reporter and the author seems to share his creation's superficial cynicism. Although his family is not religious, they generally hate *goyim* in reprisal for anti-Semitism and believe that a Jew is dead if he marries a non-Jew. But Joe is desperately in love with Mary, and after refusing to marry her for a few years, he does so at last under threat of losing her altogether. Yet he feels no different about the non-viability of intermarriage.

Joe's relationship to Jews is confused. He cannot throw off his identity, since it is part of him. Yet he hates the hostility and isolation that he believes it causes him, and the unhappiness of his marriage, and in turn hates the imputed cause of his unhappiness, his Jewishness. So far as the story shows, he has no special positive feeling for Jews, and even prefers to avoid them, especially when he is with Mary. His attitude toward Jewishness is that of a prisoner to his prison. We may conclude that this, too, is a form of self-hate, or rather, self-contempt, with the proviso that his ultimate point of view is one of tortured confusion.

Following World War II the Jewish "rogue" novel was combined with the vogue for gangsters, sex, and violence in films to produce what Meyer Levin called in a famous 1955 article, "The East Side Gangsters of the

Paperbacks." Actually some of these novels were first issued in hard cover and later reprinted in millions of copies in cheap paperback. Levin was alluding to novels like Irving Shulman's *The Amboy Dukes* (1947), Leonard Bishop's *Down All Your Mean Streets* (1952), and Harold Robbins' *A Stone for Danny Fisher* (1953). "Novels of this kind," wrote Levin, "have their source in classic impulses of Jewish self-hatred," of which he cites other examples like Weidman's Harry Bogen.[18] He was concerned about the Jewish image conveyed by these trashy novels.

While the self-hating character of Jerome Weidman's Harry Bogen in *I Can Get It for You Wholesale* (1937) and its sequel, *What's in It for Me?* (1938) is obvious, the attitude of the author—at least in the first novel—is not entirely clear. The unclarity follows from the detached tone which the author, in accordance with his naturalistic method, adopts toward the villainies of his central character. It is possible to attribute Harry Bogen's self-hate to the author. Thus Meyer Levin's frequent allusions to such novels as Weidman's as in "the tradition of self-hating Jewish literature" are ambiguous. Marie Syrkin's characterization of these Weidman novels as "a morbid literary expression of Jewish self-hatred and self-contempt" and "a pathological exhibition of masochistic self-flagellation" attributes the self-hatred to the author, even if it is "unconscious," as she says.[19] With less concern for the sociology of literature and more detachment from the motivations of the author, David Boroff designated the self-hating character as the "rogue-hero," which is at least unambiguous in attributing the self-hate strictly to the literary character.[20] Except where the evidence is clear, as in *A Jew in Love,* it is best either to recognize ambiguity or refrain from imputing self-hate to the author.

Harry Bogen of *I Can Get It for You Wholesale* is an unmitigated scoundrel who is bent on getting rich by any means, and who succeeds, for a time, by climbing over the prostrate bodies of colleagues and partners, everybody or anything barring his way. His sentimental, obsessive resort to his mother for love and comfort, although she is under no illusions as to his villainy, throws into relief his callousness toward everyone else. Even though his business practices are criminal, he contrives that others should take the punishment, and escapes scot-free. Starting at about twenty as a shipping clerk, he devises scheme after scheme—always at others' expense—to raise himself, at one time, inciting a violent strike and manipulating it to set himself up in a lucrative business.

His self-hating nature emerges from his mother's attempt to interest him in Ruthie Rivkin, her intelligent, warm young Bronx neighbor. He does not respond to his mother's coaxing, and she finally extracts the reason from him. "She's so damn Jewish-looking. You take one look at her, you see right away she's a kike from the Bronx. For crying out loud, what do you want me to do, walk down the street and have everybody giving me the horse laugh." His mother replies, "You crazy dumbell without shame!...

so *that's* what's eating you. . . . Haven't you got a little feeling in you? What are you, ashamed of what you are?. . . . Don't think you're so smart, Heshie. The world is smarter. . . . They have only to look at you to know."[21] Despite the attraction he feels for Ruthie, he rejects her, and establishes a mercenary liaison with the non-Jewish actress and singer Martha Mills whom he finally lures to bed by promises of a diamond bracelet.

The novel was immensely successful and was swiftly followed by a sequel, *What's in It for Me?* (1938). At the opening, Harry Bogen is at the zenith of his power and success. He has plenty of money, is keeping his mistress Martha, whom he has come to love and whom he supplies plentifully with money, and visits his mother for comfort. By the end of the book his whole life has collapsed: Martha runs off to Europe with his partner; the police are seeking him for funds he has embezzled; he is penniless; and his mother has died. His excesses of corruption and dishonesty have caught up with him, and his life is in ruins. It is as if Weidman were stung by the criticism with which the earlier book had been greeted, especially in the Jewish community, and tried to make amends by demonstrating that heartless, dehumanized behavior is in the end simply not viable. More specifically, Weidman creates a character who challenges Bogen's inhumanity and self-hatred and tries to make clear to him why Jews are especially vulnerable.

Weidman is a popular writer with a talent for rapid, facile narrative motion swiftly borne along almost totally by lively dialogue. While his Harry Bogen is clearly a self-hating Jew whose life and conduct are execrable, the second volume of Bogen's story quite obviously is intended to clear the author of the charge of self-hate, although the condemnation of Bogen is also implicit in the first volume in his mother's judgment on him. Meyer Levin was right when, at the end of the article mentioned earlier, he wrote that "the question becomes one of literary judgment," although "Jewish writers must recognize a particular responsibility in regard to the image of the Jew" because of their special vulnerability. He disclaimed the need for using only positive Jewish characters, pointing to his own contrary practice in *The Old Bunch*, and asked rather for "penetrating" portraits, even of Jewish gangsters, that were compatible with their humanity. He urges the Jewish writer to ask himself, "Is this true in depth? Am I merely perpetuating a myth without showing that it is a myth? Am I tailoring my writing to hot sales? Am I perhaps working out some self-hating impulses, or am I truly trying to make my characters understood?"[22] These are relevant questions, for they concern not only the sociological but also the literary aspects of the novel. In the case of the novels mentioned above, it is a question whether a finer literary talent was lacking or whether the commercial or self-hating motivations were allowed to overwhelm the literary quality.

There are novels, however, in which some readers and critics carelessly fail to distinguish the self-hatred of the central character from the attitude of the author. Budd Schulberg's *What Makes Sammy Run?* (1941) is a case

in point. The author's purpose, far from sharing Sammy's self-hate, is rather
to expose it. When the book first appeared, it was often criticized as fueling
anti-Semitism, for it came out when Hitlerism was riding high and had
supporters in the United States among many neo-fascist groups. The novel
has since often been indiscriminately grouped, because of the usual confusion between author and central character, with other novels by self-hating
authors.

To regard Schulberg as a self-hating author is to misread his novel. Sammy
does not "run" because he is a Jew. The author seeks an answer to why
Sammy runs, from his beginning as a desperately poor East Side boy, to his
development as a preternaturally shrewd operator in Hollywood who rises
from office boy to studio boss by utterly unscrupulous methods. The answer,
given by the narrator, Al Manheim, is the last sentence in the book: it is
"a blueprint of a way of life that was paying dividends in America in the
first half of the twentieth century." From beginning to end the author goes
out of the way explicitly to depart from the stereotype, as when he describes
Sammy's "little ferret face... with a nose growing large, but still straight
and sharp, giving the lie to the hook-nosed anti-Semitic cartoons." Unlike
Sammy, there were in the world, "Jews without money, without push,
without plots, without any of the characteristics which such experts on
genetics as Adolf Hitler, Henry Ford and Father Coughlin try to tell us are
racial traits. I have seen... too many Jewish nebs [nebbishes] and poets and
starving tailors and everyday little guys to consider the fascist answer to
what makes Sammy run."[23]

More common than novels with self-hating authors are those whose condemnation of their self-hating characters is unequivocal. One of the earliest
and strongest indictments of self-hate is Lewisohn's *The Island Within*. In
my opinion the treatment of his contemporary self-hating Jews has more
validity than of his central character. The novel was written in the 1920s,
the decade in which the second generation was perhaps most acutely ex-
periencing self-hatred. The young Hazel Levy responds to her father's sad,
"Are you ashamed of being Chewish?"—"Yes, I am! I'm just as good as
anybody else and I'm just like everybody else."[24] Young Joey Goldmann
early asserts, "Jewishness is a curse,"[25] and later, as a lawyer, "a very
successful lawyer now, his office full of Jewish clients,... always in love
with some blonde Gentile girl in order to transcend vicariously in conquest
of her his Jewish feeling of inferiority."[26] In a story like this one, the lines
are clearly and explicitly drawn. In fact, the contrary of self-hatred, passionate affirmation of Jewishness is the central theme of the novel.

Even more explicit in separation of the self-hate of the character from
the author is *Wasteland* (1946) by Jo Sinclair (Ruth Seid). Indeed, a central
aim of the novel is to expose what the author believes is the psychopath-
ological nature of self-hate, as Lewisohn, too, conjectured, and its exorcism
by psychoanalysis. Jake Brown (born Braunowitz), a newspaper photog-

rapher, lives in the "wasteland" of hatred for his family, which originates in and exacerbates his hatred of his Jewish identity. But he does love his mother and his sister Deborah. His sister is a lesbian who is ashamed of her sexuality and is self-denigrating. She tells Jake about her past and that her recourse to a psychoanalyst has cured her of guilt for her sexuality. She persuades him to consult a psychoanalyst about his problems, his self-hate, his unhappiness, and his excessive drinking. The body of the novel is then devoted to the unraveling of Jake Brown's neurotic situation. It is a matter of accepting his identity, both familial and Jewish. As the author conveys it, Jake's problem is the obtuseness that rises in human relations out of poverty and ignorance in father and mother. Being Jewish under these circumstances only aggravates this basic problem and gives rise to his difficulties outside the family. Jake had for years been trying to find an "identity—for himself, away from these people, who were unreal and strange to him. Away from the house, he had no identity, he was not alive, he was without framework of name, without flesh of heritage, without blood of pride or love. And yet, within the house he was without identity, too."[27] This passage states well the tensions that gave tortured ambiguity to his feelings. "Was he ashamed of being a Jew? It looked like it, didn't it! And yet, everytime he read about what was happening to Jews all over the world he wanted to smash faces, he wanted to get up and shoot faces . . . and shoot all those bastards who were doing it."[28] He had never mentioned his being Jewish at the paper for which he worked. "All right, maybe he was ashamed of being a Jew! But that wasn't the big thing he was ashamed . . . about without having to be ashamed of being a Jew."[29]

Passover Seders are represented as crucial events in Jake's rejection of his Jewish identity. As a young man, he is deeply shocked at the Seder by his hatred and contempt for his father, who "pretended to sit like this and tell a beautiful story. It was all a lie. If his father was a Jew, then he didn't want to be a Jew."[30] It was the incompatibility of the beauty of the story and the falseness of the man who was relating it which set up a contradiction. Yet it was an inescapable part of him. His solution was simply to flee from his Jewish identity, a plight smybolized by his refusal to attend Seders any longer. Jake was "ashamed that he was my father, that I was a Jew. Because he was one, the whole family—we were Jews. I blamed everything on that, I guess—on the fact that we were Jews."[31] But renunciation of Jewishness was no solution: the conflict remained. After treatment by the psychiatrist, Jake is at last ready to face his Jewishness fully, a readiness symbolized by his giving blood (during World War II), which signified to him the restoration of his identity in its several aspects. "He gave as a Jew, and as a patriot, he gave as Everyman."[32] Giving thus, most importantly, as "a member of society, a working part of it," signified restoration of mental health. For accepted as "Everyman," he was no longer "a part of wasteland."[33] While the literary psychiatry of the novel, like most attempts of this kind, is not convincing, the author does succeed in exposing the tensions and ambiguities underlying self-hate.

Several short stories of the 1940s focus on the problem of self-hate. Paul Goodman's "The Facts of Life" exposes parental evasion of Jewishness when their child reports her first encounter with anti-Semitism at school. Nine-year-old Marcia was never told she was Jewish by her parents of a mixed marriage. She discovers it when a schoolmate calls her "just an old-time Jew," and she is bewildered. She's not sure she has heard right. Did the child call her "shoe," "Jao," "Juice," or what? Her father Ronnie denies he's Jewish because he is not "racially" a Jew in appearance. The non-Jewish mother, Martha, tells Ronnie, "you Jews are not doing yourselves any favor by putting yourselves forward too much. . . . Every Jew who gets in the Supreme Court makes it so much harder for Marcia."[34] "It's true enough," thinks Ronnie. "You're a Jew, so all right!" Says Martha, "It's nothing to be ashamed of. But why bring it up in public?"[35]

Miriam Bruce wrote her *Linden Road* (1951) out of a personal need, as she said, "emotionally, compulsively," to explore the problem that "The American Jew is in constant danger of contracting anti-Semitism himself and dying of a sort of quiet soul-rot which so far nobody deems it worthwhile to discuss."[36] The Westchester, well-to-do garment manufacturer's family of her heroine, Hagar (the name is not accidental) Tobias, are trying to suppress their Jewish identity in their suburban, bourgeois, philistine existence. Hagar soon discovers in her high school years that she cannot control this process, since she is no longer invited to dances of mixed sexes. The story is so completely taken up with the problem of to be or not to be a Jew that the Depression receives no mention and Hitler scarcely any, even though the first half of the story takes place in the mid-1930s. Jewish counterpoint is supplied by an aunt who is continually critical of the family's efforts to suppress their Jewishness. Hagar even blames her aunt and other conscious Jews for the discrimination she suffers. She falls in love with a self-hating German-Jewish young man, Richard. Richard goes to England on a fellowship, and Hagar leaves home in hopes of ridding herself of the Jewish incubus. Her Aunt Vicky exclaims, "My God, what's the matter with all of you? Why do you hate yourselves so much? You've turned it into a disease, being a Jew . . . there isn't any place you can hide. It'll go with you."[37]

During World War II Hagar serves with the Red Cross in Italy; there her meeting with German-Jewish refugees modifies her attitude, and she is accepted by them. Richard has, in the meantime, served in the British army and tried to pass as a non-Jew. Hagar meets a close British army friend of Richard's, a neo-Catholic scholar, esthete, and anti-Semite, and is shocked. When she hears of a young Jewish soldier on the point of death at the hospital where no one understands Yiddish, she takes the final step in her return by volunteering to talk to him. While she is still in love with Richard, she rejects his offer of marriage at the end of the war because she refuses to deny her Jewishness. Hagar is an attractive character but a victim of her rearing. At the last she is reconciled to accepting what she is—a Jew. The writing is competent and smooth, but in the end the novel is in the manner of popular magazine fiction.

The subject returns again and again in subsequent writing because it remains an ongoing issue. In 1957 another novel, this one a great commercial success, *Remember Me to God* by Myron S. Kaufmann, is centered on the problem of self-hate. Like others, it has been criticized indiscriminately as a "self-hate" novel without noting that it is a merciless exposure of the self-hatred of its central character, Richard Amsterdam, a student at Harvard and aspirant for acceptance as a Yankee. Born and bred in Boston, Richard went to school with Yankees and believes they "don't care what my origin is,"[38] but actually judge people on an individual basis, "put aside their prejudices and accept a friend on his merits."[39] He believes that acceptance can be permanent if a Jew conforms his "manners" to what they approve.

The case for and against Richard's conformism and assimilationism is argued in several ways through his relations with characters in the novel. His father Adam is a self-made man who has risen to a judgeship through political influence. Richard has become a close friend of the Boston WASP, Hodges, and even succeeds in getting himself elected to the exclusive Hasty Pudding Club. He falls in love with Wilma Talbot, daughter of an old Boston family. Wilma's anti-Semitic father withholds consent unless Richard converts. He agrees, and "his choice to take on the Christian faith seemed an act of total freedom."[40] He asks the Reverend Todd to baptize and convert him. Todd easily perceives that Richard's reason for converting is social, not religious, and categorically refuses to comply. He tells Richard that he (Richard) has "rationalized a conversion" without any "reference to God," who "never enters your calculation at all." And he caps his refusal with the phrase, "I'm trying to bring people to Christ, not to Beacon Hill."[41] Richard's fantasies now fade. It is clear that he will now abandon his fatuous ideas. This is possible because Kaufmann has rendered Richard as possessing a peculiar kind of integrity, of honesty within the bounds of his rationalizations. And when those rationalizations are exposed for what they are, that same striving for honesty, one feels at the end, will lead him to revise his outlook.

Although the novel was a best seller, it met with an erratic variety of criticism. Some critics thought the book trashy, others considered it a memorable treatment of the problem. I share the latter view, although the novel's most serious lack is that it views the problem for the most part within a narrow religious context—viewing Jewishness as primarily a religious category.

Conclusion

The turn of the century saw the first significant entry of Jewish writers into American literature, and although there were still some years before they would produce a major literary figure, they gained in both numbers and competence as the century progressed.

In this first volume of a three-part study of the twentieth-century Jewish presence in the fiction, drama, and poetry of the United States we trace the story of the fiction from the opening of the century through the 1940s. That period ended with both critical and popular recognition of the Jewish writer's place in the mainstream of our national literature. There was also a welcome change in the image of the Jew presented by gentile novelists, although the centuries-old stereotypes still persisted. There were even in fact new forms adapted to divert attention from popular demands of the time. Although these hostile clichés lost some currency as the years wore on, they never altogether disappeared.

Instead of treating the Jewish character of an individual, fiction of this period tended to assume that all Jews were a uniform bundle of "racial" traits, like Edith Wharton's Simon Rosedale of *The House of Mirth*. All Jews, or "the Jew," were portrayed as money-obsessed or dressed in a flashy manner or deceitful and sharp in their business practices, like Potash and Perlmutter. Shylock or Barabas was the model for the Jew in some authors' work. The cliché that all Jews tried to evade military service—or dangerous service—and maneuvered to have non-Jews fight wars in their behalf while they profited was amply illustrated in war novels of both world wars. Jews were ever present scapegoats for the demagogic demands of troubled times just as the powers of the twentieth century, especially after the Russian Revolution, found the dual cliché of the Jew as Bolshevik and capitalist conspirator useful for their own profit. And for decades, charges against the Rothschilds were at hand to assuage the pain of business troubles.

The literary process which brought Jewish writers to full recognition as important American authors was a vital aspect of the acculturation of American Jews. It indicated their increasingly full participation in the country's life. In our study we have tried to show how central to American literature the work of the second generation had become. Like all writers these Jewish figures drew on their personal experience, which their integration into American life had developed in forms that contrasted sharply with the lives of their immigrant parents.

We have been concerned with the way in which Jews' writing reflected their acculturation, noting first how their mores differed from those of their Eastern European parents and, second, how they pursued professional careers or participated in labor and socialist movements. They differed in language. The parents usually spoke at best accented or ungrammatical English, while the children tended to be ashamed of their parents' speech and spoke English outside of the home. The generations' mode of life differed, too: the parents tended to continue their *shtetl* manners and diet and kept themselves largely oblivious to American forms of entertainment from movies to musical comedy to serious plays in English, and they sang different songs. Until the children became independent, they lived as little as possible in their parents' world and as much as possible in the larger English-speaking world, enjoying work and play alien to their parents. We have seen how, inevitably, tensions between the generations arose as the sons and daughters worked their way through American opportunities and the conduct of a life unknown to their parents. This study of the literature gives us a very vivid picture of the development of the Jewish ethnic group and naturally presents regrettable as well as admirable features. The story is told with increasing authenticity in the first three decades of the century through the novels of such writers as Abraham Cahan, Samuel Ornitz, Meyer Levin, Michael Gold, Daniel Fuchs, and Henry Roth.

The acculturation process took place at the time when the labor movement in the United States was beginning to express its potential power through trade unions and the Socialist party. The combination generated fiction which presented the struggles and aspirations of the Eastern European Jewish immigration. Largely concentrated in urban areas like New York and Chicago, Jewish immigrants were especially active in labor and socialist movements, and contemporary writers recounted their experience. While the second generation was growing up, their parents, many of them veterans of revolutionary or labor movements in their native Russia with extensive organizing experience there, brought that background to bear in the formation and strengthening of the unions of the hideously exploited garment workers and other industries where a large number of Jewish immigrants were employed. For some time early in the century their unions became a leading force in the general trade union movement. At the same time the second generation was receiving a free education and in large numbers trained and entered the professions as lawyers, doctors, teachers, and journalists, and many even moved into the middle class. Not only Jew but also non-Jewish authors participated in telling their story, often with considerable accuracy. But writing in this vein came to an almost complete halt in the boom years of the decade after World War I. During the 1920s the labor and socialist movements aroused little interest in the general public despite the great strikes which then took place and which, in the late 1920s, did enlist the aid of some writers, artists, and other intellectuals.

The situation was again radically changed during the prolonged Depression of the 1930s and the production of labor, socialist, and finally proletarian novels was then resumed. The term "proletarian" was used to describe those novels evincing favorable attitudes toward "revolution," attitudes most often expressed in some relationship with the Communist party. Heated literary controversy raged around this genre throughout the entire literary community. Of course labor novels which made no effort to relate to the Communist party continued to appear and other acculturation fiction still claimed its practitioners. Our study has attempted to indicate this great variety of works in their full social context.

It should have become clear that from the beginning our study has been neither purely literary nor purely social but rather socioliterary. The theses of all the books treated were closely tied to, and expressive of, their particular time and place.

Another abrupt change was ushered in when World War II put a sudden end to any radical critique of the economy. The many young writers who served in the armed forces necessarily postponed their literary careers until the mid-1940s. Then there appeared a spate of war novels, mostly by those younger writers who were beginning with their own military experiences. Among these were, of course, many young Jews. Almost all of these war novels, by both Jews and non-Jews, reported anti-Semitic events—ubiquitous in the fiction simply because similar ones had actually been experienced or witnessed by their authors. The frequency with which anti-Semitism was encountered in the army revealed the ugly paradox of American soldiers concurring with a central part of the enemy's propaganda. However, in most cases this anti-Semitism was not shared by the authors describing it. Whether Jewish or not, they clearly condemned it either explicitly or implicitly through their treatments of the episodes involved, from Norman Mailer and Irwin Shaw to the non-Jews John Horne Burns and James Jones. Of course the war novels were not unique in their accounts of anti-Semitism. Throughout our entire survey, in every period, the Jewish presence in our literature often included the presence of anti-Semitism. Yet, as the century wore on, authors less and less frequently shared their characters' prejudice. Thus, when writers like Dorothy Canfield Fisher, Sinclair Lewis, the later

William Faulkner or Thomas Wolfe, or John Dos Passos or James T. Farrell introduce anti-Semitism into their stories, they clearly disassociate themselves from it.

While exaggeration of the incidence of anti-Semitism should be avoided, its widespread existence, especially during the 1920s, 1930s, and the anti-Nazi war, must be faced. Ample evidence of its extent is available in the novels of both the Jewish and non-Jewish writers reviewed here. It is most painful to note this prejudice alive in so many of the brilliant novelists and poets writing in the post–World War I period. (One must, of course, be careful to distinguish the attitude of a fictional character from that of its creator.)

Our next volume, *In the Mainstream: The Jewish Presence in Twentieth-Century American Literature, 1950s–1980s,* discusses the Jewish presence in the fiction of the 1950s, 1960s, 1970s, and early 1980s. The final volume in the series treats the drama and poetry of the entire twentieth century in a similar fashion.

Notes

INTRODUCTION

1. Alfred Kazin, "The Jew as Modern Writer," *Commentary*, April, 1966, p. 37.

1. THE APPRENTICE YEARS: 1900–1919

1. Milton M. Gordon, *Assimilation in American Life: The Role of Race, Religion, and National Origins* (New York, 1964), pp. 71, 76.

2. Nathan Glazer and Daniel Patrick Moynihan, *Beyond the Melting Pot* (Cambridge, Mass., 1963), p. v.

3. Quoted by Gordon, *Assimilation*, pp. 116, 117.

4. Barrett Wendell, "The American Nationality," *Liberty, Union and Democracy: The National Ideas of America* (New York, 1906), pp. 10, 11, 43, 88.

5. Israel Zangwill, *The Melting Pot* (London, 1914), pp. 33, 34.

6. *American Hebrew*, Vol. 84, No. 11 (November 6, 1908), 10.

7. *American Hebrew*, Vol. 83, No. 25 (October 13, 1908), 610.

8. *American Hebrew*, Vol. 85, No. 19 (September 10, 1909), 475.

9. *American Hebrew*, Vol. 85, No. 25 (October 22, 1909), 619–20.

10. *The Maccabaean*, Vol. 23, No. 1 (January, 1913), 13, 14.

11. Zangwill, *Melting Pot*, pp. 215, 216, 203, 209–10.

12. *American Hebrew*, Vol. 85, No. 25 (Oct. 22, 1909), 620.

13. *The Maccabaean*, Vol. 23, No. 1 (January, 1913), 15.

14. Myra Kelly, *Little Citizens* (New York, 1904), pp. 126, 141.

15. Horace M. Kallen, "Democracy *versus* the Melting Pot," *Culture and Democracy in the United States* (New York, 1924), p. 94.

16. Ibid., pp. 106, 114, 116, 124.

17. Randolph Bourne, *The History of a Literary Radical and Other Papers* (New York, 1956), pp. 260, 267, 269, 270, 283.

18. Randolph S. Bourne, "The Jew and Trans-National America," *Menorah Jour-*

nal, Vol. 2, No. 5 (December, 1916), 277–78. However, Bourne imperfectly understood the way in which Jewish ethnic culture in the United States could be expressed, since he seemed to identify an imperfectly understood Jewish ethnicity with Zionism.

19. *The Maimie Papers,* historical ed., Ruth Rosen, textual ed., Sue Davidson, with an introduction by Ruth Rosen (Old Westbury, N.Y., 1977), p. 165.

20. Mary Antin, *The Promised Land* (Boston, 1969 [c1912]), p. 271.

21. Randolph Bourne, "The Jew and Trans-National America," p. 262.

22. Joseph Lebowich, "The Jew in American Fiction," *American Hebrew,* Vol. 78 (May 4, 1906), 727.

23. Rebecca Schneider, *Bibliography of Jewish Life in the Fiction of England and America* (Albany: New York State Library School, 1916).

24. Edna Ferber, *A Peculiar Pleasure* (New York, 1939), p. 8.

25. Quoted in Julie Goodman Gilbert, *Ferber: A Biography of Edna Ferber and Her Circle* (New York, 1975), pp. 115, 267.

26. Edna Ferber, *Fanny Herself* (New York, 1917), pp. 136, 188, 188–89.

27. Gilbert, *Ferber,* p. 281.

28. John Higham, "Introduction to the Torchbooks Edition," *The Rise of David Levinsky,* by Abraham Cahan, (New York, 1969 [c1917]), pp. v, viii.

29. Abraham Cahan, *David Levinsky,* pp. 201, 337.

30. Ibid., p. 3.

31. Ibid., pp. 526, 529–30.

32. John Higham, "Anti-Semitism in the Gilded Age: A Reinterpretation," *Mississippi Valley Historical Review,* Vol. 93, No. 4 (March, 1957), 571.

33. Nina Morais, "Jewish Ostracism in America," *North American Review,* Vol. 133 (1881), 269, 270, 271, 272, 275.

34. Herbert G. Gutman, "The Knights of Labor and Patrician Anti-Semitism," *Labor History,* Vol. 13, No. 1 (Winter, 1972), 65, 64, 66.

35. Rudolph Glanz, *The Jew in Early American Wit and Graphic Humor* (New York, 1973), pp. 9, 40, 32.

36. Rev. Rudolph Grossman, "The Jew in Novels," *American Hebrew,* Vol. 50, No. 7 (March 18, 1892), 123.

37. Bernard G. Richards, *Discourses of Kandinsky* (New York, 1903), pp. 129–30.

38. Robert Forrey, "The 'Jew' in Norris' *The Octopus,*" *Western States Jewish Historical Quarterly,* Vol. 7, No. 3 (April, 1975), 201–10; see also Ernest Marchand, *Frank Norris: A Study* (Stanford, Calif., 1942), pp. 214–16.

39. Owen Wister, *Philosophy Four* (New York, 1901), pp. 31, 38, 57.

40. Edith Wharton, *The House of Mirth* (New York, 1908 [c1905]), pp. 21, 23, 24, 70, 195, 283, 288.

41. Jack London, "The Yellow Peril," *Revelations and Other Essays* (New York, 1912), pp. 284–85.

42. *Jack London Reports, War Correspondence,* ed. King Hendricks (New York, 1970), p. 346.

43. Jack London, *Martin Eden, American Rebel,* ed. Philip Foner (New York, 1947), p. 105.

44. Thomas Nelson Page, *John Marvel, Assistant* (New York, 1909), pp. 9, 12, 23, 129, 133.

45. Ibid., pp. 518, 524, 552, 543–44.

46. Dorothy Canfield Fisher, *Raw Material* (New York, 1923), pp. 134, 135.

47. Dorothy Canfield Fisher, "The City of Refuge," *The Real Motive*, (New York, 1916), p. 222.

48. Dorothy Canfield Fisher, *Seasoned Timber* (New York, 1939), pp. 147, 156, 157.

49. Ibid., pp. 318, 333, 355. For a detailed study of Fisher's relation to the Jews, see David Baugardt, "Dorothy Canfield Fisher, Friend of Jews in Life and Work," *Publications of the American Jewish Historical Society,* Vol 48, No. 48 (June, 1959), 245–55.

50. Rudolf Glanz, "Jewish Social Conditions as Seen by the Muckrakers," *Studies in Judaica Americana* (New York, 1970), p. 385.

51. Upton Sinclair, *The Jungle* (Cambridge, Mass., 1946 [c1906]), p. 311.

52. Morris U. Schappes, "The Nineties—Ups and Downs of Jewish Trade Unionism," *Jewish Life,* Vol. 8, No. 12 (October, 1904), 18.

53. Walter B. Rideout, "O Worker's Revolution . . . The True Messiah," *American Jewish Archives,* Vol. 11, No. 2 (October, 1959), 158.

54. Isaac K. Friedman, "Aaron Pavansky's Picture," *The Lucky Number* (Chicago, 1896), p. 183.

55. Isaac Kahn Friedman, *By Bread Alone* (New York, 1901), pp. 91, 98, 123, 479. For further comment on Jewish characters in Friedman's earlier work, see my *Image of the Jew in American Literature*, pp. 452–53.

56. Henry Berman, *Worshippers* (New York, 1906), pp. 5, 21.

57. Rideout, "Worker's Revolution," p. 163.

58. Elias Tobenkin, *Witte Arrives* (New York, 1916), pp. 67, 256, 297, 298.

59. James Oppenheim, *Dr. Rast* (New York, 1909), pp. 50, 52, 53, 291, 292. The copy of the novel that I read, owned by the University of Vermont Library, contained the author's presentation inscription to the then socialist publicist, John Spargo: "Dear John—Here's the little work you fathered—but better, here's a token of gratitude and love, my brother—James."

60. James Oppenheim, *The Nine-Tenths* (New York, 1911), pp. 316, 49, 182, 176.

61. Ibid., p. 49.

62. Ibid., p. 168.

63. Paula Scheier, "Clara Lemlich Shavelson: 50 Years in Labor's Front Line," *Jewish Life,* Vol. 9, No. 1 (November, 1954), 8.

64. Florence Converse, *The Children of Light* (New York, 1912), p. 187.

65. Zoe Beckley, *A Chance to Live* (New York, 1918), pp. 83, 327.

66. [Arthur Bullard], *Comrade Yetta,* by Albert Edwards (New York, 1913), p. 213.

67. Griffin Mace, review of *Comrade Yetta, The Bookman,* Vol. 37 (1913), 214.

68. Ibid., p. 215.

69. Arthur Bullard, pp. 9, 212–13.

70. Ibid., pp. 29, 427.

71. David Graham Phillips, *Susan Lenox: Her Fall and Rise,* 2 vols. (Upper Saddle River, N.J., 1968 [c1915]), 2: 86, 205–6, 311, 407, 472.

2. FICTION OF THE 1920S

1. James Schroeter, "Willa Cather and *The Professor's House,*" *Yale Review,* Vol. 54, No. 4 (April, 1965), p. 495.

2. Alfred Kazin, *On Native Grounds* (New York, 1956 [c1942]), p. 204.

3. George Dobsavage, "Jews of Prominence in the United States," *American Jewish Yearbook, 1922–1923* (New York, 1922), pp. 209–12.

4. Anzia Yezierska, *Children of Loneliness: Stories of Immigrant Life in America* (New York, 1923), p. 25.

5. Anzia Yezierska, "Hunger," *Hungry Hearts* (Boston, 1920), p. 34.

6. Ibid.

7. Anzia Yezierska, "The Fat of the Land," *Hungry Hearts,* pp. 218–19.

8. Anzia Yezierska, "The Lost Beautifulness, *Hungry Hearts,* pp. 93–94.

9. Anzia Yezierska, "My Own People," *Hungry Hearts,* p. 249.

10. Anzia Yezierska, *Bread Givers,* with an introduction by Alice Kerrler Harris (New York, 1975 [c1925]), pp. 9–10.

11. Anzia Yezierska, *Red Ribbons on a White Horse,* introduction by W. H. Auden (New York, 1950), p. 218.

12. Thyra Samter Winslow, "The Cycle of Manhattan," *Picture Frames* (New York, 1923), reprinted in *A Treasury of American Jewish Short Stories,* ed. Harold U. Ribalow (New York, 1952), pp. 337–97.

13. Samuel Ornitz, *Haunch, Paunch and Jowl* (New York, 1923), pp. 30–31, 35, 38, 49.

14. Ibid., p. 78.

15. Ibid., pp. 75, 192, 200.

16. Ibid., p. 157.

17. Myron Brinig, *Singermann* (New York, 1929), p. 23.

18. Myron Brinig, *This Man Is My Brother* (New York, 1932), p. 249.

19. Paul Rosenfeld, *The Boy in the Sun* (New York, 1928), pp. 48, 57, 59, 60.

20. Lionel Trilling, Review of *The Boy in the Sun, Menorah Journal,* Vol. 15, No. 5 (November, 1928), 483–86.

21. Kazin, *On Native Grounds,* pp. 205–16, 206, 207.

22. Ludwig Lewisohn, *Mid-Channel* (New York, 1929), p. 262.

23. Ludwig Lewisohn, *The Island Within* (New York, 1928), pp. 149, 186.

24. Ibid., p. 187.

25. Ibid., pp. 258, 260, 272.

26. Ibid., pp. 161, 249.

27. Lewisohn, *Mid-Channel,* pp. 29, 303.

28. E. Digby Baltzell, *The Protestant Establishment* (New York, 1964), p. 217.

29. George Santayana, "Tradition in American Philosophy," *Winds of Doctrine* (London and New York, 1913), p. 188.

30. John Higham, *Strangers in the Land* (New York, 1974), p. 279.

31. Quoted in Baltzell, *Protestant Establishment,* p. 204.

32. F. Scott Fitzgerald, *The Great Gatsby,* in *Three Novels,* ed. Edmund Wilson (New York, 1953), p. 12.

33. "The Twenty-Third Philippic," *Harvard Lampoon,* Vol. 128, No. 10 (January 16, 1920), 408.

34. "A Divine Comedy," *Harvard Lampoon*, Vol. 134, No. 25 (September 25, 1922), 63.

35. Irving Howe, *Sherwood Anderson* (New York, 1957), p. 32.

36. Sherwood Anderson, *A Story-Teller's Story* (New York, 1924), p. 394.

37. *The Sherwood Anderson Reader*, ed. with an introduction by Paul Rosenfeld (Boston, 1947), p. 337.

38. Sherwood Anderson, *Dark Laughter* (New York, 1925), p. 278.

39. Howe, *Sherwood Anderson*, p. 188.

40. C. David Heymann, *Ezra Pound: The Last Rower, a Political Profile* (New York, 1976), pp. 297, 298.

41. Quoted in Ibid., p. 66.

42. Hugh Kenner, *The Pound Era* (Berkeley, Calif., 1971), p. 465.

43. E. E. Cummings, *The Enormous Room* (New York, 1934 [c1922]), pp. 191, 193, 194. For other instances of Jews described as the ugliest possible men, see Louis Harap, *The Image of the Jew in American Literature*: by Hawthorne, pp. 109–10; by George Lippard, p. 49; by Henry Harland, p. 469.

44. E. E. Cummings, *Complete Poems, 1913–1962* (New York, 1972), pp. 244, 438, 644.

45. Justin Kaplan, review of Richard E. Kennedy, *Dreams in the Mirror* (New York, 1979), *New York Times Book Review*, January 13, 1980, p. 28.

46. William Faulkner, *Mosquitos* (New York, 1927), pp. 324, 325.

47. Ibid., p. 325.

48. William Faulkner, *The Sound and the Fury* (New York, 1929), pp. 97, 204.

49. William Faulkner, "Death Drag," *Collected Short Stories of William Faulkner* (New York, 1950), pp. 185, 187, 192.

50. Joseph Blotner, *Faulkner, A Biography*, 2 vols. (New York, 1974), 1: 683.

51. Irving Howe, *William Faulkner*, 3rd ed. (Chicago, 1975), p. 220.

52. Faulkner, *"Death Drag,"* p. 187.

53. William Faulkner, *Sanctuary* (New York, 1931), p. 219.

54. Ibid., p. 223.

55. Blotner, 2: 1146.

56. Ibid., p. 1529.

57. Faulkner, "The Fable," *Collected Short Stories*, p. 551.

58. William Faulkner, *The Mansion* (New York, 1959), p. 109.

59. Ibid., p. 178.

60. Alfred J. Kutzik, "Faulkner and the Jews," *Yivo Annual of Jewish Social Science*, Vol. 13 (1965), p. 224. The entire article was helpful in my section on Faulkner.

61. Elizabeth Nowell, *Thomas Wolfe, a Biography* (New York, 1960), p. 86.

62. Thomas Wolfe, *Look Homeward, Angel* (New York, 1952 [c1929]), pp. 100, 101.

63. Thomas Wolfe, *Of Time and the River* (New York, 1937 [c1935]), p. 468.

64. Thomas Wolfe, *The Web and the Rock* (New York, 1952 [c1939]), pp. 322, 323.

65. Ibid., pp. 547, 548.

66. Ibid., p. 565.

67. Ibid., pp. 590, 591.

68. Ibid., p. 601.

69. Nowell, *Thomas Wolfe*, p. 98

70. Thomas Wolfe, *You Can't Go Home Again* (New York, 1940), p. 705.

71. Thomas Wolfe, "I Have a Story to Tell," *The Short Novels of Thomas Wolfe*, ed. with an introduction by C. Hugh Holman (New York, 1961), p. 272.

72. Ibid., p. 274.

73. F. Scott Fitzgerald, *The Beautiful and the Damned* (New York, 1951 [c1922]), p. 82.

74. Ibid., p. 120.

75. Ibid., p. 183.

76. Ibid., pp. 269–70.

77. Ibid., p. 388.

78. F. Scott Fitzgerald, *The Great Gatsby*, in *Three Novels*, p. 53.

79. Ibid., p. 86.

80. Ibid., p. 130.

81. Milton Hindus, "F. Scott Fitzgerald and Literary Anti-Semitism," *Commentary*, Vol. 3 (1947), 509, 510.

82. William Goldhurst, "Literary Anti-Semitism in the 20's," *Congress Biweekly*, December 24, 1962, p. 11.

83. F. Scott Fitzgerald, *The Last Tycoon*, in *Three Novels*, p. 15.

84. Ibid., p. 28.

85. Ibid., p. 42.

86. Ibid., p. 45.

87. Ibid., p. 150.

88. Ernest Hemingway, *The Sun Also Rises* (New York, 1926), p. 4.

89. Ibid., p. 3.

90. Ibid., p. 45.

91. Ibid., pp. 96, 98.

92. Ibid., p. 95.

93. Ibid., p. 101.

94. Ibid., p. 142.

95. Ibid., p. 145.

96. Ibid., pp. 182, 184.

97. Carlos Baker, *Ernest Hemingway, a Life Story* (New York, 1969), p. 133.

98. Ibid., p. 154.

99. Robert Alter, "Eliot, Lawrence and the Jews: Two Versions of Europe," *Defenses of the Imagination* (Philadelphia, 1977), p. 151 (originally published in *Commentary*, Vol. 50, No. 4 [October, 1970], 86). For other illustrations of Alter's thesis, see Louis Harap, *The Image of the Jew in American Literature*, for Hawthorne, pp. 107–17, and for Melville, pp. 118–32.

100. Phyllis C. Robinson, *Willa: The Life of Willa Cather* (New York, 1983), p. 48. On the whole question of Willa Cather's anti-Semitism, see Robinson, passim; and James Schroeter, "Willa Cather and *The Professor's House*," *Yale Review*, Vol. 54, No. 4 (April, 1965), 494–512. Schroeter does not mention the extremely respectful treatment of the Rosens in Cather's short story, "Old Mrs. Harris."

101. Robinson, *Willa*, p. 259.

102. E. K. Brown, *Willa Cather, A Critical Biography*, completed by Leon Edel (New York, 1953), p. 292.

103. Ibid., p. 33.

104. Robinson, *Willa*, p. 48.

105. Willa Cather, "The Marriage of Phaedre," *The Troll Garden* (New York, 1905), p. 98.

106. Robinson, *Willa*, p. 206.

107. Willa Cather, "Scandal," *Youth and the Bright Medusa* (New York, 1920), p. 166.

108. Ibid., p. 171.

109. Robinson, *Willa*, p. 48.

110. Willa Cather, *The Professor's House* (New York, 1925), p. 43.

111. Ibid., p. 86.

112. Schroeter, "Willa Cather," pp. 500, 503.

113. Willa Cather, "The Old Beauty," *The Old Beauty and Others* (New York, 1948).

114. T. S. Eliot, *The Complete Poems and Plays, 1909–1950* (New York, 1962), p. 21.

115. T. S. Eliot, *After Strange Gods* (London, 1934), pp. 19–20.

116. On the interpretation of "Burbank with a Baedeker, Bleistein with a Cigar," see Robert Alter, "Eliot, Lawrence and the Jews." See also Hyam Maccoby, "The Anti-Semitism of T. S. Eliot," *Midstream,* May, 1973, pp. 68–79.

117. J. Mitchell Morse, "Prejudice and Literature," *College English,* Vol. 37, No. 8 (April, 1967), 782.

118. James Joyce, *Ulysses* (New York, 1934), pp. 34–35.

119. Edmund Wilson, *I Thought of Daisy* (New York, 1929), pp. 290, 291, 292.

120. Sinclair Lewis, "That Passage in Isaiah," with an introduction by Arthur A. Chiel, *American Jewish Historical Quarterly,* Vol. 64, No. 3 (March, 1975), 258–67.

121. Mark Schorer, *Sinclair Lewis* (New York, 1961), p. 305.

122. Sinclair Lewis, *Arrowsmith* (New York, 1925), pp. 228, 387.

123. Sinclair Lewis, *It Can't Happen Here* (New York, 1935), pp. 76, 192.

124. Malcolm Goldstein, *The Political Stage: American Drama and the Theater of the Great Depression* (New York, 1974), p. 270.

3. THE DEPRESSION YEARS: THE 1930S

1. Allan Nevins and Henry Steele Commager, *A Short History of the United States* (New York, 1945), p. 468.

2. Ray Allen Billington, Bert James Lowenberg, and Samuel Hugh Brockanier, *The United States: American Democracy in World Perspective* (New York, 1947), p. 649.

3. Matthew Josephson, *The Infidel in the Temple* (New York, 1967), p. 407.

4. Joseph Freeman, "Introduction," *Proletarian Literature in the United States,* ed. Granville Hicks, Michael Gold, Isidor Schneider, Joseph North, Paul Peters, Alan Calmer, with an Introduction by Joseph Freeman (New York, 1935), p. 25.

5. Quoted by Daniel Aaron, *Writers on the Left* (New York, 1963), p. 21.

6. *Proletarian Literature in the United States* (New York, 1935).

7. Waldo Frank, "Forward," *American Writers Congress,* ed. Henry Hart (New York, 1935), p. 5.

8. Marcus Klein, *Foreigners: The Making of American Literature* (Chicago, 1981), p. 181.

9. E. Digby Baltzell, *The Protestant Establishment* (New York, 1964), pp. 52–53.

10. Michael Gold [Irwin Granich], "Toward Proletarian Art," *The Liberator*, Vol. 4 (February, 1921), 23; also cited in Walter B. Rideout, *The Radical Novel in the United States, 1900–1954* (Cambridge, Mass., 1956), p. 125.

11. Cited in Walter B. Rideout, "O Worker's Revolution. . . . The True Messiah," *American Jewish Archives*, Vol. 11, No. 2 (October, 1959), 125.

12. Joseph Freeman, *An American Testament* (New York, 1973 [c1936]), pp. 160–61.

13. Mike Gold, "Thornton Wilder: Prophet of the Genteel Christ," *The Mike Gold Reader* (New York, 1954), pp. 47, 49 (this review originally appeared in *The New Republic*, October 22, 1930).

14. Edmund Wilson, *The Shores of Light* (New York, 1952), pp. 535, 539.

15. Michael Gold, *Jews Without Money* (New York, 1935 [c1930]), p. 158.

16. Ibid., p. 309.

17. Michael Gold's reply is contained in Wilson, pp. 537–38.

18. Henry Roth, *Call It Sleep* (New York, 1964 [c1934]), p. 417.

19. Isidor Schneider, *From the Kingdom of Necessity* (New York, 1935), pp. 164–65.

20. Ibid., p. 45, 48.

21. Ibid., p. 73.

22. Ibid., p. 430.

23. Edwin Seaver, *Between the Hammer and the Anvil* (New York, 1937), pp. 198, 228.

24. Ibid., p. 228.

25. Ibid., pp. 228–29.

26. Ibid., pp. 313–14.

27. Edward Dahlberg, *Those Who Perish* in *The Novels of Edward Dahlberg* (New York, 1976), p. 574.

28. Waldo Frank, *The Death and Birth of David Markand* (New York, 1971), p. 258.

29. John Dos Passos, *Manhattan Transfer* (New York, 1925), pp. 203–6.

30. Ibid., pp. 261–62.

31. Ibid., p. 348.

32. Ibid., p. 22.

33. Ibid., p. 313.

34. Ibid., p. 356.

35. Ibid., p. 101.

36. Ibid., p. 397.

37. John Dos Passos, *USA:* I. *42nd Parallel*, II. *Nineteen Nineteen*, III. *The Big Money* (3 vols. in one) (New York, 1937), 1: 423, 424.

38. Ibid., 1: 428.

39. Ibid., 1: 432.

40. Ibid., 2: 437.

41. Ibid., 2: 439.

42. Ibid., 2: 441.

43. Ibid., 3: 445.

44. Ibid., 3: 111, 111–12, 113.

45. Ibid., 3: 543.

46. Hyman and Lester Cohen, *Aaron Traum* (New York, 1930), pp. 124.

47. Ibid., pp. 208–9.

48. Ibid., p. 277.

49. Ibid., p. 286.

50. Ibid., p. 281.

51. Ibid., p. 368.

52. Konrad Bercovici, *Main Entrance* (New York, 1932), p. 62.

53. Ibid., p. 170.

54. Joseph Gollomb, *The Unquiet* (New York, 1935), pp. 373, 400–401.

55. Ibid., pp. 122, 123. For an extended fictional treatment of nihilistic attitudes toward Jewishness among Jewish revolutionaries in Russia in the 1880s, see my discussion of Abraham Cahan's *The White Terror and the Red,* in Louis Harap, *The Image of the Jew in American Literature,* 2nd ed. (Philadelphia, 1978), pp. 509–13.

56. Leslie A. Fiedler, *The Jew in the American Novel* (New York, 1959), pp. 25, 26.

57. Daniel Fuchs, *Three Novels: Summer in Williamsburg, Homage to Blenholt, Low Company* (New York, 1961).

58. Fuchs, *Summer in Williamsburg,* p. 13.

59. Ibid., p. 256.

60. Ibid., p. 257.

61. Ibid., pp. 176–77

62. Ibid., p. 377.

63. Fuchs, *Low Company,* p. 92.

64. Ibid., p. 311.

65. Ibid., p. 2.

66. Walter B. Rideout, *The Radical Novel in the United States, 1900–1954* (Cambridge, 1956), p. 189. The notice appeared in *The New Masses,* Vol. 14 (February 12, 1935), 27.

67. Rideout, *Radical Novel,* p. 190. Edwin Seaver's review appeared in *The New Masses,* Vol. 14 (March 5, 1935), 21.

68. Marie Syrkin, "The Cultural Scene: Literary Expression," *The American Jew: A Composite Portrait,* ed. Oscar Janofsky (New York, 1942), pp. 101–2. Strangely Miss Syrkin forgot all about Roth when fifteen years later she wrote "The American Jewish Novel," *Jewish Frontier,* November, 1957, pp. 5–9.

69. Rideout, *Radical Novel,* p. 186. Rideout lists *Call It Sleep* as published in 1935 (p. 297) and Leslie Fiedler follows him in *The Jew in the American Novel,* p. 38. The copyright date is 1934.

70. Henry Roth, "On Being Blocked and Other Literary Matters: An Interview," interviewed by John S. Friedman, *Commentary,* Vol. 64, No. 2 (August, 1977), 34. Roth there says that "the book came out in 1934."

71. Henry Roth, *Call It Sleep* (New York, 1964), p. 227.

72. Ibid., p. 253.

73. Ibid., p. 257.

74. Ibid., p. 330.

75. Ibid., p. 405.

76. Ibid., p. 419.

77. Ibid., p. 437.

78. Ibid., p. 441.

79. Ibid., p. 161.

80. Ibid., p. 49.

81. Ibid., p. 175.

82. Ibid., p. 40.

83. Ibid., p. 80.

84. Ibid., p. 163.

85. Ibid., p. 198.

86. Ibid., p. 224.

87. Ibid., p. 228.

88. Ibid., p. 374.

89. Ibid., p. 183.

90. William Freedman, "Henry Roth in Jerusalem: An Interview," *The Literary Review,* Vol. 23, No. 1 (March, 1979), 19.

91. Roth, "On Being Blocked," p. 23.

92. Ibid., p. 34.

93. Ibid., p. 35.

94. Ibid., p. 36.

95. Ibid., p. 38.

96. Freedman, "Henry Roth," p. 16. A useful bibliography is "Henry Roth: A Bibliographical Survey," *Studies in American Jewish Literature,* Vol. 5, No. 1 (Spring, 1979), 62–71.

97. Meyer Levin, "What Is a Jewish Book?" *American Judaism,* Rosh Hashana, 1957, p. 14.

98. Meyer Levin, *In Search* (New York, 1950), pp. 75, 76.

99. Frederick Morton, "Meyer Levin: A Talk," *New York Times Book Review,* February 19, 1978.

100. Meyer Levin, *The Old Bunch* (New York, 1937), pp. 227–28.

101. Ibid., p. 229.

102. Ibid., p. 320.

103. Ibid., p. 641.

104. Ibid., p. 704.

105. Levin, *In Search,* pp. 93, 97.

106. Ibid., p. 145.

107. Lionel Trilling, review of *By the Waters of Manhattan,* by Charles Reznikoff, *Menorah Journal,* Vol. 19, No. 1 (October, 1930), pp. 88, 91, 92. Reznikoff's novel should not be confused with his volume of the same name of his "Selected Verse" published in 1962.

108. Charles Reznikoff, *By the Waters of Manhattan* (New York, 1930), p. 91.

109. Trilling, review, p. 89.

110. Irving Fineman, *Hear, Ye Sons* (New York, 1933), p. 33.

111. Ibid., p. x.

112. Nat J. Ferber, *One Happy Jew* (New York, 1934), p. 12.

113. Louis Zara, *Blessed Is the Man* (Indianapolis, 1935); Louis Zara, *Blessed Is the Land* (New York, 1954), p. 393.

114. Aben Kandel, *Rabbi Burns, A Novel* (New York, 1931), p. 13.

115. John Higham, *Send These to Me* (New York, 1975), p. 198.

116. Oscar Handlin, *Adventures in Freedom* (New York, 1954), p. 208; Baltzell, *Protestant Establishment*, p. 231.

117. Bernard Berelson and Patricia J. Salter, "Majority and Minority Americans: An Analysis of American Fiction," *Public Opinion Quarterly*, Vol. 10 (1946), 160.

118. Ibid., p. 173.

119. Ibid., p. 186.

120. Ibid., p. 188.

121. James T. Farrell, *Young Lonigan*, in *Studs Lonigan*, Modern Library ed. (New York, 1968), p. 19.

122. Ibid., pp. 174, 179.

123. Ibid., pp. 180, 183.

124. James T. Farrell, *The Young Manhood of Studs Lonigan*, in *Studs Lonigan*, pp. 73, 74.

125. Ibid., p. 128.

126. Ibid., p. 133.

127. Ibid., p. 376.

128. James T. Farrell, *Judgment Day*, in *Studs Lonigan*, p. 77.

129. Ibid., p. 418.

130. Ibid., pp. 424–25.

131. Henry Miller, *Tropic of Cancer* (New York, 1961), p. 3.

132. Ibid., p. 8.

133. Ibid., p. 109.

134. Michael Gold, "The Dreiser I Knew," *The Mike Gold Reader* (New York, 1954), p. 161. This article, published in 1950, does not allude to Dreiser's anti-Semitism.

135. W. H. Swanberg, *Dreiser* (New York, 1965), p. 267.

136. Ibid., p. 354.

137. Ibid., pp. 363–64.

138. "Editorial Conference," *American Spectator*, No. 11 (September, 1933).

139. *Letters of Theodore Dreiser*, ed. Robert E. Elias, 3 vols. (Philadelphia, 1959), 3: 715.

140. Swanberg, *Dreiser*, p. 427.

141. Hutchins Hapgood, "Is Dreiser Anti-Semitic?," *The Nation*, Vol. 140 (April 17, 1935), 436–38.

142. "Dreiser Denies He Is Anti-Semitic," *The New Masses*, April 30, 1935, pp. 10–11.

143. *The Nation*, Vol. 140 (May 8, 1935), 523.

144. "Letters About Dreiser," *Nation*, Vol. 140 (May 15, 1935), 572–73.

145. Mike Gold, "The Gun Is Loaded," *A Literary Anthology*, ed. Michael Folsom (New York, 1972), pp. 230, 224, 228.

146. *Letters of Theodore Dreiser*, 3: 747.

147. *Letters of Theodore Dreiser*, 3: 763.

148. Swanberg, *Dreiser*, p. 462.

149. F. O. Matthiessen, *Theodore Dreiser* (New York, 1951), pp. 224–25, 227.

150. Swanberg, *Dreiser*, p. 465.

4. THE JEW AT WAR: THE 1940S

1. Morris U. Schappes, *Documentary History of the Jews in the United States, 1654–1875* (New York, 1950), p. 5.

2. See Louis Harap, *The Image of the Jew in American Literature,* 2nd ed. (Philadelphia, 1978), pp. 354, 356.

3. Quoted in Simon Wolf, *The American Jew as Patriot, Soldier, and Citizen* (New York, 1895), p. 1.

4. Morris U. Schappes, *The Jews in the United States: A Pictorial History, 1654 to the Present* (New York, 1958), p. 179.

5. John Dos Passos, *Three Soldiers* (New York, 1932 [c1921]), p. 119.

6. James T. Farrell, *The Young Manhood of Studs Lonigan,* in *Studs Lonigan* (New York, 1968), p. 11.

7. William Faulkner, "Death Drag," *Collected Stories of William Faulkner* (New York, 1950), p. 192.

8. Harold U. Ribalow, "The Jewish GI in American Fiction," *The Menorah Journal,* Vol. 37, No. 2 (Spring, 1949), 266.

9. Schappes, *The Jews in the United States,* pp. 248, 250.

10. Ibid., p. 231.

11. Irwin Shaw, "Act of Faith," *A Treasury of American Jewish Short Stories,* ed. Harold U. Ribalow (New York, 1952), pp. 302–3.

12. Delmore Schwartz, "A Bitter Farce," *The World Is a Wedding* (Norfolk, Conn., 1948), pp. 105, 96, 98, 99, 101, 104.

13. Louis Falstein, *Face of a Hero* (New York, 1950), pp. 42, 44.

14. Norman Mailer, *The Naked and the Dead* (New York, 1948), p. 284.

15. Stefan Heym, *The Crusaders* (Boston, 1948), pp. 35, 37.

16. Irwin Shaw, *The Young Lions* (New York, 1948), p. 302.

17. Saul Levitt, *The Sun Is Silent* (New York, 1951), p. 105.

18. Mailer, p. 492.

19. Ibid., p. 72.

20. Ibid., pp. 265, 666.

21. Ibid., pp. 667, 672, 682.

22. Heym, *The Crusaders,* p. 425.

23. Ibid., pp. 503, 5.

24. Shaw, *The Young Lions,* p. 330.

25. Ibid., pp. 321, 322, 343, 344.

26. Ibid., p. 328.

27. Falstein, *Face of a Hero,* pp. 42, 44, 308.

28. Ibid., pp. 104, 105, 296, 76, 121–22, 292.

29. Levitt, *Sun Is Silent,* pp. 302, 35, 50.

30. Ibid., pp. 131, 266, 106.

31. James Landon, *Angle of Attack* (New York, 1952), pp. 74, 123.

32. Herman Wouk, *The Caine Mutiny* (New York, 1951), p. 448.

33. Ibid., p. 446.

34. James Jones, *From Here to Eternity* (New York, 1953), p. 569.

35. Ibid., p. 498.

36. John Horne Burns, *The Gallery* (New York, 1965 [c1947]), p. 372.

37. Ibid., p. 341.
38. Ibid., p. 344.
39. Ibid., p. 358.
40. Ibid., p. 358.

5. JEWISH ANTI-SEMITISM: THE PROBLEM OF SELF-HATE

1. Clement Greenberg, "Self-Hatred and Jewish Chauvinism," *Commentary,* Vol. 10, No. 5 (November, 1950), p. 426. Kurt Lewin's essay "Self-Hatred among Jews" is in *Resolving Social Conflicts,* ed. Gertrud Weiss Lewin (New York, 1948), pp. 186–200.

2. Vera Caspary, *Thicker Than Water* (New York, 1932), pp. 13, 149.

3. Ben Hecht, *A Jew in Love* (New York, 1931), p. 5.

4. Ibid., pp. 3–4.

5. Ibid., pp. 3, 45.

6. Ibid., p. 117.

7. Ibid., p. 139.

8. Ibid., pp. 21–22.

9. Ibid., p. 24.

10. Ibid., p. 142.

11. Ben Hecht, *A Guide for the Bedevilled* (New York, 1944), p. 61.

12. Ben Hecht, *A Child of the Century* (New York, 1954), pp. 371, 380–81.

13. Ibid., pp. 380–81, 382.

14. The opinions and citations concerning West's attitude toward his Jewishness are based upon and drawn from Jay Martin, *Nathanael West: The Art of His Life* (New York, 1970), pp. 78–91.

15. Nathanael West, *A Cool Million,* in *Miss Lonelyhearts and a Cool Million* (London, 1961), pp. 116, 134.

16. Nathanael West, *Miss Lonelyhearts,* pp. 48–49.

17. West, *A Cool Million,* pp. 100–101, 114, 165, 165–66, 167.

18. Meyer Levin, "What Is a Jewish Book?" *American Judaism,* Rosh Hashanah, 1957, p. 15.

19. Marie Syrkin, "The Cultural Scene: Literary Expression," *The American Jew: A Composite Portrait,* ed. Oscar I. Janowsky (New York, 1942), p. 103.

20. David Boroff, "An Authentic Rogue-Hero," *Congress Bi-Weekly,* Vol. 21, No. 9 (May 25, 1960), cited in Bernard Sherman, *The Invention of the Jew: Jewish-American Education Novels, 1916–1964* (New York, 1969), pp. 155ff.

21. Jerome Weidman, *I Can Get It for You Wholesale* (New York, 1937), pp. 232–33.

22. Meyer Levin, "The East Side Gangsters of the Paperbacks," *Commentary,* Vol. 16 (1953), 339, 342. This article was reprinted in *Mid-Century: An Anthology of Jewish Life and Culture in Our Times,* ed. Harold U. Ribalow (New York, 1955), pp. 350–64. Levin reiterated his critique in "What Is a Jewish Book?" *American Judaism,* Rosh Hashanah, 1957, pp. 14–16, and responses from Harold Robbins and Leonard Bishop are appended to the article.

23. Budd Schulberg, *What Makes Sammy Run?* (New York, 1941), pp. 303, 16, 119.

24. Ludwig Lewisohn, *The Island Within* (New York, 1956 [c1928]), p. 100.

25. Ibid., p. 96.
26. Ibid., p. 185.
27. Jo Sinclair [Ruth Seid], *Wasteland* (New York, 1946), p. 20.
28. Ibid., pp. 27–28.
29. Ibid., p. 28.
30. Ibid., p. 64.
31. Ibid., p. 67.
32. Ibid., p. 289.
33. Ibid., p. 290.
34. Paul Goodman, "Facts of Life," *Collected Stories* (New York, 1978), p. 47.
35. Ibid., p. 59.
36. Miriam Bruce, "Why I Wrote a Novel," *Mid-Century*, p. 332.
37. Miriam Bruce, *Linden Road* (New York, 1951), p. 68.
38. Myron S. Kaufmann, *Remember Me to God* (Philadelphia, 1957), p. 128.
39. Ibid., p. 140.
40. Ibid., p. 413.
41. Ibid., p. 563.

Bibliographical Note

Since World War II research material relating to the Jew in American literature, including both studies of individual authors and surveys of various aspects or phases of the general subject, has proliferated in numerous books and periodical articles. A student entering the field should supplement the primary texts of literary works with political, social, and economic histories of the period. One cannot otherwise understand the full socioeconomic life of fictional characters or the effect that life has had on their individual modes of thinking and feeling. An acquaintance with American-Jewish history is also essential in judging the authenticity of fictional Jewish characters in the United States. Useful background material is offered in Morris U. Schappes's *Jews in the United States: A Pictorial History, 1654 to the Present* (1958, 2nd ed. with corrections and a supplementary chapter updating the history to 1965, 1965). This book is based on original research. The readable *World of Our Fathers* by Irving Howe assisted by Kenneth Libo (New York, 1976) is also very useful although mainly drawn from secondary sources.

For an analysis of problems of ethnicity the student is referred to John Higham's classic *Strangers in the Land, Patterns of American Nativism 1860–1925,* corrected, with a new preface (New York, 1974). E. Digby Baltzell's *The Protestant Establishment* (New York, 1964) scrutinizes the effect of Anglo-Saxon dominance and recession of influence that so strongly influenced the acculturation of Jewish immigrants. Milton M. Gordon's *Assimilation in American Life: the Role of Race, Religion and National Origins* (New York, 1964) offers a guide through the maze of ethnicity theories.

While the present volume covers only the period from 1900 to the 1940s it is essential for the serious student to become acquainted with the past treatment of the Jew in earlier literature in the United States. Some knowledge of the treatment of the Jew by English writers is also important, since so much nineteenth-century and early twentieth-century American practice was derived from patterns developed in England. The most comprehensive work on this subject is Montagu Frank Modder's *The Jew in the Literature of England to the End of the Nineteenth Century* (Philadelphia, 1939; New York, 1960). More selective than Modder, and brilliantly written with irony and insight is Edgar Rosenberg's *From Shylock to Svengali* (London, 1961). The comparable American volume to Modder's is Louis Harap's *The Image of the Jew in American Literature: From Early Republic to Mass Immigration* (Philadelphia, 1974; 2nd ed., 1978). Although the cut-off date for this work is 1900 it ends with a forty-page chapter surveying the entire English fictional achievement of Abraham Cahan, extending into the twentieth century. Sol Liptzin's *The Jew in American Literature* (New York, 1966) provides a short and rather spotty account concluding with the 1940s. A brief introductory view of the subject is contained in Leslie Fiedler's pamphlet, written for the Herzl Institute, *The Jew in the American Novel* (New York, 1959). This treats a small number of selected figures. A concise history of the Jewish religion in this country is presented in Nathan Glazer's *American Judaism* (Chicago, 1959). Finally, since so many of the novels are located in New York, and since the New York experience generally sets the pattern of early immigrant experience for Jews, the student would do well to consult Moses Rischin's study in depth of that experience, *The Promised City* (Cambridge, Mass., 1962).

By far the best work on labor, socialist, and proletarian fiction is Walter Rideout's *The Radical Novel in the United States* (Cambridge, Mass., 1956). His article on Jewish writers of the radical novel in "O Workers Revolution ... The New Messiah," *American Jewish Archives*, Vol. 2, No. 2 (October, 1959), pp. 157–75, is also valuable. Bernard Sherman's *Invention of the Jew: Jewish-American Novels, 1916–1964* (New York, 1969) is a useful study, and Marcus Klein's *Foreigners: The Making of American Literature* (Chicago, 1981) is an exceptionally stimulating one. One can, of course, also find a large number of works on special aspects of the Jew in literature.

There is still, to my knowledge, no comprehensive authoritative study of the history of anti-Semitism in the United States but sections of some of the books listed above, notably Higham's and Baltzell's, are informative on the subject for specific periods.

The files of the monthly magazines *Commentary* and *Midstream* contain many studies of specific Jewish writers and of particular problems concerning the Jew in literature. Occasional articles also appear, in greater numbers of later years, in the general scholarly and critical journals.

The primary works of fiction in our field from 1900 to the mid-1940s are discussed in detail in the foregoing pages so that it would be redundant to list them here. A reader has only to consult the index to ascertain where to find all the necessary information about each of these, including publication data.

Index

About the Author

LOUIS HARAP received his A.B. and Ph.D. from Harvard University. He is the former editor of *Jewish Life* and is currently on the editorial board of *Jewish Currents*. He is the author of *In the Mainstream: The Jewish Presence in Twentieth-Century American Literature, 1950s—1980s* and *Dramatic Encounters: The Jewish Presence in Twentieth-Century American Drama, Poetry, and Humor and the Black-Jewish Literary Relationship* (both published by Greenwood Press, 1987), *Social Roots of the Arts*, and *The Image of the Jew in American Literature: From Early Republic to Mass Immigration* (1974). His articles have appeared in *Journal of Ethnic Studies, Science and Society, Jewish Currents*, and numerous other journals.